GRANNIES' REMEDIES

****

GRANNIES' REMEDIES

By MAI THOMAS

Gramercy Publishing Company • New York

A WORD OF CAUTION

Grannie was at best an enlightened amateur. Before actually using any of her remedies, you should consult your doctor.

This edition published by Gramercy Publishing Company
a division of Crown Publishers, Inc.,
by arrangement with James H. Heineman, Inc.

i j k l

Library of Congress Catalogue Card No. 66–27823
© MCMLXV Wolfe Publishing Ltd.
British Publisher: Wolfe Publishing Ltd.

CONTENTS

An Introduction to
Grannie

AROUND the turn of the century, when life was a great deal simpler, my grandmother lived in a grey stone cottage in a village on the borders of England and Wales.

It was a pleasant dwelling-place, which had stood in its overgrown garden of roses, hollyhocks, sweet peas, lavender, gooseberry bushes and gnarled old fruit trees since the days of the first Queen Elizabeth. The four small bedrooms had sloping floors, low ceilings, and little leaded windows that looked across lush pastures and a winding river to the blue Welsh hills. There was a kitchen with an enormous black-leaded range and a mass of shining copper pans, and a sink where the water came out of a hand-pump. And, heart and centre of all, there was the big, sunny sitting-room which seemed to the eyes of one small girl, at least, the most fascinating treasure-house on earth.

On the wall above the fireplace hung a bell-mouthed blunderbuss with which, so legend said, my grandfather had once driven off a highwayman. White china dogs stared glassily from either end of the chimney-piece, flanking a porcelain mandarin whose head nodded entrancingly at the gentlest touch. On the window-ledge, between the old-fashioned potted plants, there were great spiky sea shells brought in some clipper ship from the South Seas. When you put them to your ear, you could distinctly hear the roaring of the waves. There was a glass-fronted cabinet filled with Dresden shepherdesses, eggshell coffee cups, ivory Buddhas and elephants, and a globe which, when shaken, produced a most satisfactory snowstorm around a miniature pagoda.

This was the domain of my grandmother, a stately old lady dressed invariably in a black silk gown, with a shawl about her shoulders and a scrupulously laundered white lace cap atop her grey hair.

She was a small, slim woman, very graceful and unashamedly proud of her small hands and feet. Her dark eyes and warmly brown skin, coupled with the high cheekbones, betrayed the strain of Romany in her blood. Except for a touch of rheumatism in her hands, she was perfectly fit and active and would accept no help either with the housework or with the gardening.

She lived alone. Her husband, my grandfather, had been lost with his ship many years before I was born. She had reared her children and seen them settled in their own homes. Now, perfectly content and fiercely independent, she busied herself with the life of the village and the surrounding farms.

When she went out, if the weather were not too inclement, she wore what I believe was called a dolman and a perky little bonnet with an osprey plume and broad purple ribbons tied beneath her chin. In winter, she affected a close-fitting, red-squirrel jacket with a kind of mutton-chop sleeve and red woollen mittens. Almost invariably she carried a long, slim umbrella, the handle fashioned like a bird's head, but I never saw her open it, even when the rain was teeming down.

The villagers held her in almost awed respect. Some even whispered that she was a "white" witch. Whatever the truth of that claim (and she never troubled to deny it), certain it is that as soon as crisis hit the village—whether childbirth, death, measles, mumps, or some ailment among the livestock—within minutes somebody would be knocking on her back door.

She had, of course, no medical training in the accepted sense, yet for miles around people had very much more faith in her treatment than in the conventional skill of the local doctor with his top hat, wooden stethoscope and mysterious little black bag. Grannie's remedies *worked*, they said.

* * *

The origin of those remedies, which my grandmother had been collecting throughout her long life, is obscure. Some undoubtedly were handed down from her Romany forebears; others might well have had an ancestry dating back to the Druids. Some were so spartan, even terrifying, that the very thought of undergoing treatment might have produced an instantaneous "cure."

To cure whooping cough, my grandmother said, some people recommended that you skin a mouse, roast it, and give it to the sufferer to eat. If the patient were "finnicky," they suggested the treatment be disguised by baking the mouse in a patty.

Fortunately, Grannie didn't favour this remedy, but she told me that a common method of getting rid of tapeworm was to make the patient fast for three or four days. Then, in the same room, a large steak would be cooked and held in front of the patient's mouth, whereupon the ravenous tapeworm would shoot out of the patient's mouth, eager to get at the meat!

Less drastic was her treatment for ague. First, she said, you must cut an apple into three parts, on which you must write *Deus Pater*, *Deus Filius*, and *Deus Sanctus Spiritus*. The patient must fast for three days. At midnight on the first day, he must eat the section inscribed *Deus Pater*, and at midnight on the second day, the piece marked *Deus Filius*. At midnight on the third day, he ate the remaining portion, and the fever would leave him immediately.

Foolish? Well, the basic management for some fevers today is a starvation diet—which was just what my grandmother ordered. And no doubt the "mystic" words helped the cure along.

In this atomic age, thousands of people believe firmly that whooping cough can be cured by taking the sufferer for a trip in an aeroplane. Is that more credible than Grannie's mouse patty story?

My grandmother died quietly and without fuss at the age of 95. After her death I found in the old cottage a collection of school exercise books, each filled with her careful copper-plate handwriting. Through the years she had patiently compiled a pharmacopeia of folk-medicine for the guidance of those who should come after her.

This book is a selection of Grannie's remedies. It is also a memorial to a very good and great old lady, whose like we shall never see again.

I
Grannie's Medicine Chest

RANNIE'S "dispensary" was a large Georgian mahogany press, which stood in its own alcove in the sitting-room. Its contents might not have won a vote of confidence from any Medical Association, but they were undoubtedly comprehensive.

These, according to a list in her own firm handwriting, were the medicines and appurtenances essential in every home:

Three thermometers
Condy's Fluid and carbolic fluid
Lint, old rags, and gutta-percha
    tissue
Carron oil
Linseed meal
Flour of mustard
Rigollet's mustard leaves
Flannel for compresses
Bandages
A spatula
Castor oil
Quinine

Chlorodyne
Carbolic smoke ball
Sal volatile
Camphorated spirits
Hazeline
Ammonia
Diachylon
An india-rubber hot-water
    bottle
An enema
Elliman's Embrocation
Syringes
A feeding cup

11

Medicine glasses with
    measurement

Cotton wool
Arnica liniment

At the bottom of the list was this note:

Medicine Stains

"Medicine stains may be removed from silver spoons by rubbing them with a rag dipped in dilute sulphuric acid and washing it off with soapsuds."

Domestic Measures

Domestic measures can be approximately gauged this way:

A wine-glassful (ordinary size)	= 1 fluid oz. and a half
Two tablespoonsful	= 1 fluid oz.
One tablespoonful	= half-fluid oz.
One dessertspoonful	= two drachms
One teaspoonful	= one drachm

These measurements apply solely to fluids—never to solids. A tablespoonful of some solids, as powders, would weigh two or three ounces, some granules one ounce.

Somewhat ahead of her time in this respect at least, Grannie firmly believed in dealing with germs before they had time to get into the human system, as the following notes show:

Disinfectant

Dissolve together in a gallon of water 4 oz. of zinc sulphate and 2 oz. of common salt.

Disinfectants for Rooms

To disinfect a room, etc. close the room windows and doors and chimneys to exclude outer air. Break roll sulphur in small pieces; place on a metal dish, and set this on a pair of tongs over a metal pot in which there is water, or over a large box of sand, to avoid danger of fire. Light it with a few hot coals or methylated spirit poured around the sulphur. Leave the room and shut the door. A pound and a half of sulphur is sufficient for 1,000 cubic feet of space. Keep the room closed three hours after the burning has ceased, then air well for six hours. Clothing and bedding may be hung on lines and left in the room.

Similarly, she was convinced that flies, bugs and such "varmints" had much to do with the spread of sickness, and had her own drastic methods of dealing with them:

To make an Ant Trap

Soak a sponge in water and wring it near-dry. Sprinkle with sugar and lay on a plate by the ants' haunts. As soon as it is full, plunge it into boiling water.

Ants, to Exterminate in Gardens

Mix a tablespoonful of carbolic acid with a basin of water and apply to nests. In the house, place cayenne where they are most seen, and scrub shelves, etc., with carbolic soap.

Another way is to boil 1 lb. of Cape aloes in a gallon of water and add 6 oz. of powdered camphor. Excavate an ant-hill, pour a quart of this into it, and cover as much area as possible, then fill the excavation. When the nest cannot be found, mix this *largely* with water and sprinkle on the leaves, etc., through the rose of a watering can.

Crickets

Put cucumber peel on the floor at night near their hiding-places. This will destroy them. It also destroys beetles.

Emetic Mixture

(For children): The safest emetic is ipecacuanha wine.

Give doses of half a teaspoonful to a teaspoonful in sweetened water, followed by draughts of tepid water. Repeat every 10 minutes till vomiting results.

(For adults): 1—Take 1 to 2 teaspoonsful powdered mustard. Mix in a tumblerful of warm water.

2—Take 20 grains of sulphate of zinc and a tumblerful of water. Mix, and give as an emetic, to be followed by long draughts of tepid water. This is good in cases of drug poisoning.

Emulsion of Gum Arabic

Take 2 drachms gum arabic powder, sweet almonds, blanched, white sugar, half an ounce of each. Warm a pint of barley water, dissolve the gum in it, and when almost cold, pour slowly on the almonds, which should have been previously beaten to powder with the sugar to form a milky mixture, then strained. This is useful for common colds.

Epsom Salts

Adult dose is half an ounce, taken first thing in the morning with a warm drink afterwards. An excellent saline purgative.

Flies

The best remedy for getting rid of flies is Myocom or fly-gum. Also a piece of flannel saturated with turpentine put on a plate will get rid of the flies. Pyrethrum or Persian insect powder will free a room of flies if blown about with a small bellows. Wood ashes thrown into drains and on rubbish heaps destroys the flies' eggs. A ⅞ oz. of quassia chips boiled in a pint of water and mixed with 4 oz. of treacle draws flies and kills them. Fried camomile flowers scattered about gets rid of fleas. They can't tolerate the smell.

To protect yourself from flies and gnats, sponge weak carbolic acid on the skin, and sometimes, clothing. The solution should not contain more than 7 per cent carbolic acid.

Mustard

If you've got some English mustard handy, you have always got an efficient emetic. A full teaspoonful in a tumblerful of warm water generally produces vomiting. If it doesn't act within 10 minutes, it can be repeated. If still ineffective, a third dose can be given in another 10 minutes.

It is particularly useful for drunkenness, narcotic, and other poisoning, as well as in all cases where the stomach is overloaded with indigestible food and it is necessary to empty the stomach without depressing the system.

Mustard Poultices

Usually made with the flour of mustard mixed to the consistency of a poultice with water or vinegar, spread on a piece of thick brown paper or rag, and apply to the skin. Cold water should be used in their preparation. It is wrong to use, as some do, hot water or vinegar.

For anyone with a delicate skin it is advisable to place a piece of thin muslin between the poultice and skin. Always remove if it produces redness, whether it causes pain or not. A poultice should be instantly removed if it causes severe pain, otherwise it is liable to blister the skin and cause difficult-to-heal ulcers.

Some mustard poultices are made of a combination of one part mustard and four parts linseed meal. Mix the mustard with warm water in a separate vessel. Mix linseed meal with boiling water, add the mustard mixture, and stir with the meal. Spread on linen, and apply for 3 or 4 hours.

Poultices are seldom used nowadays because they are heavy, messy, and generally inferior to fomentations. Never use them for infants with chest affections, as they affect the breathing.

Linseed Poultice

Pour boiling water into a previously warmed basin and sprinkle in the meal, stirring constantly with a broad-bladed knife, until thick paste is formed. Spread the paste on a piece of linen or a layer of tow, and turn in the edges all round. A piece of fine muslin dipped in olive oil can be laid on the paste to prevent it sticking to the skin. Secure it to the affected part with bandage. Change every 3 or 4 hours.

Bran Poultices

Are lighter than linseed, and can be used several times. Make a flannel bag to the size required and fill with bran. Wrap loosely in a towel, pour boiling water over it, and wring out as with a fomentation.

Another good and very simple poultice is a piece of soft thick sheet-lint, doubled, squeezed out in hot water, and laid over the part, covered with a larger piece of thin rubber-sheeting.

Bread Poultice

Put half a pint of boiling water over a sufficient quantity of bread-crumbs; stir until a soft mass; spread a half-an-inch thick over a large cloth, and apply.

Yeast Poultice

Made by mixing a pound of flour or linseed meal with half-a-pint of yeast. The mixture should be heated and carefully stirred.

Charcoal Poultice

For charcoal poultice soak 2 oz. of bread-crumbs for 10 minutes in ½ pint of boiling water, then mix. Gradually add half-an-ounce of powdered wood charcoal, and 1½ oz. of linseed meal. The whole should be well stirred, and spread and applied in the ordinary way.

Insects and Vermin

Dissolve 2 lbs. of alum in 3 quarts of water. Wait until the alum is dissolved, then with a brush apply boiling hot to every joint and crevice infested by bugs, earwigs, or other insects. Keep it boiling whilst using. Strong boiling hot tea of cayenne used with a brush is also a good remedy.

Leather (to Vermin-proof)

Castor oil mixed with tallow will vermin-proof leather.

Lint

Can be quickly made by nailing a piece of old linen on a board, and scraping its surface with a knife. Scraped lint is the fine filaments from ordinary lint, and is used to stimulate ulcers and absorb discharges.

Moths

Anything moth-infested should be damped with benzine. It harms nothing but the moth.

A brick kept damp, and raised one-eighth of an inch from the floor, will collect moths under it. Once weekly, raise the brick and crush the moths or, take a small bunch of red wool, place on a piece of paper on the floor of a cupboard, and the moths will collect. Every few days, if the wool is shaken, moths will drop on the paper and can be destroyed. When clothes are infested, take a large linen cloth and wet thoroughly. Lay it folded two or three times over the affected part, and press with a very hot iron. This will destroy the larvae and eggs.

Moths in feathers can be destroyed by making openings in the bed-pillow, or whatever article they may be in, and placing lumps of camphor among them, or by putting the feathers in sacks, washing them, and drying well for days in sunlight.

Moths like the turnings and corners of carpets. Wring a cloth out of hot water, lay over the bindings and edgings, and iron with a very hot iron. Hold the iron on until the cloth is dry.

Another way is to wipe floors with a cloth wrung out of strong, hot cayenne tea, leaving the carpet turned back long enough for the floor to dry before replacing, wring a clean cloth dry out of this hot pepper tea, and wipe the binding and carpet edge rubbing hard. Salt sprinkled on pieces of cotton wool dipped in turpentine, put under the carpet edges can also be successful.

Finally, for a good moth preventative, mix 12 drops of oil of cloves, 12 drops of caraway, 6 drops of oil of lavender, a glass of whisky, and a piece of camphor. Sprinkle with it. Cedar-wood shavings are also death to moths.

Slugs

Put cabbage leaves in an oven till soft; rub with fresh dripping and lay wherever the slugs are. The leaves will soon be found covered with slugs and snails.

Smell of Paint

Paint smell can be removed by shutting the room; placing in the middle of it a pan of lighted charcoal on which some juniper berries have been thrown.

A handful of hay in a pail of water is another effective method.

From health contentment springs . . .

The best physicians are Dr. Diet, Dr. Quiet, and Mr. Merryman

A handful of good life is better than a bushel of good learning

He that would have a clear head, must have a clean stomach

By examining the tongue of a patient physicians find out the diseases of the body, and philosophers the diseases of mind

*Reason's whole pleasure, all the Joys of Sense
Lie in three words, Health, Peace and Competence
But Health consists in temperance alone
And Peace, oh Virtue! Peace is all thy own*

You should not touch your eye but with your elbow

The man who spends his energies deliberately, has the most inexhaustible bank to draw upon, and will draw the longest

2

Grannie's First-Aid Service

LIFE in a country village can be fuller and more hazardous than the city dweller would suspect, and hardly a day passed without Grannie being called out in a hurry. Her accident cases were varied and colourful, as the following "stock" remedies show:

Antidote

For alcohol, opium, prussic acid, strychnine and all poisoning.

Take a heaped teaspoonful each of common salt and ground mustard stirred quickly in a glass of warm water, and swallow immediately. This causes instant vomiting. When vomiting stops, swallow the whites of two eggs, then drink plenty of strong coffee.

Bleeding

To stop bleeding, use powdered rice sprinkled on lint and

applied to the wound, or put a handful of flour over the cut. If there is a cobweb handy, bind it on the wound and bleeding will stop. An application of Hazeline also stops it.

Bruises

Rest and bathe in cold water. If skin is unbroken, apply half-a-teaspoonful of arnica lotion to a tumbler of water. Wet soft linen rags with this lotion, and apply and change

as often as they dry. Alternatively, wring out a cloth in hot water and lay on the affected part. Renew frequently till pain eases.

Bruises of the Finger

The fastest way of getting relief after the occurrence of the accident is to plunge the finger into water as hot as can be borne. By so doing, the nail is softened and allows the blood to pour out beneath it, thereby soon relieving the pain. The finger may then be wrapped in a bread and water poultice.

For bruises, sprains, contusions, and local inflammations, diluted vinegar is also a popular and useful application.

Or, you can immediately apply treacle spread on brown paper. Or a plaster of chopped parsley mixed with butter.

To prevent a bruise swelling, instantly apply a cloth, 5 or 6 times doubled, dipped in cold water, and re-dip when it gets too dry and warm.

To cure a bruise swelling, foment it half-an-hour, morning and night, with cloths dipped in water as hot as you can bear.

Burns (slight)

Immediately apply pulverised charcoal and linseed oil. Common soda moistened with water applied quickly is effective. Freely use soft soap, then linseed oil and sift over the burn, wheaten flour. When this dries hard, repeat the oil and flour till a complete covering is obtained. Let this dry till it falls off and a new skin forms.

> [*Important: Ideas on the treatment of burns have changed radically since Grannie's days. You are now strongly advised that the only dressing you should apply is a dry clean piece of linen—and to get the doctor's advice immediately. You should not remove clothes unless it is impossible to reach a hospital or doctor.*]

To dress a burn, mix equal parts of linseed oil and lime water, saturate a cloth with it, and bind on the burn. This is the carron oil used by surgeons.

Instantly, in the case of scald or burn, cover the injury with a sheet, or a portion of sheet, or wadding, taking care not to break any blister that may have formed.

Envelop every part of the injury from all access of the air, laying one or two more pieces of wadding on first to effectually guard the burn or scald from atmospheric irritation.

A light bandage should finally secure the dressings in place. Exclusion of air from a burn or scald is the best, quickest, and least painful treatment.

To treat burns, take chalk and linseed, or common olive oil, and mix into a compound as thick as honey.

Add vinegar to reduce the thickness if necessary. Apply with a soft brush and renew the application from time to time.

Choking from Fish Bone

When a person has a fish bone in the throat, insert the forefinger, press upon the root of the tongue, so as to induce vomiting; if this does not do, let him swallow a large piece of potato or soft bread; and if these fail, give a mustard emetic.

Convulsions

Throw cold water on the face and sponge the head with it. Put the child into a hot bath of mustard and water (100° F). Keep the child in the bath 15 minutes or until better. Rub thoroughly dry and wrap warmly. Your doctor should be summoned immediately and his advice taken.

Dog Bites

If there is doubt about the dog, suck the wound and plunge a lighted vesuvian into the wound. For ordinary dog-bites, spread a thick paste of carbonate of soda and water over the wound and bind. Lance the surface around the wound and let it bleed freely in tepid water, to which pink Condy has been added.

Rabies

If bitten, take immediately 1½ oz. of the root of the elecampane plant (the green root is preferable). Slice or bruise it, put into a pint of fresh milk, boil down to half-a-pint, strain, and drink when cold. Fast at least 6 hours afterwards. Next morning repeat the dose and fast, using

2 oz. of the root. On the third morning take a third dose. Remember, eat nothing for 6 hours after each dose.

A man was said to have been cured of hydrophobia by being put in a cellar alone with nothing to drink but brine left in a meat-barrel. After having several fits his thirst was so intense that he drank the brine. He had no more fits. It is impossible to check the truth of this story.

Mad Animals (Bites)

Tie string tightly over the part, cut out the bite and cauterise the wound with carbolic fluid. Then apply a piece of spongio-piline; give a purgative and plenty of warm drink.

Ears

To remove insects from the ear, gently use a warm-water syringe. But this is a job for a doctor or nurse.

Eyes

To remove substances from the eyes, bathe with luke-warm water till clear. If stubborn, raise the lid gently and pass a soft camel-hair brush along it.

When dust gets into the eyes, dash cold water into them. If this doesn't do the trick, you can either syringe the eye with lukewarm water or, placing your forefinger upon the cheek-bone, slightly bend the finger to draw down the lower lid, and you will probably be able to remove the dirt. If not, repeat the operation with a cleaned matchstick over the upper lid; ask the patient to look down, then turn the lid upwards over the needle. This will turn it inside out, and should enable you to remove the trouble with the corner of a handkerchief. As soon as the substance is removed, bathe the eye with cold water, drop in a drop of castor oil, and, if very sore, exclude the light for a few hours.

For inflamed eyes use the white of an egg beaten to a

froth and add 2 tablespoonsful of rosewater. Apply on a soft rag and change as often as it dries.

Face-ache

Apply with a flannel a mixture of 2 drs. ether, 2 drs. laudanum, 2 drs. camphorated spirits of wine, 2 oz. of sal-volatile. For external use only: laudanum is dangerous.

Faintness

Take 1 or 2 teaspoonsful of compound tincture of lavender whenever symptoms appear.

Fainting is due to failure of the heart's action, and can be caused by emotion; by breathing heated impure air; by loss of blood and other causes of shock; by diseases of the heart and digestive organs.

Treatment: Place the patient flat on his back, and loosen clothing. Give him fresh air by opening windows and making bystanders refrain from crowding round. Rub limbs briskly in an upward direction. If able to swallow, diluted brandy, sal volatile, or Eau de Cologne may be given by the mouth. If the attack shows signs of long duration, apply a mustard plaster or poultice over the heart. When recovery has taken place, do not allow him to attempt to stand for some time after he is conscious.

* * *

For faintness and prostration, take the whites and yolks of 3 eggs and beat them up in 5 oz. of plain water; add slowly 3 oz. of brandy with a little sugar of nutmeg. If the stomach is very irritable, take a tablespoonful of cream and beat it up thoroughly with the white of a new-laid egg. Add slowly to the frothy mixture one tablespoonful of brandy in which a lump of sugar has been dissolved.

Fits

These can be either epileptic or apoplectic. In the former, the unhappy person afflicted gives a scream, becomes deathly pale, falls on the face, becomes convulsed, then insensible.

Clothes should be loosened and a doctor summoned. In apoplectic fits, the person falls, goes purple in the face, and breathes in a snoring manner. Raise the head, apply cold water to it, and call a doctor.

Flea-bites

Rub the bites with Thilum, which is an Indian remedy.

Hiccough

Put some drops of vinegar on a piece of loaf sugar and eat slowly. Or, moisten brown sugar with vinegar and take a few grains to a teaspoonful. The effect is almost instantaneous.

Hysterics

Put the hysterical person on a bed, loosen clothing; slap the chest and face smartly with the end of a towel dipped in cold water. Don't be hard in your manner. Open-air exercise, strengthening diet, cheerful surroundings, with the removal of all care and perplexities is important as well as proper regularity of the bowels. Iron pills help. Strong tansy tea, taken cold and in small quantities, is good.

A long, narrow strip of strengthening-plaster, worn the entire length of the spine during cold weather, is also good. This may be made by mixing by heat, dark resin with half its proportion of beeswax, adding a few drops of olive oil.

Itching

Use a cone of cacao butter impregnated with 2 per cent cocaine. This should be rubbed over the affected part. The warm skin melts a layer of the cacao butter, to form a soothing emollient shield. This is good for irritating affections of the skin, and for insect bites.

Itch or scabies is due to a parasite which causes intense itching which is aggravated when the body becomes warm, as on first going to bed. Rub soft soap all over the body, and then take a hot bath and scrub with a nail-brush. Dry the skin, and then rub in sulphur ointment, which must not be washed off for 12 hours. Clothes must be baked.

To soothe itching skin, a weak carbolic acid lotion, two grains to the ounce, diluted vinegar or alcohol, bicarbonate of soda solution, a teaspoonful or so to the pint.

Mosquito Stings

Apply a mixture of 50 grs. of powdered alum, 10 grs. or aromatic vinegar, 10 grs. of glycerine immediately. It soothes itching and pain.

Nettle Rash

Rub the parts with parsley.

Nettle-rash – Hives

Local remedies are important. They are conveniently applied in the form of lotions or baths; among the former are vinegar and water and alcohol and water. Bay rum may be used, soda, a drachm to half a pint of water, and weak solutions of carbolic acid.

Nettle Sting

Rub the part with juice of nettles.

Nose Bleed

Small pieces of ice may be sucked and inserted into the nostril, and a piece held against the side of the nose and forehead.

Or, firmly grasp the nose with the finger and thumb of the right hand for fully 10 or 15 minutes, thus completely stopping the movement of air through the nose.

Bleeding from the nose sometimes yields to a piece of rag saturated with vinegar introduced into the nostril. This may also generally be stopped by putting a plug of lint into the nostrils. If not, apply a cold lotion to the forehead, raise the head, and place over it both arms, so that it will rest on the hands; dip the lint plug in friar's balsam, or tincture of kino. Heat should be applied to the feet; and, in obstinate cases, the sudden shock of a cold key or cold water poured down the spine, will often instantly stop the bleeding. If the bowels are restricted, take a purgative.

*   *   *

Hot Packs

Are valuable in cases where it is necessary to sweat. The bed should be protected with a mackintosh, and a blanket laid over it. The patient should be stripped, and a blanket dipped in hot water and wrung out as dry as possible, thrown over him, with plenty of blankets overall.

Warm milk or barley-water will promote perspiration. After an interval of about half-an-hour, remove the wet blanket and rapidly swathe the patient in hot, dry blankets.

Wrapping a patient in hot blankets, giving him warm drinks, and the placing of hot-water bottles or heated bricks, well wrapped to prevent burning, in the bed is another means of promoting perspiration.

GRANNIES' REMEDIES

Dislocated Thumb

Frequently produced by a fall. Make a clove hitch by passing two loops of cord over the thumb, placing a piece of rag under the cord to prevent it cutting the thumb. Pull in the same line as the thumb. Apply a cold lotion, one part spirit to 3 parts water.

Dry Heat

Wool may be heated against a can containing boiling water and laid on affected parts. This is a useful way of applying heat in inflammations of the eye and joints. Heating wool in front of a fire is dangerous. A layer of dry, hot wool wrapped round a joint and covered with oiled-silk, rapidly becomes saturated with perspiration, and gives great relief in acute inflammation, such as gout and rheumatism. Change the wool frequently.

Noses

If a foreign substance gets up a child's nose, open the child's mouth, place your mouth over it, and blow gently to expel the substance. But better to get a doctor.

Poisons and Antidotes

Use the following treatments if no doctor is at hand:

Oil of Vitriol-Aquafortis-Muriatic Acid—Magnesia, chalk, soap and water every two minutes.

Tartar Emetic—Oily drinks and warm water.

Prussic Acid—Pump water on back, put strong-smelling salts to nose.

Arsenic—Emetics of mustard and salt, some water and sweet oil or milk.

Mercury-Corrosive Sublimate—Whites of eggs and milk in large quantities.

Opium-Laudanum—Strong coffee, emetic draught, vinegar and water, dash cold water on the face, walk up and down for 2 or 3 hours.

Lead—Castor oil and emetics, plus whites of eggs.

Verdigris—Whites of eggs, gruel, castor oil.

Henbane-Hemlock-Nightshade—Emetics and castor oil, brandy and water.

Poisonous food—Emetics and castor oil.

Carbolic Acid—Flour and water and glutinous drinks.

Chloral Hydrate-Chloroform—Pour cold water over head and face.

Strychnine—Emetic of mustard and warm water.

Oxalic Acid—Magnesia dissolved in water every 2 minutes.

Snake-bites

Snake venom produces symptoms of shock, nausea, and faintness, often accompanied by vomiting, followed by intense lethargy, lapsing into coma. The bite of the English viper is rarely fatal.

Treatment: Immediately tie a ligature tightly above the wound, then suck the wound. This may be safely done provided there are no cracks or sores on the mouth or lips. Encourage bleeding. Wash the wound as soon as possible with strong ammonia (such as sal volatile), Condy's fluid, or tincture of iodine. The shock should be treated by giving large doses of stimulants, preferably sal volatile, and the patient must somehow be kept awake and from yielding to lethargy.

In the tropics, the following drastic treatment is sometimes adopted: Tissues around the bites are pinched up and cut away; a paste is then made of gunpowder and blood and the wounds filled with it. The paste is then ignited and the tissues consequently cauterised.

Sore Throat

An effective remedy for sore throat, especially when accompanied by hoarseness—onions boiled in molasses.

In relaxed, ulcerated, and other forms of sore throat benefit is often derived by inhaling the vapour of hot vinegar.

Sores and Cuts

Bathe with one part whisky and 3 parts water.

Sore or blistered heels should be prevented by wearing well-made boots for rough work, and by keeping the leather pliant with dubbin, tallow, or castor oil. Socks should be changed after a day's work, feet washed, and the skin hardened with surgical spirit. Strong salt and water may be used. Before starting in the morning, the feet should be greased with lanoline, petrol jelly, castor oil, tallow or mutton-fat.

If chafing or blistering occurs, the condition must be treated as in bed sores. The blister can be pricked, but the skin must not be removed. Blisters from rowing can be similarly prevented and treated.

Sprains

The injured member should be elevated and cold applications made to the joint either with cloths wrung out in cold water, or by powdered ice in towels or in a rubber bag. The best way of keeping cloths wet without changing them is to fill a jug with water, place it higher than the limb; moisten a strip of linen, place one end of it in the water, and let the other end hang on the outside. Rest it on the cloths that cover the injured place so that the water is continuously conducted to the linen.

As the sprain improves, it will require gentle rubbing with liniment.

Sunburn

Wash the face with sage-tea.

Sunstroke

Often affects people through severe muscular exertion in

hot sun. An attack is frequently sudden. The victim falls insensible, but usually there is headache, dizziness, and gradual loss of consciousness. The face flushes, the pulse is rapid, and temperature high.

Treatment: Loosen clothing and immediately pour cold water over the patient. Strip clothing, and if you have any ice, rub the body with it, otherwise cover the patient with a sheet and keep it drenched with cold water. As

consciousness returns, lots of cold water drinks should be given.

If still insensible, apply mustard-leaves to the nape of the neck, arms, and leg calves. After recovery, the patient is very sensitive to heat and should refrain from exposure to hot sun or exertion in hot weather for some time.

Stings and Bites

Bees, wasps and hornets: Extract the sting, if left in the flesh, and apply ammonia or bicarbonate of soda. You can also apply honey to a bee sting.

Gnats, mosquitos and ants: Ammonia or bicarbonate of soda.

Scorpions, centipedes, tropical spiders: Place a ligature above the wound, encourage bleeding, and apply ammonia, vinegar, or turpentine, followed by hot fomentations. Give stimulants if there are symptoms of shock.

Bee stings are best treated after the removal of the sting itself (which should be squeezed out by firm pressure of the thumb-nail), first by cooling, then by hot compresses. Covering the swelling with damp, cold earth is a good cure.

Jelly fish

Sea-bathers stung by them suffer nausea and faintness, as well as pain in the affected limb. A warm bath and a teaspoonful of sal volatile in water should be administered if there are signs of shock. On the sting itself, use bicarbonate of soda or ammonia.

An excellent lotion for such cases can be made with equal parts vinegar, arrack, and water. This is also good applied to the head for headache and fever delirium. The pains of venomous bites or stings is often speedily relieved by constant application of a piece of vinegar-moistened rag.

Weevers and Rays

Inflict troublesome wounds with their sharp spines. Suck the wound to promote bleeding, then wash the wound with Condy's fluid, ammonia, or bicarbonate of soda, and dress with olive oil.

Teething

Dill water is frequently administered to children during teething, when they appear to be griped by wind in the stomach and bowels. Attack the cause, as wind is usually the result of something more serious. Some magnesia can be given with the dill water, which should be used in doses of a teaspoonful or more to a year-old child.

Warts

Rub them daily with radish, or with juice of marigold flowers. It seldom fails. Or, rub the wart on a piece of raw meat.

Small doses of sulphate of magnesia taken internally can also remove warts. Three grains of Epsom salts taken morning and evening is a known cure in France. Apply twice or thrice daily some aromatic vinegar, dab on the skin with a fine camel-hair brush, taking care not to touch the surrounding skin, when most probably the wart will shrivel away.

A good ointment for warts, which should be applied daily, is made from a mixture made of 2 drs. muriate of ammonia, 1 oz. powdered savin, and 1½ oz. of lard.

Wounds

Before dressing a wound examine the colour of the blood. If it flows regularly and is dark, it can be dressed. If it is bright scarlet and spurts out in jets, put on a tourniquet and wash the part well with cold water, bring the edges of the wound together, and keep them together with strips of sticking plaster. Place some lint wet with friars' balsam on the cut, and secure with a bandage. Remember a tourniquet should never be left on too long at a time. A doctor must be consulted in the case of arterial bleeding and a note made of the time when the tourniquet was applied.

Where the wound is the plaster must be . . .

Music helps not the toothache

Nor love they life nor hate: but what thou livest
Live well: how long or short, permit to heaven

The grand secret seems to be, to contrive that the
exercise of the body and that of the mind may serve
as relaxations to each other

Those who are candidates for health, must be as
circumspect in the task they set their mind as in the
exercise they give to their body

The patient can oftener do without the doctor than the
doctor without the patient

What we have been longest used to is most likely to
agree with us best

Who steals an old man's supper does him no wrong

3

Grannie's Herbal

HE BASIS of Grannie's healing powers was—apart from a shrewd if untutored use of practical psychology—an encyclopaedic knowledge of the curative use of herbs and plants.

What follows was carefully written into one of her notebooks, though whether it was her own or some older practitioner's composition, I have no means of knowing:

In the book of Ecclesiasticus we read: "The Lord hath created medicines out of the earth, and he that is wise will not abhor them." Gypsies, descended from ancient Egyptian tribes, believe that for every ill we suffer there is a plant growing somewhere to cure it.

They used the herbs of the fields and hedgerows, and the homely ones growing in their cottage gardens. They ate sage leaves with their daily bread and cheese, for it was said: "How can a man die with sage in his garden?" They drank good nettle ale, cider and mead.

GRANNIES' REMEDIES

Wise mothers dosed ailing daughters with the homely mugwort tea, believing the old proverb:

"If they would drink nettles in March
And eat mugwort in May,
So many fine maidens
Wouldn't go to clay."

For perfumes country folk used sweet musk, gilly flowers, cabbage roses, lad's love and rosemary.

* * *

Camomile is a comforting herb. The specific name of this well-known field plant is Anthemis, from anthos, a flower; meaning in this case that it is not only a flower, but one well worthy of notice. It is said that every part of the plant has healing properties.

* * *

Balm tea is another old favourite. Mothers used to give it to lazy children because it was said to stimulate them.

* * *

Young nettles grow thickly everywhere in the Spring. Herbalists claim there is no Spring medicine so purifying for the blood.

* * *

Coltsfoot is another prolific herb, appearing early in the year. This plant has been used for centuries as a remedy for Spring coughs. It was so well thought of that apothecaries honoured it by painting its flowers on the doorposts of their shops. Its leaves, shaped like a colt's foot, were dried and used as tobacco, while its silky, white seeds were collected by housewives as pillow stuffing.

* * *

Dandelion is very valuable for diseases of heart and liver. It was sometimes called "heart-fever grass." Its young leaves give flavour and goodness to salads.

* * *

For many, many centuries, the elder has been a famous

medicine, believed to cure everything. Country folk looked upon elder as a sort of apothecary's shop conveniently growing in the hedgerows. Its flowers, leaves and berries, made into cordials, teas, and wines, were drunk hot at bedtime to cure colds. Most of us know Hans Andersen's story of the little boy who got his feet wet—"The Elder Tree Mother."

The boy's mother put him to bed and into a teapot she put some elder flowers to make a warm, comforting cup of elder tea: "The little boy looked at the teapot; he saw the lid rise and the elder flowers spring forth, so fresh and white they were, and they shot out long, thick branches—even out of the spout they shot forth—spreading on all sides, and growing larger and larger, till at last there stood by the bedside a most charming elder bush, a perfect tree, some of its branches stretching over the bed and thrusting the curtain aside. Oh, how full of blossoms was this tree, and how fragrant were those blossoms! And in the midst of the tree sat a kind-looking old dame, wearing the strangest dress in the world. It was green like the elder leaves, with a pattern of large white elder flower clusters spreading all over it—one could not be sure whether it was actually a gown or real, living green leaves and flowers."

The Tree-Eaters

Slippery elm—as a healing nourishing food—was discovered by early colonists in North America. They knew little of the terrible, long winters in that country, and when the first frost came they hadn't enough food and faced starvation. They had to eat roots and gnaw the bark of trees. One of the trees was the Canadian elm, and the people who ate this bark found that it not only satisfied their hunger, but gave them strength and vigour.

Although we are told there is healing in every herb that grows, it is dangerous to experiment with them. The herbalist, learning his art, must be wary, and never taste the berries, or any part of a plant, unless its properties are known to him, for certain parts of healing plants are often poisonous.

Balm was popular as a physic herb and for its sweet scent, and was also used for rubbing on furniture to pleasantly perfume a house. In "The Merry Wives of Windsor," Anne Page bids the elves:

"The several chairs of order look you scour
With juice of balm and every precious flower."

Decoctions

The usual method of giving a herbal medicine is by means of what is known as a decoction. To make decoctions, herbs are simply boiled in water. They should be prepared fresh daily. Sometimes herbs and water are boiled, strained and the liquor used to cover fresh herbs and again boiled. Decoctions should be made over a clear flame, free from smoke, in a covered vessel; and, in the case of herb leaves, brought to the boil, then strained into a jug and covered till cold.

Decoctions are solutions of the active principles of vegetable substances obtained by boiling. This method is adopted to obtain principles which cannot be separated by simple infusion in cold or even boiling water. Small quantities only should be made at a time, as they are apt to change.

Decoction of oak bark—Take an ounce of oak bark and a pint of water. Put into a covered vessel and boil for 10 minutes, then strain. The dose of this preparation is from 2 to 6 tablespoonsful. It is a fine astringent, and used as a gargle for relaxed throat.

Decoction of barley—Take 2 oz. pearl barley and 5 pints of water. Wash the barley in cold water, reject the washings, and having poured over it half-a-pint of water, boil for 5 minutes. Repeat, then after adding the remainder of the water boiling, let the whole boil down to 2 pints, then strain. Barley water made this way is serviceable in all cases of fever and inflammation, and can be taken in any quantity. To this, various substances are sometimes added, such as sliced figs, raisins, liquorice root, slices of lemon, and sugar-candy.

*   *   *

Decoctions are valuable for illnesses connected with stomach, bowels and kidneys, because this fluid passes quicker into these organs than any other medicine. They can be sweetened with sugar but are better without. If roots, barks, leaves, flowers and seeds are boiled together, let the roots boil first for some time, then add the bark and bring to the boil again; and so with leaves, seeds and flowers, each in the order mentioned. Figs, quince seeds, and linseed, should be tied in a muslin bag—all need long boiling—then should be removed before straining the liquid. Decoctions must be kept covered. The usual dose is from 1 to 5 liquid ounces, according to the strength of the decoction and the age of the patient.

Rosemary Decoction
A decoction of rosemary, made with wine instead of water, used to be taken as a remedy against giddiness. A decoction of a good handful of the leaves, covered with cold water, brought to the boil and strained, is an excellent hair tonic to be rubbed into the scalp till the skin glows.

Balm

A stimulant for use in fevers, you should try a compound spirit of balm. This spirit—almost as good as a liqueur—is distilled from 8 oz. of balm, 4 oz. of lemon peel, 2 oz. each of nutmeg and carraway seeds, and 1 oz. each of angelica root, cinnamon and cloves. Add a quart of brandy, keep the liqueur in stoppered bottles, and use as a stimulant.

Infusion of balm is prepared by covering an ounce of leaves with one pint of boiling water, and letting it stand for 15 minutes.

Strain, then take freely in wine-glassful doses as a tonic, and to induce perspiration.

Beans

Are good for a variety of ailments. For boils, reduce haricot beans to a powder, mix with an equal quantity of fenugreek and honey, and apply outwardly to boils, bruises, or blue marks caused by a blow.

You can also usefully treat eye troubles with beans. Mix bean flour with equal quantities of rose leaves, frankincense and the white of an egg. Apply to eyes that water or are swollen.

Sciatica can be eased by burning bean husks to ashes, and mixing into an ointment with unsalted lard. Apply for old pains, sciatica, and gout.

Celery

This is excellent for rheumatism. Cut celery into pieces and boil in water until soft, then drink the water. Put new milk, with a little flour and nutmeg, into a saucepan with boiled celery, and serve warm with pieces of toast. Eat with potatoes, and the rheumatic aches and pains will ease.

Camomile Lotion—for skin and hair

Place 5 or 6 dried camomile flowers in a bowl and pour a half-pint of boiling water over them. Cover the bowl for 10 or 12 minutes. When the lotion has slightly cooled, sponge it on the skin with a small pad of cotton wool. Camomile lotion is credited with astringent properties, is used for closing enlarged pores and toning-up relaxed muscles. This lotion also makes an excellent hair tonic. Cleanse the scalp with it twice a week.

Cold Cream

To make a simple cold cream, take 1½ oz. olive oil, 6 drachms of white wax, 2 drachms of spermacetti, and 3 drops of oil of lavender. Melt the wax and spermacetti in the oil in a double saucepan or a jar standing in a pan of boiling water over a flame. Stir vigorously with a porcelain or bone spoon until the ointment is well mixed. Remove from the fire and beat gently until it becomes stiff and sets, when it should be potted for use.

Coltsfoot

Coltsfoot syrup is a first-class remedy for coughs, colds, giddiness and headache.

For coughs and colds make a decoction from a handful of the leaves in 2 pints of water. Boil down to 1 pint, strain and sweeten with a syrup made of sugar-candy. The dose is an occasional teacupful.

Dandelion

Dandelion extract acts on the liver and has a slight aperient action.

Boil down a decoction of the *fresh* root, sliced—1 oz. to 1 pint of water—to half-a-pint, and strain; add 2 drachms of cream of tartar. Dose: a wine-glassful taken two or three times daily.

An excellent liver tonic is made with 4 oz. of fresh dandelion roots boiled in 2 pints of water until the liquid is reduced to 1 pint. Strain off and take a wine-glassful twice a day.

This is also good for rheumatism.

Ointment for Obstinate Ulcers

Bruise a pound of primrose leaves with half-a-pound of the flowers, simmer them in an equal quantity of lard without salt until the primroses become crisp, then strain through a coarse sieve.

Elecampane

This root is aromatic, tonic, and stimulating. It is used for dyspepsia and pulmonary affections.

The infusion of elecampane is made from the dried root covered with boiling water.

Dosage is 1 fluid ounce.

Hart's Tongue

A cure for hiccough. The distilled water of the hart's tongue fern is good for stopping hiccough. Used as a gargle, it cures bleeding gums.

Lotion for Soothing Heat and Skin Irritation

2 oz. lettuce juice, 2 drs. of Eau de Cologne, 2 oz. distilled vinegar, 4 oz. elder flower water, well mixed. Dab the skin with it frequently.

Lotion to Soothe General Body Irritation

Bathe with grains of boracic acid diluted with an ounce of water, and powder with talcum powder.

Linseed Lotion

For unbroken chilblains and rheumatism, apply lotion made of 4 tablespoonsful each of pure linseed oil, and oil of turpentine. Add 2 drachms of spirits of camphor and shake well until mixed.

Marshmallow Ointment

Highly prized for soothing effects and for allaying inflammations. Made by macerating equal weights of marshmallow leaves and pure unsalted lard together in a double saucepan, or jar standing in a pan of boiling water. Simmer for an hour to extract all soluble parts of the leaves before the ointment is strained and potted.

Or, you can boil the leaves for 45 minutes, strain and evaporate the liquid to a thin extract, and then mix with lard.

Physicians rarely take medicine

'Tis the great Art of Life to manage well the restless mind

The surest way to health, say what they will
Is never to suppose we shall be ill
Most of those evils we poor mortals know
From doctors and imagination flow

A man as he manages himself may die old at thirty, or young at eighty

God and the doctor we alike adore
But only when in danger, not before
The danger o'er, both are alike requited
God is forgotten and the doctor slighted

Children and chickens must be always picking

The head and feet keep warm; the rest will take no harm

4
Grannie's
Invalid
Diets

Arrowroot

TAKE a tablespoonful of arrowroot and mix into thin paste with a little water. Gradually add half-a-pint of boiling water, stirring the whole time. Put on the stove for 3 or 4 minutes, continuing to stir until the whole is evenly mixed.

Remove from the stove and add grated nutmeg, sugar, etc., to taste. A little lemon juice is an effective alternative to the nutmeg. It is more nourishing if made with milk, but it can be too rich for a weak stomach, then water is preferable. It should always be prepared fresh as required.

Although arrowroot is a valuable and easily digestible food for invalids and children, remember that it isn't very nourishing.

"As a vehicle for wine," said Miss Florence Nightingale, "and as a restorative quickly prepared, it is all very well. But it is nothing but starch and water. Flour is both more nutritive and less liable to ferment, and is preferable wherever it can be used."

Arrowroot Pudding

Rub a tablespoonful of arrowroot in a basin with a little cold water, and add, stirring constantly, a pint of boiling milk. Mix in the contents of one egg and three teaspoonsful of powdered, refined sugar, which have previously been beaten together. Boil in a basin, or bake. This is good for early convalescence.

Arrowroot Blancmange

Take three tablespoonsful of arrowroot, make into a mucilage with water, then add milk in sufficient quantity, and boil until of a proper consistence. Pour into a mould, and allow to cool and set. Eat with currant jelly or with lemon juice and sugar. Milk or beef-tea may be used instead of water in the preparation of arrowroot mucilage. It should be boiled 20 minutes. This again is excellent for early convalescence.

Arrowroot-water

Take 2 teaspoonsful of arrowroot, and make into a smooth paste with a little water. Add a pint of water, and simmer for 5 minutes, stirring constantly.

Strengthening Jelly

Soak overnight 2 oz. of isinglass or prepared gelatine, 1 oz. of gum arabic, 5 oz. of sugar-candy, and a grated nutmeg in a bottle of port wine. In the morning, simmer on stove till dissolved. Strain and set aside in a cool place till it forms firm jelly. A piece the size of a nutmeg may be taken 5 or 6 times a day. This is good for debility when the stomach is unable to bear normal food.

Strawberry Tea

Strawberries contain citric acid, and "strawberry treatment" is said to be effective for gout, stone in the bladder, kidney trouble, worms in the intestines.

In fever cases, strawberries squeezed in water make a cooling, refreshing beverage. Delightful-tasting tea can be made from dried leaves of the wild strawberry. May and June are the best months to collect the leaves. At the same time, collect young blackberry leaves and young wood-roof leaves, and dry in the same way as the strawberry leaves. From a mixture of these three kinds of leaves you can produce a drink equal in taste and aroma to Chinese tea.

Young blackberry leaves possess the same taste as pure, good Chinese tea, and better than most other teas. Leaves must be put in a dry place, not in the sun, then stored for use in a closed jar. To make about 6 cups of tea, use as much as can be taken up with the tips of the fingers of one hand. Pour boiling water on it, and leave for 5 or 10 minutes. Add a little sugar, but no milk, and you have a very pleasant-tasting drink.

Honey

Honey is an excellent "pick-me-up" for older folk. It is laxative, purifying, strengthening. Mixed with tea, it is a remedy for catarrh and phlegm. It is also good for external sores if you take half-parts of honey and flour, and mix well together by adding a little water. Honey ointment should be thick, not fluid. Used internally, honey acts efficaciously in many other ailments.

If difficulty of swallowing is felt, boil a teaspoonful of honey with half-a-pint of water. This makes a delicious throat-gargle for singers; and if a drop is swallowed, there is no risk of tummy upset.

Honey-water is wonderful for the eyes as a purifier

and strengthener. Boil a teaspoonful of honey in half-a-pint of water for 5 minutes, and the decotion is ready for use.

Grandmother knew a man of over eighty who added a teaspoonful of pure honey to some boiling water, and allowed it to boil for a time. He soon had a tasty wine which was also invigorating. He used to say: "I owe my strength and vigorous old age to honey-wine." Its effects are aperient, purifying, nourishing and invigorating. It is reminiscent of the "mead" of ancient times.

Honey is excellent for healing ulcerated throat. Boil a spoonful of honey with two pints of water for a few minutes, then take 2 to 4 spoonsful of it every hour.

Half-a-spoonful of coriander boiled with a spoonful of honey in 2 pints of water. A spoonful taken hourly cleanses the stomach.

Weak, delicate children should be given a cupful or two of boiled milk daily to which has been added a little honey. Never use raw honey for a cough as it can be too sharp, but if boiled in either water or milk, the cough will be soothed or clear up completely.

Brandy Mixture

Take brandy and water—4 tablespoonsful each; 2 egg yolks, and a half-ounce of powdered white sugar. Beat the yolks and sugar together; add the spirit and water, flavour with grated cinnamon or nutmeg and you have a stimulant and restorative for anyone feeling run-down.

Adult dose is from one to three tablespoonsful repeated according to need. Children should be given a teaspoonful to a tablespoonful according to age.

White Wine Whey

Take a pint of milk, add mace, nutmeg and cinnamon, with sugar to taste. Boil until the milk is on the point of boiling. Remove and add in one or two wine-glassfuls of sherry or white wine. Put back on the boil, stirring gently one way until it curdles. Remove, and strain through a teacloth or some muslin. Make sure the patient is warmly tucked in bed, give him the White Wine Whey and it will make him perspire profusely. This is excellent for catarrh and influenza.

Wine Whey

Pour half-a-pint of sherry to a pint of boiling milk; stir thoroughly until it coagulates. Strain off the whey, and sweeten to taste.

Egg Nog

Beat an egg yolk with 6 oz. of milk. Add some brandy or whisky, and some sugar. Add a beaten egg white.

A tablespoonful of lime-water added to Wine Whey and Egg Nog makes them more easily digestible.

Egg Jelly

Take 3 new-laid eggs; separate whites from yolks, and beat separately. Dissolve half-an-ounce of isinglass in a quarter-pint of warm water and add the juice of half a lemon. Mix together and add 2 tablespoonsful of brandy. Pour into a mould, and cool.

Pish-Pash

For invalids, it comprises fresh meat cooked in rice. Cut a chicken into small pieces, place in a small pan, add 3 tablespoonsful of rice. Pour over it 2 breakfast-cupsful of cold water, and cook slowly. You can add spices during cooking. The rice part alone, which will have absorbed most of the strength of the meat, can be used if the patient is very ill.

Water-Souchy

Take 2 flounders, soles, whitings, or haddocks, and boil in a quart of water so that the fish are reduced to pulp. Strain, and removing the fins from 4 more fish, put them into the liquid. Add salt and cayenne pepper to taste and a little chopped parsley. Boil well and eat with the sauce. This is very digestible.

Macaroni Pudding

To 4 tablespoonsful of cinnamon water add 2 oz. macaroni. Simmer until the macaroni is tender. Add 3 egg yolks, white of an egg, an ounce sugar, drop of oil of bitter almonds, a glass of raisin wine, beaten into half-a-pint of milk. Bake in a slow oven.

Rice Pudding

Add 2 tablespoonsful of rice to a pint-and-a-half of milk and simmer until the rice is soft. Add 2 eggs, beaten with half-an-ounce of sugar. Bake for three quarters-of-an-hour in the oven.

Rice and Apples

Take some rice and boil quickly in hot water. Strain through a colander; expose for 15 minutes. Stew separately some apples; mix with the rice and sweeten to taste.

Rennet-Whey

Take a piece of rennet and infuse it in some boiling water, removing all soluble matter. After pouring off the liquid, take a tablespoonful of it, and mix with 3 tablespoonsful of milk. Place the mixture near heat, covering with a piece of clean cloth. When a uniform curd forms, remove it, divide into small pieces with a spoon, and separate the whey with gentle pressure. This is good for feverish conditions.

White Wine Whey

Put a-half-pint of new milk into a deep pan. Place on the stove and as soon as scum rises to the edge of the pan, pour in a glass of sherry, or other white wine, then sweeten with a teaspoonful of refined sugar. Boil again, stirring constantly, then place aside until the curd forms a lump. Strain the whey through a sieve or piece of muslin. It can be taken cold or tepid and is an excellent moderate stimulant.

Egg Brandy

Take 3 eggs and beat them with 5 oz. plain water. Slowly add 3 oz. of brandy, also a little sugar and nutmeg. Two tablespoonsful of this can be given at a time. This is good for prostration cases.

Another useful stimulant is made by taking the white of a new-laid egg and stirring with a tablespoonful of cream. Add a tablespoonful of brandy in which a lump of sugar has been dissolved.

Milk and Soda Water

Sweeten half-a-pint of milk with a teaspoonful of refined sugar. Bring almost to boiling point and pour over it a bottle of soda water. For stomach acidity, this is the way to administer milk.

Boiled Flour and Milk

Wheaten flour, kneaded with water, is put into a linen cloth and tied firmly. Next place in a pan of water and boil slowly for 12 hours. Dry, then take the thick rind away on removing the cloth, and again dry. A tablespoonful of this grated and boiled with a pint of milk, is excellent for recovery from diarrhoea or dysentery.

Boiled Bread Pudding

Pour a pint of hot milk over half-a-pound stale bread, and allow the mixture to soak for an hour in a covered basin. Beat with 2 eggs. Put it all into a covered basin, tie a cloth over it, and place in boiling water for half-an-hour. Eat with salt or sugar.

Batter Pudding

Beat the contents of 2 eggs with half-an-ounce of sugar. Mix this with a tablespoonful of wheaten flour and a pint of milk. Put in a basin of boiling water and boil with a cloth tied over it.

Tapioca Pudding

Make a pint of tapioca mucilage with milk. Beat 2 egg yolks with half-an-ounce of sugar, and stir into the mucilage. Bake in a slow oven. Sago and arrowroot can be made into similar puddings.

Mashed Carrots and Turnips

Peel the carrots and turnips; boil separately in 3 successive waters; press the water out through a clear, coarse cloth, mash together with sufficient milk to make into a pulp. Season with salt. Place before heat till the surface dries.

Vermicelli, or Macaroni Soup

To a quart of beef-tea boiled to a third, add an ounce of vermicelli or 2 oz. of macaroni previously well boiled in water. Boil the whole to one pint. Add salt to taste. Instead of vermicelli or macaroni, you can use rice. It should be added to the soup after its concentration. Previously prepare the rice by boiling and slightly drying.

Chicken Broth

Beat the yolk of an egg with 2 oz. of water. Add with parsley or celery to chicken tea, and boil to a half. Rice, vermicelli, or macaroni, fully boiled, can be mixed in.

Mutton Broth with Vegetables

Slowly boil in a pan for 2 hours a pound of fat-free mutton chops. Remove the chops, and to the remainder add 3 carrots and 3 turnips, peeled, sliced, boiled, with the water drained, plus 2 onions, sliced and boiled. Season with salt and celery. Simmer slowly for 4 hours. Put the chops in again, and simmer for another hour.

Tripe

Boil some onions in 2 waters, and partially boil some tripe. Boil together slowly till the tripe is soft and tender. Add salt and a few grains of cayenne pepper. Tripe is easily digested and very good for a convalescent.

Grit-gruel

Wash grits in cold water. Pour off the fluid and add fresh cold water. Boil slowly, until the water is reduced by half. Strain through a sieve. An ounce-and-a-half of grits should make a pint of gruel.

Oatmeal Gruel

Take 2 or 3 tablespoonsful of oatmeal and rub in a basin with a little cold water. Repeat the process, adding fresh water each time until milkiness stops reaching the water. Put the washings into a pan, and boil till a thick mucilage forms. These gruels contain more nourishment than sago, arrowroot, or tapioca, as they contain a small quantity of gluten. Sweeten and mix with milk, if preferred.

Iceland Moss Jelly

Iceland moss contains a bitter principle which should be cleared before use. To do this, pound dry; soak in tepid water with a little bicarbonate of soda for 24 hours, then press in a coarse cloth. Add an ounce of the prepared moss to a quart of water and let the mixture boil to a half. Strain through a sieve, and sweeten, or mix with milk, according to taste.

More die by food than famine

Diet cures more than the lancet

Feed sparingly and defy the physician

Cheese is a peevish elf:
It digests everything but itself

We seldom repent of having eaten too little

Better lose a supper than gain a hundred physicians

Many a pie has cost an industrious husband a twenty-pound note in doctor's bills; and many a human life has paid for an apple dumpling

Over exertion, or anxiety of mind, disturbs digestion infinitely more than fatigue of body—the brain demands a much more abundant supply of the animal spirits than is required for the excitement of mere legs and arms

5

Grannie's Invalid Drinks

Invalid Orgeat

BEAT 2 oz. of almonds with a teaspoonful of organe-flower water and a bitter almond or two. Pour a quart of milk and water to the paste. Sweeten with sugar or capillaire. This is good for those with a tender chest. It is also good for gout. By adding half-an-ounce gum arabic, it allays the pain.

Cranberry Drink

Mash a teacupful of cranberries into a cup of water. Boil 2 quarts of water with a large spoonful of oatmeal and a bit of lemon peel. Add the cranberries and some sugar, then about ¼ pint of sherry, or less. Boil the whole for half-an-hour and strain off.

Egg Milks

Beat a fresh-laid egg, and mix well with ¼-pint of warm

milk, a tablespoonful of capillaire, the same of rosewater, and a little scraped nutmeg. Do not warm it after the egg is mixed in. Take first thing in the morning and last thing at night and it will be found strengthening and particularly helpful for anyone suffering from a cough.

Add the beaten yolks of 3 eggs to 2 tablespoonsful of powdered white sugar, 3 cloves, the rind of half-a-lemon, and half-a-pint brandy. Pour over it a quart of warm milk, stirring rapidly. Serve immediately.

Convalescent Strengthening Drink

Beat an egg white to a froth, then beat the yolk in a tablespoonful of cold water. Put a tablespoonful of cold water in a wineglass, add a tablespoonful of sherry, then make it hot. Pour in the egg, stir constantly, put in a saucepan and on a slow flame. Stir one way till it thickens. Do not let it boil. When hot, put in the whipped white to set. The drink can be taken hot or cold.

Parsley Tea

Stimulates the kidneys and is good for rheumatism. Take a handful of freshly gathered leaves or a tablespoonful of dried parsley, and wash in cold running water. Put into an earthenware jug and pour over a pint of boiling water. Cover the jug with a cloth. Let it get cold, then strain into a glass jug. Drink plenty of it an hour before meals.

Peppermint Tea

Infuse a large handful of mint leaves in $\frac{1}{2}$-pint of boiling water, then add a teaspoonful of honey. A wine-glassful taken hot at bedtime is excellent for a cold.

For cases of nausea and flatulence, add an ounce of mint leaves to a pint of boiling water. Let stand till cold, strain, and take a wine-glassful frequently.

Betany Tea

Gathered when about to flower, Betany has the taste of tea when brewed the same way. It cures headaches.

Hawthorn Tea

Mix hawthorn leaves together with one part of balm and sage. They make an excellent and pleasant sanative tea, particularly good for nervous people.

Irish Moss Jelly

An ounce of carrageen, or Irish moss, should be boiled in a pint-and-a-half water, then sweeten and acidulate, or mix with milk as in Iceland Moss Jelly.

Ground Rice Milk

Mix a tablespoonful of ground rice with a pint-and-a-half milk, add half-an-ounce candied lemon-peel cut into slices, boil for half-an-hour; strain while hot. This is nutritious during acute disease and early convalescence.

Rice Milk

Boil a tablespoonful of ground rice with a pint-and-a-half milk, or equal parts of milk and water. Stir smooth, and boil 2 minutes. Flavour with sugar and nutmeg. Very nourishing for children.

Bread Panada

Grate a piece of stale bread and mix into sufficient water to form a thick pulp. Cover, and after it has soaked an hour, beat with 2 tablespoonsful of milk and a little sugar, then boil for 10 minutes, stirring constantly.

Sago

Add a tablespoonful of the best sago to a pint of water, and let it stand for two hours, then boil for a quarter-of-an-hour, stirring constantly until it forms a clear, uniform jelly.

Remove from the stove, and flavour with sugar, nutmeg, as in the case of arrowroot. Instead of water you can use milk. Sago is frequently employed where a non-stimulating diet is required.

Sago Milk

Soak an ounce of sago in a pint of water for an hour. Pour off the water and add a pint-and-a-half milk. Boil slowly until the sago is well incorporated with the milk.

Sago Posset

Put 2 tablespoonsful of sago into a pint of water and boil until a mucilage forms. Take lemon rind and rub a quarter-ounce of loaf sugar on it. Put in with half-a-teaspoonful of tincture of ginger into 5 oz. of sherry wine. Add the mixture to the sago mucilage and boil 5 minutes. A wine-glassful may be taken at a time and is excellent for debility from acute diseases of a non-inflammatory nature.

Tapioca

Prepare the same as sago, only, being more soluble in water, it requires half the time for maceration and boiling. Sweeten and flavour like sago.

Tous-les-mois

This should be prepared like arrowroot. It has the same value.

Motherwort Tea

A full tablespoonful of dried motherwort should be put in a jug and poured over a cupful of boiling water. Cover the jug with a cloth and leave to cool. Strain, then divide into two doses and take at half-hour intervals. This is a good stimulant for tired mental workers.

Sage Tea

Boil equal parts of sage, rosemary, honeysuckle and plantain in water. Be sure the water covers. Add a tablespoonful of honey to each pint of liquid and use as required. This makes a good hairwash; a gargle for sore throat, or will heal a sore mouth.

Yarrow Tea

Brew as you would ordinary tea with a tablespoonful each of dried leaves mixed with dried elder-flowers. Drink hot on retiring if you have a bad cold.

Lime Water

Excellent to give children with their milk when there is tendency to acidity, or when the bowels are too relaxed. A tablespoonful should be mixed with 3 tablespoonsful of milk.

Apple Water

Slice 2 large apples and pour a quart boiling water on them. Strain in 2 or 3 hours, and sweeten with honey.

Linseed Tea

Take 2 drachms of bruised liquorice-root and an ounce of linseed, and put into a pint of boiling water. Allow the jug to stand near a warm stove for 4 hours, then strain through muslin or calico. Don't bruise the linseed. This is good for coughs.

Egg Wine

Beat an egg (yolk and white) with a tablespoonful of cold water. Pour on it a mixture of a glass of sherry or white wine, and half-a-glass of water previously heated together (not boiling), stirring all the time. Sweeten with white sugar, and add a little grated nutmeg, to taste. Taken in this form it is more digestible, but flavour is improved by heating ingredients in saucepan (not to boiling), stirring one way for a minute till they thicken. With a slice of toast or biscuit, this can be advantageously taken by invalids twice daily.

Egg wine, made as above, without warming the egg, is lighter on the stomach, but isn't so pleasant.

Lemon Wheys

Pour as much lemon juice into boiling milk as will make a small quantity quite clear. Dilute with hot water to an agreeable acid, and put in a lump or two of sugar. This promotes perspiration.

Egg Emulsion

Rub a yolk of 2 eggs and a little sugar with a pint of cold

water. Add afterwards a glass of wine and a little lemon juice for flavour. This is very restorative in cases of debility, and for recovery from severe illness when mild stimulation is required. With wine, the emulsion is as good for coughs, hoarseness, and constipation.

Toast and Water

Slowly toast a thin piece of bread until extremely brown and hard. Plunge it into a jug of cold water and cover for an hour before use. It should be a brown colour before drinking and is good for weak bowels.

Toast Water

Toast very brown, one pint of white or brown bread-crusts. Add a pint of cold water, and let stand an hour. Strain, then add cream and sugar.

Apple Tea

Roast 2 large sour apples and cover with boiling water. Cool and strain, pour, and add sugar to taste.

Rice Water

Two tablespoonsful of rice; one quart of cold water; cook an hour, or until dissolved. Add salt and sugar to taste.

Flaxseed Lemonade

Pour a quart of boiling water over 4 tablespoonsful of cold flaxseed. Steep 3 hours, strain, add juice of 3 lemons, and sweeten to taste.

Orange Whey

The juice of an orange to a pint of sweetened milk. Heat slowly until curds form. Strain and cool.

Egg Lemonade

Take the white of an egg, one tablespoonful of pulverised sugar, juice of one lemon, one glass of water, then beat together.

Baked Milk

Put half-a-gallon of milk in a jar, and tie it down with paper. Let it stand in a moderate oven 8 or 10 hours. It will be like cream, and very nutritious.

Cranberry Jelly Juice

Mix cranberry jelly with cold water.

Redcurrant Whisky

For a cold, add a little redcurrant jelly to a glass of hot whisky punch. Drink before going to sleep.

Cooling Draught

Fifteen grs. of sulphate of magnesia, 20 grs. sulphate of soda, 2 drs. syrup of orange peel, and 2 oz. distilled water. Taken every morning before breakfast for a week, soothes skin irritation.

Lemonade

Hot, strong lemonade at bedtime will often break-up a bad cold.

Imperial Drink

To a quart of boiling water add 2 teaspoonsful cream of tartar, the juice of 2 lemons, and sweeten with honey or sugar. It should be ice-cold.

Barley-water

Add one tablespoonful of pearl barley to a pint of water, and boil for a few minutes, stirring constantly to wash the grain. Pour off the water, and add one pint-and-a-half of clean water; simmer gently for an hour, and strain. Sugar and lemon juice may be added. Extremely good for colds and other illnesses.

Beef Essence

Take a pound of gravy beef, free from skin and fat, and chop fine. Mix with 3 tablespoonsful of water and pound it.

Allow to soak for 2 hours. Put into a covered earthen jar with a little salt. The edges of the jar should be sealed and a cloth tied over the top. The jar should be placed in a pot half-full of boiling water, and kept on the stove 4 hours. Now strain through a coarse sieve, so that the fluid and the smaller solid particles of the meat can pass. Two teaspoonsful or more can be given at a time for serious debility.

Beef Tea

Take a pound of beefsteak or gravy beef free from fat; mince or cut into small pieces; put in a well-covered jar with a pint-and-a-half of cold water or barley-water. Now place the jar in a saucepan of water and simmer for 3 hours, or leave the jar in a not too hot oven overnight. Strain, and remove fat.

Or, take some good-quality gravy beef or beefsteak, beat well, rub pepper and salt over it, place on a flat tin punched with small holes (an onion grater could be used), pour some port wine over the meat, then cover with a plate and place some weights on it.

Increase the weights a couple of times to help press all the juice from the meat.

Chicken Tea

Take a small chicken. Remove the skin and fat between the muscles, divided into two long halves. Remove the lungs and everything adhering to the backbone and chest walls; cut into thin slices. Place the slices in a pan with some salt, then pour over it a quart of boiling water. Cover the pan and boil slowly 2 hours. Allow to stand for half-an-hour, strain off the fluid through a sieve. Beef-tea and chicken-tea are excellent during sickness if animal diet is admissible, and, by adding flour, or other thickening substance, are good convalescence nourishment.

Mutton Tea

A pound of mutton, free from fat, should be cut into thin slices. Pour a pint-and-a-half of water over it, allowing it to macerate, as in beef-tea. Afterward, boil for half-an-hour and strain.

Veal Tea

A pound of fillet of veal, free from fat, should be sliced, then boiled for half-an-hour in a pint-and-a-half of boiling water.

Stokos

Put ¾ lb. fine oatmeal, 6 oz. sugar, and half-a-lemon cut into slices into a pan. Mix together with a little warm water. Add a gallon of boiling water, stir thoroughly, and use cold. This is a very nourishing drink, as is the next suggestion.

Cokos

Mix into a thin batter 6 oz. of sugar, 6 oz. of fine oatmeal, 4 oz. of cocoa. Add a gallon boiling water; put into a stone bottle and cork. This is a very good drink after strenuous athletics or exercise.

Mustard Bath

And, for the convalescent, a *mustard bath* is also an excellent stimulant. Two tablespoonsful of mustard are required for every gallon of water in the bath. The mustard should first be made into a paste in a basin, then gradually added to the water in the bath. Temperature 100° F.

Eat a bit before you drink

Be temperate in all things

Eat at pleasure, drink by measure

He that goes to bed thirsty rises healthy

Temperance is reason's girdle and passion's bridle

The intemperate die young and rarely enjoy old age

Against diseases here the strongest fence
Is the defensive virtue abstinence

All sick people want to get well, but not always in the best way. Said a wealthy man, Doctor, strike at the root of the disease, and smash went the decanter under the faithful physician's cane

6

Grannie's Keep-Fit Rules

REVENTION, Grannie believed, was better even than her own well-tried remedies. She had small patience with invalids who had, as she put it, "brought their troubles on themselves." Her favourite rules, as she recorded them, were simple and effective.

Hints for Health

Never lean the back against anything cold.

Never begin a journey till breakfast has been eaten.

Never take warm drinks and go straight into the cold.

Keep the back, especially between the shoulders, well-covered, and the chest well protected.

Never go to bed with cold or wet feet.

Bathe daily to keep the skin in active condition, and the pores well open.

Never ride in an open carriage or on a bicycle when warm from exercise.

When hoarse, speak as little as possible until the hoarseness has gone.

When sleeping in a cold place, breathe through the nose, and keep your mouth shut.

When going from a hot atmosphere into a cold one, keep the mouth closed so that the air may be warmed in ·its passage through the nose before it reaches the lungs.

Never stand on ice or snow where there is too much exposure to cold wind.

Never stand still in cold weather, especially after exercise.

When sewing or writing, change position from time to time.

*   *   *

My grandmother used to tell me of the experiences of a Mr. George Catlin, an American artist. During years of association with American Indian tribes, he concluded that one of the main causes of ailments affecting civilised peoples is their habit of breathing through the mouth.

The Indian child, he observed, was never allowed to sleep with its mouth open. The mother always pressed the baby's lips together as soon as it fell asleep, to form a lasting habit. So, when the child grew, sleeping or waking, it kept its mouth shut. Mr. Catlin claimed that this habit was the reason why native races of North and South America used to enjoy such good physical perfection and escape so many of the diseases of civilised communities. Among millions of natives, he never saw or heard of a hunchback or crooked spine, or an idiot or lunatic, and premature death was also uncommon.

It is plain that nostrils are for breathing, and are the natural outlet of the lungs. The sides of the air passages are lined with hairs which, to some degree, prevent ingress of noxious matters. You are healthier if you breathe through the nose. Some people who lived in malarious districts for years without suffering from any of the fevers that haunt such neighbourhoods, ascribe their exemption entirely to the habit of breathing properly. Air comes in contact with the membranes of the nose, and these are supposed to have some power of neutralising malarious and contagious poisons. It is also to be noticed that, by drawing in our breath only through the nostrils, the air is warmed by contact with the membranes before it reaches the lungs, and so inflammation and congestion of these organs are avoided.

Perfect sleep cannot be obtained with the mouth open. "Contrast," said Mr. Catlin, "the natural repose of the Indian child, educated to keep its lips closed, with the uncomfortable slumbers of the child of civilisation, with its little mouth wide open and gasping for breath. The firmly shut mouth, too, promotes good looks. Who ever yet saw an open mouth that was not insipid and unattractive? Keep your mouth shut, then, when you read, when you write, when you listen, when you are in pain, when you are walking, when you are running, and by all means when you are angry."

All crooked or constrained bodily positions affect respiration. Reading, writing, sitting, standing, speaking, or working with the trunk of the body bent forward is extremely hurtful, by overstretching the muscles of the back, compressing the lungs, and pushing downward and backward the stomach, bowels, and abdominal muscles.

There is no time of life at which warmth is of more

importance than in infancy. To plunge a child into cold water, with the idea of making it hardy, as is done in some countries, and even in our own, by some ignorant people, is the height of cruelty and folly. Bowel complaints, croup, and convulsions are likely to result.

A baby should be kept at a temperature above what is suitable for an adult. It should be warmly, but not heavily, clothed.

The room in which it is kept should be maintained at a good but not oppressive heat, and it should never be put into other than tepid water.

Sea-sickness

To prevent sea-sickness, eat well before starting. If sickness comes, it is far better not to retch on an empty stomach. When sea-sickness is prolonged, one of the safest things to take is the white of an egg, beaten in cold water. This will pave the way for a whole egg, with the addition of a little brandy.

Bovril is also good and also, with Brand's essence of chicken, to eat cold.

There's nothing better than antipyrine tablets. Don't take too many, and choose a seat near the centre of the craft to prevent sea-sickness. A teaspoonful of Worcester sauce often relieves.

Cucaine is also very good for sea-sickness. A teaspoonful of a solution of cucaine of the strength of one-in-a-thousand, administered every 2 or 3 hours. For children, give half-drachm doses.

Slimming

To slim, it is necessary to reverse the process by which slim persons become fat. The main principle is withdrawal from the diet of food, such as bread, potatoes, sugar, fat and butter. But diminish the quantities, not suddenly leave off anything to which you have been accustomed for years.

Here is a good diet to follow:

Breakfast (about 8.30 a.m.): Four or 5 ounces of kidneys, boiled fish, bacon, or cold meat (pork or veal excepted), or 2 eggs (not hard-boiled), a large cup of tea or coffee (with neither milk nor sugar), a little biscuit, or an ounce of dried toast, brown bread, or crust off a loaf.

Lunch (about 1 p.m.): Five or 6 ounces of fish (any sort, except salmon, herrings, or eels), any meat (pork or veal excepted), any vegetable (except potatoes, parsnips, beetroot, turnips or carrots), an ounce of dry toast, a crust cut from the loaf, fruit out of the pudding (omit the sugar), any kind of game or poultry, and 2 glasses of dry sherry, or 3 of good, sound claret (no champagne, port or beer to be taken).

Tea (about 5 p.m.): Two or 3 ounces of fruit, a rusk or two, and a cup of tea (without milk or sugar).

Dinner (about 8.30 p.m.): Three or 4 ounces of fish or meat, and a glass or two of wine, if you like.

It is always well for the busy man, who has rushed home to his dinner, to pause a quarter-of-an-hour or so before sitting down to it. Fatigue is not good for digestion.

"A man's body and his mind are like a jerkin and a jerkin's lining; rumple the one, you rumple the other." Brain and stomach must be free from any mutual disturbance, for either to perform functions properly. A state of gentle and pleasurable excitement of the mind is favourable to digestion. "Chatted food," according to the old proverb, "is half digested."

Athletic Training Diet

For athletic training the object is to reduce the fat and

increase the size and hardness of the muscles and the power of endurance. The finest food for athletes is:

Lean and rare beef or mutton
Stale flour bread
Potatoes and other vegetables, in moderation
Tea, coffee, beer or wine, in great moderation.

As this kind of diet contains little or no fat, and little starch or sugar, it cannot feed fatty tissue. Its leading element is nitrogen, which is contained in the beef and mutton. The quantity of tea or coffee allowed is limited to not more than a cup at each meal. Tea is preferable to coffee. Only a glass or two of beer or wine is permissible.

Dyspepsia

To enjoy a good appetite and eat 3 meals a day without discomfort is a blessing, yet millions in good health cannot eat a meal without it being followed by painful dyspepsia. Dyspepsia, grandmother assured us, can be cured, and avoided, by sticking to these rules:

Eat three times a day
No between-meal snacks
*Nothing after lunch except a biscuit or slice of bread
    and butter, and a cup of hot drink*
Spend at least half-an-hour at each meal
Cut up all the food into small pieces
*Never eat so much as to cause the slightest
    uncomfortable sensation afterwards*
*Try not to work or study hard within half-an-hour
    of eating.*

If there is one rule on eating about which most agree, it is that meals should be taken at regular periods. People may differ about what they eat, but you never meet people who say it is as well to take 2 meals today and 5 tomorrow; to take dinner at 1 o'clock today, 3 tomorrow, and 5 next day.

Grandmother used to say that dyspeptics should avoid the following errors: Never weaken the digestive organs by giving them too little to do. Never confine themselves to coarse, loosening foods.

Essential to cure dyspepsia is exercise and particularly out-door exercise.

Those whose health is generally good can cure mild stomach upsets by total abstinence. Abstinence is easily best for disorders arising from indigestion and intemperance.

A king of Persia sent to a tribe of Bedouins a celebrated physician, who inquired how they lived. "We never eat till we are hungry, and then not to repletion," was the answer. "I may retire, then," said the doctor; "I have no business here."

And then there was the famous nobleman who called on a great physician and surgeon. "Doctor, I wish you would examine this eye; I fear some deadly mischief is at work here."

"If you will sit there in my patient's chair, and let me do the talking I will soon find out what is the matter with you." After a few questions, the doctor concluded:

"Your difficulty is not where you think it is, in your eye, but"—pointing his finger at the patient's enormous abdomen—"it is there, in your kitchen. Of course, when the kitchen is out of order, the garret and all the other rooms in the house are likely to be more or less affected. Now all you need to do is to clean the kitchen, and your garret will require no special purification. Your lordship must do as the famous Duke of Wellington did on a well-known occasion—cut off the supplies and the enemy will leave the citadel."

A woman was cured of severe dyspepsia with hard bread and beer. She said: "A German physician was called in; but heart and stomach were on a strike, and refused to assimilate food. In great perplexity, he said: 'Can you take beer?' I could try, and he went on to prescribe:

'You get the General to get you some coot peer, fresh from the prewery. Dake von leetle half-a-glass mit a pit of hart pread and leetle pit uv cheese. Chew de pread slow, and sip de peer. Do not culp it like some beebles do—schust sip schlow, and eat the pread and cheese mit it. I dinks maype dat set de stoomach do vork vonce more!' "

The prescription worked like a charm.

* * *

In the latter part of the last century, a New York man attained so high a reputation for curing dyspepsia that he obtained 500 dollars for each case he undertook, payable in advance. Patients were bound by solemn oath not to reveal his treatment; after his death many, considering themselves free from their obligation, revealed the secret. It mainly consisted in slapping the abdomen or bowels with the palms of the hand for 5 or 10 minutes on rising in the morning; for a quarter-of-an-hour or more about 11 o'clock; in the forenoon, and in the evening before retiring. This is excellent for chronic indigestion. Rubbing and kneading is a very old idea.

In addition to slapping and kneading the abdomen, and exercising freely out of doors, a dyspeptic should eat only when hungry, select digestible food and chew it well. Dyspepsia can also be cured by living on egg yolks beaten with potatoes and water. Try this: Beat an egg in a bowl; add 6 tablespoonsful of cold water; mix the whole together; add 2 tablespoonsful of the farina of potatoes mixed thoroughly with the liquor in the bowl. Pour in as much boiling water as will convert the whole into a jelly. Mix well.

Take it either alone or with a little milk and sugar, not only for breakfast but for stomach debility and at other meals. The dish is light, easily digested, extremely nourishing. Bread or biscuits may be eaten with it as the stomach condition improves.

After dinner sit awhile :
after supper walk a mile . . .

Alternate rest and labour long endure

An ounce of prevention is worth a pound of cure

Go to bed with the lamb and rise with the lark

One hour's sleep before midnight is worth two after

Early to bed and early to rise
Make a man healthy, wealthy and wise

The only rule for a rich man to be healthy is by exercise
and abstinence to live as if he were poor

Employment is Nature's physician, and is essential
to human happiness

Be not solitary; be not idle

7

Grannie's Sickness Remedies

RUNNING through Grannie's legacy of notebooks, it is difficult to believe that there was
any disease or ailment with which she had not
done battle in her time. Some of her remedies
were too spartan for inclusion here; a few appear to have
no firmer basis than superstition, and the recovery of the
patient doubtless owed more to Grannie's firmness of
purpose than to her medication. Nevertheless, in the
majority of cases, "it worked."

Abscesses and Sores

Make a yeast poultice by mixing 5 oz. of yeast with an
equal quantity of hot water; with these stir up a pound
of flour to make a poultice, place it on the stove until it
swells, then use. This is a stimulating, emollient poultice.

Ankles (sprained)

Take some caraway seeds, pound, and place into a tin basin with a little water. Put on the stove and stir till the mixture thickens, then bind on the ankle. It will ease pain and inflammation.

Or, foment with warm vinegar, 4 or 5 minutes every 4 hours.

Or, shower hot water poured from a few feet over it.

Ankles (weak)

Take a raw oyster in the palm of right hand, and massage the ankles with it until the oyster is almost rubbed away. Do this every evening at bedtime, and the ankles will become stronger.

Asthma

Cut an ounce of stick liquorice into slices. Steep for 24 hours in a quart of water and drink when you are worse than usual.

For asthma, the best drink is apple water—boiling water poured on sliced apples.

Food should be light and easily digestible. Ripe fruits baked, boiled, or roasted, are good; but strong liquor, especially beer or ale, are bad. Supper should be very light.

Baldness

The best baldness preventive is care of the hair during ill-health.

The head should be washed at least once a week. An egg yolk, or a piece of quillaia bark, may be added to the water to produce a lather.

Or, put 4 lb. of unadulterated honey into a still, with 12 handfuls of the tendrils of vines and the same quantity of rosemary-tops. Distil as cool and as slowly as possible.

The liquor may be allowed to drop till it begins to taste sour.

Or, use a pomade made of one part of pilocarpine in 200 parts of petroleum jelly. Regularly used, it will prevent baldness and give great glossiness to the hair.

When the hair is thin, to restore the scalp to a healthy condition, scurf should be cured by bathing with tepid water night and morning, plus the constant application of glycerine and lime-water in between. No fats or oils should be used at this stage as they are liable to go rancid and irritate the scalp still more. Glycerine and lime-water, or fresh olive oil and lime-water, may be used.

A good compound for gentle action on the hair follicles is obtained by adding a few drops of tincture of cantharides to toilet vinegar, then gently damping the scalp after washing well with the compound.

If you are already far gone, you may revive some hair roots by brushing the scalp till redness and a warm glow are produced, then rubbing into the roots of the hair the following lotion: 2 oz. of Eau de Cologne, 2 drs. of tincture of cantharides, 10 drops of oil of lavender, and the same of rosemary. Apply to the head once or twice daily.

Bed-wetting

The child should be prevented from sleeping on its back by threading an empty reel of cotton with tape, and attaching it to the back of the nightdress over the loins. The bed-covering should be light. Iron is beneficial in many cases.

Boils

As soon as a boil appears, bathe it with repeated and continuous applications of ice-cold water, and apply carbolic, camphor, iodine, or solution of caustic. If the boil is obstinate, bring to a head with poultices of camomile flowers.

Boils can result from over-rich diet, or from being run down. For the first, rhubarb, black draught, magnesia, with restricted diet, should be taken. For the second, tonic foods and medicines, soups, fish, eggs, milk, etc., with cod liver oil and mild iron preparations.

Half a wine-glassful of fresh yeast, taken night and morning, often acts like a charm in stopping the formation of fresh crops of boils.

A grain of sulphide of calcium, taken three times a day as a pill, is good.

The boils should be frequently bathed with very hot water, or painted with tincture of iodine or glycerine of belladonna, once or twice daily. If this doesn't succeed, constant poulticing is needed to bring them to a head. After breaking, they should be covered with a piece of lint thickly smeared with salicylic ointment, and fomented frequently with hot water.

Body Odour

Wash twice a day with carbolic or coal tar soap, dry, then dust with boracic acid. The powder should be thoroughly rubbed into the skin. Change stockings twice a day, and they should be dipped in boracic lotion and hung to dry. Inside of shoe and the feet of the stockings should be freely dusted with boracic whenever they are worn. If perspiration is profuse, cork-soles should be worn inside your shoes. The soles should be soaked in boracic lotion, then dried. An iron tonic is also helpful.

Bowel Complaints

A little camphor dissolved with a little clove oil is an excellent remedy for incipient bowel complaints. Repeated doses of a few drops at a time should be taken.

Breath

Rinse mouth and throat with 10 grs. of carbolic acid to

1 oz. of water, 1 dr. each of tincture of calamus and tincture orris root, 1 oz. spirit of nutmeg and 2 oz. of rosewater. For impure breath arising from weakness, a tonic should be taken as well; made of equal parts of wild cherry and cinchona bark.

For acidity of stomach causing bad breath, drink a glass of cold water every morning before getting out of bed, and a glass of hot water before going to bed at night. Rinse the teeth and mouth and gargle the throat well, morning and evening, with a few drops of Condy's ozonised water, in plain water. After each meal take a powder containing 10 grs. powdered vegetable charcoal and 5 grs. of bicarbonate of soda.

Bronchitis

The following prescription is recommended: Carbonate of ammonia 35grs., ipecacuanha wine 2 drs., spirit of choroform 1 dr. (1 to 7), paregoric 2 drs., water ad 8 oz. Mix and take one tablespoonful three times a day, or oftener if the cough is troublesome.

Bilious

Before going to bed take a gill of hot water and the juice of a lemon.

Blackheads

Wash with good soap several times a day. Afterwards rinse the soap off and dry with a rough, coarse towel. Take plenty of exercise and avoid rich food.

Blushing

Take half a wine-glassful of compound infusion of gentian twice a day.

Bunions

Shoe pressure must be avoided.

Paint them every second day with iodine till the soreness disappears.

Alternatively, belladonna and glycerine can be painted on.

Camphor Inhalations

Pour half-a-pint of boiling-hot water over a drachm of pulverised camphor, and inhale the vapours for 10 to 20 minutes. This gives great relief for a cold.

Carbuncle

Treatment must be both constitutional and local. Strength must be kept up by giving raw eggs, cream, milk, beef-tea, mutton-chops.

Alcohol should be given with the food, but over-stimulation must be guarded against. The bowels must be kept open.

Painting the surface with tincture of iodine three times a day hastens the formation of the openings in the skin, but if the pain is severe, painting with belladonna and glycerine, and hot compresses of dry wool, give more relief.

Hot fomentations are best avoided, as they encourage the formation of boils. When the openings form, a wet dressing of boracic lint the exact size of the swelling may be applied, covered with cotton wool and changed frequently.

When the discharge has diminished, the salicylic ointment dressing may be used.

Castor Oil

The best method for taking it is to float it on milk and, before taking, eat a piece of orange or lemon peel.

Catarrh

Take 25 parts roasted coffee, 1 part menthol, 25 parts of sugar, grind them together to a fine powder, and use as snuff. Glykaline is also beneficial.

Chapped Hands

Take the fat of mutton, melt and strain, and pour it into a basin to harden. Before it is hard, work it into a ball. To apply it, first hold before a fire until the surface is soft, then rub this soft tallow on the chaps, working it gently into the skin.

Or, mix a ¼ lb. of unsalted hog's lard, which has been washed in spring water and then rosewater, with the yolks of 2 new-laid eggs and a large spoonful of honey. Add as much fine oatmeal or almond-paste as will work into a paste.

Always dry the hands thoroughly after washing.

You can alternatively rub in boracic ointment or simple lanoline. Glycerine is effective in some cases, but causes much smarting.

Chapped Lips

Put a ¼-oz. of gum-benjamin, storax and spermaceti, some Alkanet-root, a chopped apple, bunch of bruised black grapes, a ¼-lb. unsalted butter and 2 oz. of bees-wax into a new tin saucepan. Simmer gently till the wax, etc., is dissolved, then strain through a linen cloth. When cold, melt again, and pour into small pots or boxes; or, if to make cakes, use the bottoms of teacups.

Charcoal Powders

This often arrests putrid sores. It is placed above the dressings, and, not infrequently, quilted loosely in a little cotton wool.

Chilblains on Hands

In France, to treat this condition they take a piece of alum about the size of a nut, and melt it in enough hot water to cover the hands. When the alum is melted, soak your hands in the liquid for nearly a quarter-of-an-hour, then cover your hands at once with gloves, which you keep on all night, and as long as you can manage to do so during the day.

Chilblains

If they are broken, mix 2 fluid ounces of tincture of catechu, one ounce of honey, and 7 oz. of water, and treat them with this mixture.

You should do some active exercise, such as skipping, for a few minutes before going to bed and directly they are dressed in the morning.

Chilblain Liniment

Mix together 2 oz. of methylated chloroform, 8 grains of cocaine hydrochlorate, 3 oz. of compound camphor liniment, 5 oz. of liniment of soap, colour with cochineal, and filter.

Chilblain Ointment

Take 20 minims of oil of lavender, 10 minims liquid carbolic acid, and 1 oz. of oxide of zinc ointment, mix together to make an ointment, and apply at night.

For broken chilblains, take black oxide of iron bole and oil of turpentine, each 1 dr., rub together and add mixture to 1 oz. melted resin cerate.

A Russian remedy is to dry the peel of cucumbers and, when required, soften the inner part with water and apply to the affected part.

Colds

In the earliest stages, such old-fashioned, time-honoured remedies as a hot mustard foot-bath, hot sleeping draughts, or the like, taken to provoke abundant sweating, are excellent, but must be taken at the outset to do good.

An old piece of cold-prevention advice called for habitual, persistent attention to the following rules:

"Walk with the toes turned outward. Walk with the chin slightly above the horizontal line, as if looking at the top of a man's hat in front of you, or at the eaves or roof of a house. Walk a good deal with your hands behind you. Sit with the lower part of your spine pressed against the chair-back."

Keep handy an inhaler. Add 5 drops of eucalyptus oil to the water in the inhaler; inhale for 7 minutes, drawing the gas up through the mouth and letting it out through the nostrils, and afterwards through each nostril in turn.

Five drops of spirit of camphor, on sugar, will often prevent a cold if taken at once.

To relieve a chest cold, wring out a piece of flannel in boiling water, and sprinkle it with turpentine and lay it on the chest.

To cure a head cold, inhale constantly with chloride of ammonium in which 4 drops of oil of eucalyptus have been put.

There are many ways in which a cold may be arrested. A good dose of quinine, 6 to 10 grs., is an effective remedy. Bathe the feet in hot water and drink a pint of hot lemonade, after which sponge with hot water and stay in a warm room, and bathe the face constantly with hot water.

Snuff hot water up the nostrils every 3 hours.

Inhale ammonia or menthol.

Take 4 hours' active exercise in the open air.

More than a century ago, the web of the black spider was thought to cure ague. Cobwebs were a popular remedy for fever.

In some country districts, there are still many folk who believe that swallowing a spider will cure them. Pepper is also a popular remedy, and many take a teaspoonful of pepper in a glass of gin.

Grandmother knew a man who claimed to have cured himself of the 'flu by putting into his boots a half-gill of hot whisky and putting the boots instantly on. The very first day he tried it the fever came as usual, but there was no chill; the second day the symptoms were modified; and after the third application there was no return of fever.

He said: "I well remember, when a boy, there being a tavern in our neighbourhood where teamsters stopped to rest and water their horses, of seeing the carters instead of drinking their half-gill of whisky, pouring it into their boots cold, as a protection against the frost. They told me there was nothing equal to it to warm the feet; that it was better than fire, for the feet remained warm for a long time and prevented sickness. It is also excellent for a cold, or when from exposure, the feet got wet or damp, and a cold or other disease may be apprehended. I have known it to act like a charm."

When it comes to generally looking after health, many notable men have been convinced that habitual moderation in eating and drinking was essential to the full and healthy employment of their intellect. Sir Isaac Newton, when he applied himself to the investigation of light and colour, to quicken his faculties and enable him to fix his attention, confined himself all the time to a small quantity of bread, with a little sack-and-water. He took a little whenever he felt his strength flag.

Grandmother used to point out that some will wrap

the head on going to bed in a flannel nightcap, and take a glass of negus warm, whey, or gruel: another will take a tumbler of cold water with or without a spoonful of sal volatile. A very good way to stop catarrh on its accession is to go to bed early, to take a warm drink with a mild aperient pill, half-an-ounce Epsom salts, or a Seidlitz powder, early the following morning.

Generally, an abstemious diet should be observed, and drinks such as barley-water, freely taken. A mild aperient should be administered—a dose of compound senna mixture, followed by a dose of saline mixture, and at bed-time, 5 grains of Dover's powder taken and the legs bathed as high as the knees in warm water for 10 minutes. If the catarrh is severe, it is better to stay in bed, but not keep too warm, or be wrapped in too much clothing. This may accelerate cure of the cold, but will increase susceptibility to a recurrence of the attack.

A cold must be broken within the first 48 hours, or it will run its course. As soon as a person discovers he has a cold, he should stay in a room of uniform temperature, drink warm drinks, bathe his feet in hot water, and take 4 compound cathartic pills at bed-time, and a drachm of Epsom salts in the morning. He shouldn't eat meat for a few days, and if the chest is painful, apply a porous plaster.

* * *

Another school recommends abstinence from food, or not to eat anything except a piece of dry bread for breakfast and dinner, and nothing for supper; and liberal indulgence in cold water, drinking at least 2 tumblers on going to bed and on rising in the morning.

A cold can often be broken if the person, as soon as he gets the first symptoms, abstains from food for, say, 36 hours, goes to bed in a warm room, wraps up well, and drinks plenty of hot drinks.

The majority of colds are caught by cooling off too quickly after exercise. Persons exercise until perspiration is produced, then try to cool off.

Anyone exposed to cold or wet through the day should bathe his feet and hands in warm water at night, and they will escape many colds and serious illnesses.

An "old woman's bath" will do good, too. This is an old-fashioned "sweat" brought about by being tucked up in bed in warm blankets, and drinking hot teas until a most profuse perspiration is induced and kept up for hours. Even after you have run the risk of taking cold you can often escape by removing all damp clothes as quickly as possible, soaking the feet for 10 minutes in hot mustard-water, applying a large mustard plaster to the back and covering up well with warm blankets in a warm room to produce free perspiration. Perspiration is promoted by drinking one or two cups of hot tea—camomile tea, for example. Home remedies, promptly applied, can prevent serious illness.

For the cough attending a common cold the following is an excellent cough syrup: Take an ounce thoroughwort, an ounce of slippery elm, an ounce of stick liquorice, and one ounce of flax seed. Simmer together in a quart of water until the strength is entirely extracted. Strain carefully, add a pint of molasses and half-a-pound of loaf sugar. Simmer them together and, when cold, bottle tight.

Generally, it is better not to stop a cough—especially in children. A cough is Nature's way of bringing up phlegm which would otherwise accumulate.

Ipecacuanha wine will, by loosening the phlegm, loosen the cough, which is the right way to get rid of a cough.

Constipation

Finely chop 1 lb. of figs and 2 oz. of senna leaves; add a cupful of treacle; mix well and put into well-covered earthenware pots. Dosage for an adult, $\frac{1}{2}$ teaspoonful; for a child, $\frac{1}{4}$ teaspoonful.

For habitual constipation, obtain pills made of $4\frac{1}{2}$ grains of resin of podophyllin; the same of soap and of extract of hyoscyamus; divide into 10 pills. A grain-and-a-half of extract of rhubarb added to each pill makes them still more effective.

Corns

Most corn remedies contain potash or acetic acid, substances which soften the epidermis, combined with various resins and pitch. They are good but do not cure the trouble if bad shoes are worn. Soft corns can be helped by daily washings with soap and water, and occasional use of spirits of camphor to harden the skin. Also wear cotton wool saturated with oil or glycerine between the toes.

Or, apply fresh every morning the yeast of small beer spread on a rag.

After paring the corns close, apply bruised ivy-leaves daily. Within a fortnight, they will drop out.

Apply chalk, powdered and mixed with water. This is also a good remedy for warts.

Corns can be eased by soaking the feet in hot water in which oatmeal has been boiled. This also soothes dry and hot feet.

For a corn caustic, use 4 drs. of tincture of iodine, 12 grs. of iodide of iron, 4 drs. of chloride of antimony; mix, and apply with a camelhair brush after paring the corn. Three applications should do the trick.

Yet another corn cure is effected by soaking a piece of bread in strong vinegar and applying as a poultice to the corn; the corn gets softened and can then be easily removed.

Or, soak the leaf of the common ground ivy overnight in strong vinegar, and keep it on the corn with the stocking. After wearing all day a fresh-soaked leaf should be used.

For especially persistent corns mix 1 dr. salicylic acid, 2 drops lactic acid, and 1 oz. of flexile collodion. Apply daily and you will soon be able to get the corns out. Soak the feet occasionally in water in which salt has been dissolved. Dry the feet carefully then powder them.

Alternatively, you should bathe the feet in lukewarm water for quarter-of-an-hour; take a razor blade and pare away the upper part of the corn. Then apply a mixture of 2 parts salicylic acid, 4 parts flexile collodian, 1 part creosote, and allow to dry.

Coughs

Make a hole through a lemon and fill it with honey. Roast it and catch the juice. Take a teaspoonful frequently.

Or, try ½-teaspoonful grated fresh horseradish, 2 teaspoonsful of honey. Take a dessertspoonful of this mixture at a time.

Or, cut a hole through the middle of a swede and fill the hole with brown sugar. Leave overnight, then drink the juice.

Or, take a teaspoonful every 3 hours of a mixture made with 1 teaspoonful castor oil, 1 teaspoonful glycerin, 1 teaspoonful lemon-juice.

An ancient remedy for coughing is to boil 2 or 3 snails in barley-water, but don't tell the patient.

Nervous coughing can be stopped by pressing on the nerves of the lip in the neighbourhood of the nose. Pressure there can prevent a cough at the outset. Sneezing can be stopped the same way. Pressing hard on the roof of the mouth can also stop coughing. Willpower can do wonders, too. There was a doctor who used to say, whenever he entered hospital wards: "The first patient who coughs will be deprived of food today." Patients rarely coughed then.

Effective relief can also be obtained by surrounding the neck with an envelope of wetted linen or cotton, oil-silk, and thick flannel in the order mentioned. This, too, is good for the croupy cough and breathing with which children are often attacked at night. As there is always dryness of the throat, water should also be given. A tea-spoonful of salt in a tumbler of water is a good gargle. Ordinary coughs seldom require more than frequent sipping of linseed tea. For bad chest coughs, application of a fomentation, prepared like the envelope of linen, oil-silk, and flannel for the throat, is best.

Cough Emulsion

Take 2 drachms gum ammoniac and half-a-pint water. Rub the ammoniac well, gradually adding the water, until well mixed, then strain through linen. This emulsion is good for coughs and asthma if no inflammatory symptoms are present. Dose is from 1 to 2 tablespoonsful taken with an equal quantity of almond emulsion.

Emulsions soothe irritation in the lungs, or alimentary canal, and are vehicles for substances that couldn't otherwise be so conveniently taken in liquid form.

Another useful cough mixture is made with 5 oz. honey, $\frac{1}{4}$-lb. treacle, 7 oz. vinegar. Mix and simmer for 15 minutes. When warm, add 2 drachms of ipecacuanha wine. Dose a tablespoonful every 4 hours for adults.

A purge at the outset of a cough can help. Also, a low diet, avoidance of exposure to cold, hot drinks of lemonade or elder-bloom tea, stimulating foot-baths—anything to secure free perspiration, and the relief of congestion by the inhalation of steam.

Coughs respond particularly well to water treatment. Night and morning wash feet and legs up to the knees in cold water, then rub very briskly with a rough towel until the skin glows. You should also frequently sniff tepid water up the nostrils and sip a tumblerful of hot water before each meal and just before retiring. This treatment can break a cold at the onset and prevent bronchitis developing.

Cough Lozenges

A very effective prescription uses 25 grs. ipecacuanha,

50 grs. Kermes mineral, 8 grs. codeine phosphate, 1½ oz. white sugar, 1½ oz. gum arabic, 1½ oz. extract of liquorice, 20 drops oil of aniseed, and some syrup of tolu to work into the mass. Form, roll, and cut into 160 lozenges. Take one three times a day.

Cough Mixture

Take some liquorice sticks, ½-pint flaxseed, and the rind of a lemon; put into a quart of water and allow to simmer for two days. Then add the juice of a lemon and ½-lb. brown sugar. Boil for 3 hours and strain. Add, when cool, ½-pint rum. Shake well and take a wine-glassful every morning fasting.

Or, mix 3 drs. pure terebene, 2 drs. ol. eucalypt. globul, 2 drs. syrup of tolu, and 2 oz. listerine. Shake the bottle and take a tablespoonful every 2 or 3 hours.

Croup

At the first croupy sound, wrap the child warmly and put its feet in mustard-water as warm as can be borne. At the same time give small doses, from 15 to 30 drops (according to age), of syrup of ipecac, repeating half-hourly till free vomiting takes place. Bathe neck and chest with camphorated oil, and keep warm with layers of flannel. After vomiting, a teaspoonful of a cough mixture (less for an infant), should be given every 3 or 4 hours until symptoms disappear. The cough mixture is simply a mixture of equal parts of sweet oil, paregoric, and syrup of ipecac. Equal parts of goose oil and honey rubbed on the throat and chest is first-rate if the patient is kept well covered and out of draughts. Alternatively, give a teaspoonful of ipecacuanha wine. If vomiting doesn't soon follow, give half the dose again. Keep the patient in bed. Warm a brick and when hot put it into a bucket of water placed at the bedside. This will cause warm vapour to rise and will help the patient breathe. Apply a warm poultice to the throat and use warm fomentations. Milk is the best diet. If this doesn't relieve, send for the doctor.

Some cases of pleurisy can be stopped if the patient, at the beginning of an attack, takes an alcohol or vapour bath to perspire freely, drinks plenty of strong tea made with catnip, and keeps well covered in bed.
(Casual treatment for this is now considered dangerous. —Editor.)

Turpentine may be applied over the seat of the pain and mustard on the feet. Rubbing the arms and legs with dry flannel helps to moderate the severity of the attack. Call a doctor if relief isn't obtained in a few hours.

Dandruff

Take an ounce of sulphur and a quart of water; shake constantly every few hours and saturate the head every morning with the liquid. Dandruff will disappear in a week or so, and the hair become bright and glossy.

Or, you can wash the head with coaltar soap, and sponge with boracic lotion. A weak sulphur and lanoline ointment can be used.

Dry Lips

When lips, gums and tongue are dry and coated with mucus in acute illness, they should be washed several times daily with glycerine diluted with an equal quantity of water. A little lemon-juice or a few drops of rosewater can be added to make it pleasanter.

Dysentery

Use an enema of an ounce of starch gruel in which you have put 2 grs. of iodoform.

Ear-ache

Wet a bit of cotton wool in corn oil; gather into it a pinch

of black pepper, and insert in the ear.

Ear Wax

At bedtime, put a few drops of olive oil into each ear, then close with a piece of cotton wool. A doctor or nurse will clear the loosened wax with a proper syringe.

Eyes

Bathing the eyes several times a day in cold water makes them bright.

*   *   *

If you have any discoloration around the eyes, get the fresh root of Solomon's seal, scrape it like horseradish, moisten with vinegar, and apply to the injury.

*   *   *

For a stye in the eye, bathe frequently with warm milk and water, or in warm poppy water if very painful. When the stye bursts, smear along the edge of the eyelid with one part of citrine ointment and four parts of spermaceti, well mixed.

*   *   *

Hot boracic fomentations can help burst the stye.

*   *   *

If an eyelash is seen situated in the centre of a stye it should be pulled out. Give quinine and iron tonics to improve your general resistance.

*   *   *

To treat weak eyes, play a jet of weak salt water (a teaspoonful of salt to a half-pint of water) on the eyelid. This is a strengthener. Bathing the eyes with cold water before washing preserves and keeps them strong.

Feet

People suffering with cold feet should put them into hot

water for 10 minutes before going to bed, then plunge them into cold water for a second; wipe dry and rub till warm. Put on a pair of cotton socks wrung out of cold or tepid water, draw over them a pair of thick lamb's wool stockings, and sleep in them.

For perspiring feet, dip them in cold water a minute every morning and sprinkle pulverised tannin at the bottom of the shoes every other day. Wash the feet in warm water nightly, after which, dip them into cold water a moment.

Or, a foot-bath of salt and water is first-rate for perspiring feet. Or, dust the feet every night for a week, and afterwards once a week, with the following application: Mix 2 parts salicylic acid and 3 parts burnt alum. If the perspiration causes the feet to be unpleasant, an application of subnitrate of bismuth should be rubbed over them.

Alternatively, wash the feet every night with water containing a little ammonia, and rub them with ammonia, especially between the toes. Woollen stockings should be worn and the feet powdered with perfumed talcum powder.

For swollen, sore, or blistered feet, use 3 parts of salicylic acid, 10 parts of starch, and 87 parts of finely pulverised soapstone, and dust into shoes and stockings.

For tired feet, immerse them for 10 minutes in 2 quarts of cold water, 2 tablespoonsful of ammonia and 1 tablespoonful of bay rum. Bathe the water over the limbs to the knees, then rub dry with a towel. The tired feeling will go.

Fomentations

Flannel, spongio-piline, or "gamgee-tissue," should be wrung out in boiling water as follows:

The material should be wrapped in a towel folded lengthwise and placed in a basin with the ends of the

towel hanging over the edge. Pour boiling water into the basin, and seize the ends of the towel and twist in reverse ways to wring out the water. Untwist the towel and the fomentation—be sure it is not too hot—should then be placed on the part, covered with oiled silk, then a layer of cotton wool, and secured with flannel bandage.

Headache

For many types of headache, a towel wrung out of water as hot as can be borne and wound round the head gives relief.

Or, take a wide-mouthed, glass-stoppered bottle; half fill with fine sponge, and pour on 3 drs. of a solution of bisulphide of carbon. Apply the mouth of the bottle to the temple or as near as possible to the seat of pain, close so that none of the vapour can escape, and keep it there 5 minutes or so.

After a minute or two, tingling is felt, which in 3 or 4 minutes increases. It subsides if the bottle is removed, as will any redness of the skin. This is especially good for neuralgia and nervous headaches.

A saline wash for headaches is made by mixing a half-ounce of salt, 4 fluid ounces each of vinegar and soft water, 2 fluid ounces of brandy. Be sure the salt is fully dissolved. This is an effective cooling wash for headaches and can also sometimes be used tepid.

Heartburn

Take 2 tablespoonsful 3 times a day between meals of a mixture made with 3 drs. sulphite of soda, 3 drs. sal volatile, 2 drs. of tincture of ginger, 8 oz. infusion of quassia. Take a tablespoonful of whisky in warm water with your meals.

Or, immediately after meals, take a teaspoonful of

wheat charcoal plus a tablespoonful of glycerin just before or after meals.

Housemaid's Knee

Is due to prolonged kneeling and inflammation of the bursa over the ligament of the knee-cap. The elbow, buttock, and back of the knees are also sometimes affected, especially in rheumatic and gouty persons.

Use soft pads to kneel on. When inflamed, the joint must be rested and cold applied. After acute symptoms, or in cases of slow formation, paint with iodine and apply pressure with strapping or a bandage, and avoid further irritation.

Indigestion

A quarter-of-an-hour before meals, take 2 tablespoonsful of a mixture made of $1\frac{1}{2}$ dr. of carbonate of bismuth, $1\frac{1}{3}$ dr. of carbonate of magnesia, $1\frac{1}{2}$ oz. of mucilage of tragacanth, and 8 oz. of water. Or, drink a teacupful of very hot water when going to sleep; in the morning half-a-cupful of milk filled up with boiling water, and eat whole wheatmeal bread.

If you have severe stomach pain through indigestion, drink the juice of half a large lemon, or sweet orange, every day immediately after dinner.

Influenza

Go to bed in a warm, well-ventilated room. Diet should consist of soda and milk, alternated with beef-tea or broths. Old people require stimulants, best given in the form of brandy, egg, and milk mixture. Give plenty of fluid. During the profuse perspirations a flannel night-dress, frequently changed, should be worn.

Ingrowing Nails

Rarely occur if nails are properly attended. Toe nails

should never be cut too short, and always square across, with corners carefully preserved and not rounded. Skin debris, forming a soft pad under the nail, should never be picked out with a knife or scissors.

The foot should be soaked in hot water. Thin the nail by scraping. If very painful, apply a linseed poultice. When irritation has subsided, cotton wool should be pressed between the flesh and the nail, and after, saturate it with iodine: do this for several days. If it is necessary to raise the end of the nail, press cotton wool between it and the toe.

Liver

If your liver is sluggish, drink a glass of hot water with the juice of half-a-lemon squeezed into it, night and morning, without any sugar.

Lumbago

For lumbago or sprains, mix a beaten raw egg with ½-pint of vinegar, an ounce of spirits of turpentine, ¼-oz. of spirits of wine, and the same of camphor. Beat together, bottle, and shake for 10 minutes. It must be tightly corked. In half-an-hour it will be ready. Rub in well 3 or 4 times daily after warming the affected part with a hot-water bottle or in front of a fire.

For similar pains and rheumatic conditions, mix 2 oz. of mustard with ½-pint of spirits of wine and 2 drs. of camphor. Let the mixture stand 2 or 3 days, corked in a bottle. Strain off and keep closely bottled for use.

Mustard Plaster

To make a soothing mustard plaster, mix mustard with the white of an egg instead of water. This plaster will draw without blistering.

Mustard Poultice

Should be made the same way as linseed, except by adding a tablespoonful of mustard to the linseed. It can also be made of the mustard powder alone, or in combination with bread crumbs or linseed meal. When only mustard is used, the powder should be moistened with water and the paste produced spread on a piece of linen and covered with muslin as a protective between the mustard and the skin. When mixed with linseed, the powder and the meal may be incorporated before water is added, or the meal may be moistened and spread on linen for application and the mustard then spread on the surface. Mustard leaves can be used in the place of mustard poultices, only require wetting before application, and are both clean and economical.

Another recipe requires the poultice, made in the usual way. Dip a sponge into it, wrap it in a soft handkerchief, and apply to the part. By warming the sponge again and moistening it afresh, it can be re-applied and the strength is preserved.

Nails

To whiten nails, mix 2 drs. of diluted sulphuric acid, 1 dr. tincture of myrrh, and 4 oz. filtered water. Cleanse the hands with soap and then dip the fingers into this mixture.

Nausea

A cup of hot water before meals will prevent nausea.

Milk

To increase mother's milk, drink a pint of water going to bed, or drink largely of soup made with lentils.

Neuralgia

An excellent liniment for neuralgia is made by mixing a

pint of methylated spirits, 2 oz. each of cedar bark, sassafras, and origanum, 1 oz. of powdered carbonate of ammonia.

Mix well and apply with lint to the gums round the teeth, or to the face in neuralgic pain, by wetting brown paper and laying on the parts. Never too long for fear of blistering.

This is also good for rheumatic pains.

Another remedy is made by mixing 1 part of iodoform to 10 to 15 of collodion. Spread thinly and repeatedly on the neuralgic surface, it is usually effective. If not, the application should be repeated.

Onions

If your breath smells strongly after onion eating, a cup of strong coffee will remove all smell of onions from the breath.

Perspiration

People who perspire a lot should use a teaspoonful of cloudy ammonia in the bath. Some alum, borax, or ammonia in the water is very good, then powder the most affected parts with talcum or rice powder.

Or, melt as much boracic acid as half-a-pint of water will dissolve, and apply to the parts which perspire, and keep well powdered with talcum. When perspiration under the arms stains clothing, put thick pads of cotton wool over dress preservers near the skin, bathe with Eau de Cologne and water, and rub plenty of talcum powder well in.

Eau de Cologne dabbed under the arms after washing or bathing helps to close the pores and to reduce profuse perspiration.

Piles

Eat a large boiled leek.

Rheumatism

Salicylate of soda. Start with 5 grs. in a wineglass of water, and increase the dose to 20 grs. This is not for those with weak hearts.

A lotion for rheumatism is made with a tablespoonful of cayenne, 4 tablespoonsful of salt. Pour on a pint of boiling vinegar. When cold, take 2 oz. of tincture of myrrh and 1 dr. of essential oil of spearmint, sassafras and origanum; shake the oils well together with the tincture of myrrh before mixing with the vinegar, cayenne and salt. Bathe the parts affected, or rub gently. Take 2 pills 3 times a day made of 1 oz. powdered poke root, the same of gum guaiacum, ½ oz. of lobelia.

Rheumatism: Pine Baths

Excellent for gout and rheumatism. Prepare by emptying a bottle of pinol extract into an ordinary bath for adults, and half-a-bottle for children. Pinol is good as a deodoriser in sick rooms.

Ringworm

Shake ½ dr. red iodide of mercury; 1 dr. iodide of sodium, and 3 drs. of water in a bottle till dissolved. Cork and keep ready for use. When required, take a spoonful and add to it 3 of water. Mix well and apply to the parts with a camel-hair brush. Do not repeat for several days.

Ringworm can also be cured in 10 days by cutting the hair off the affected spot; rubbing in turpentine and washing off with carbolic soap. Then wash the whole head with hot water and touch the spots with diluted iodine, repeating once or twice a day.

Rough Skin

Use tepid filtered water with lanoline soap. This should

be applied with rubber gloves. Very soft towels are necessary for drying the skin gently. The roughness should then be treated with a little cold cream. Rub into the skin every night some borax ointment. A little Hunyadi water taken occasionally and a dose of Bourbole water twice a day after food is beneficial.

Sleeplessness

Warm, easily-digested food is the most valuable of all sleeping draughts. Mental work should always be stopped half-an-hour before retiring and some relaxation indulged in, such as a short walk, exercise, or a not too exciting book. A sedentary life and intense mental work should be countered by periods of active exercise. Over-fatigue is best treated by a tepid bath or sponging, and a long draught of water before going to bed. A teaspoonful of salt in a pint of hot water is also useful.

When sleeplessness is due to worry, try to divert the thoughts by taking deep breaths and breathing out gently and slowly through the nostrils and fixing attention on the outflowing stream of air; counting sheep; repeating a nursery rhyme over and over; watching, in imagination, a sailing ship.

Drugs should never be taken except under medical advice.

Sleep will do much to cure irritability. It restores vigour to an over-worked brain. It builds and strengthens a weak body. It cures headache. Sleep is Nature's greatest cure-all.

A remedy for insomnia suited to almost everybody is eating onions. Common raw onions should be taken, but Spanish onions, stewed, will do. This is due to a peculiar essential oil in onions. This oil has great soporific powers. Eat 2 or 3 onions, and the effect is magical.

Take onion soup or syrup of onions every night. Onion jelly is also very soothing. To make it, shred 2 or 3 good-sized onions in a little stock and stew till tender. Add a squeeze of fresh lemon to make the onions digestible for the most delicate stomach, then pour in enough hot water for the quantity and thickness of the soup. Boil ten minutes. Season and add a small piece of butter.

When awakened and unable to sleep easily again, get out of bed, beat and turn your pillow, shake the bed-clothes well, then throw the bed open and leave it to cool. Meanwhile, walk about awhile, then return to bed. You will soon fall asleep.

If you don't want to get out of bed, lift up your bed-clothes, draw in fresh air, and let them fall, forcing it out again. Repeat 20 times.

Old people examined to assess the causes of their longevity agreed on one thing—all went to bed early and rose early.

> Early to bed, and early to rise,
> Makes a man healthy, wealthy, and wise.

Snoring

Sometimes due to thickening and partial stoppage of the nostrils. In such cases little can be done. Smoking may cause it; sometimes it is because the stomach is out of order, and a mild laxative should be taken. Heavy dinners, too many bedclothes, and unventilated rooms, can all cause snoring.

Stiffness

A remedy for stiffness after exertion is a good soaking for 10 minutes in a bath of the hottest water that can be borne. Follow with vigorous rubbing all over with coarse, hot towels. Afterwards rub a little camphorated oil into the skin and knead all the muscles thoroughly with the hands for 15 minutes. Then take 10 grs. of salicylate of soda in a wine-glassful of water at bedtime, and enjoy a brisk walk next morning.

Tapeworm

A draught containing bitter aloes should be taken in the morning. The evening before, take a laxative saline draught. This works every time.

Throat Soreness

Mix $\frac{1}{4}$-oz. finely pulverised sulphur with 3 oz. of pure honey. Dilute with vinegar and use as a gargle.

Make a quart of red pepper tea, strain and add a tablespoonful of salt. Sweeten with honey. Gargle often with this lukewarm.

Get 2 large lemons, put in the oven until warm, peel and squeeze out the juice. Add $\frac{1}{4}$ lb. of best honey, mix well and add 2 dessertspoonsful of best glycerine. Mix well and bottle. Take a teaspoonful as often as necessary.

Throat Ulceration

Mix an ounce of powdered alum with the whites of 4 eggs and 2 oz. tincture of camphor. Use night and morning.

Toothache

Mix 60 drops of creosote or spirits of tar, 60 drops of brandy, 120 drops of sweet spirits of nitre. A piece of lint dipped into this and applied to the tooth can effect a cure.

Another toothache relief mixture is made by mixing 1 part bryonia liniment in 10 parts of warm water. Put a teaspoonful in half a wine-glassful of warm water and hold in the mouth over the aching tooth.

Voice

To strengthen the voice, take 2 drs. beeswax, 3 drs. balsam, 4 drs. powdered liquorice root. Melt the balsam with the wax in an earthen jar; when melted, remove from the stove, and while in a melted state, mix in the powder. Make pills of 3 grs. each and take 2 occasionally 3 or 4 times a day.

Whooping Cough

To allay paroxysms, try the following remedy:

Carbolic acid ⎱ each		7½ drops
Alcohol ⎰		
Tincture of iodine		5 drops
Peppermint water		750 drops
Tincture of belladonna		15 drops
Syrup of diacodium		150 drops

A tablespoonful should be given every 2 hours till paroxysms stop.

A valuable remedy for whooping cough is to get a long-spouted kettle to spread steam into the room. Fill the kettle to the spout-hole. When the water boils put in a tablespoonful of carbolic acid, then let the steam from the kettle fill the room. This relieves.

Whooping cough can be helped if the child takes, morning, noon and night for four days, a dose of finely-ground alum mixed in a small quantity of powdered sugar.

The dose varies from 1 to 2 grains according to the age of the child. If necessary, after the fourth day a child 8 years old must take 7 grains of ground alum 3 times a day. Milk diet is forbidden, and cold air avoided.

To relieve whooping cough, you can obtain a preparation called "Crysolyne" made from tar. Place a little in a saucer and put a nightlight under it. The "Crysolyne" will evaporate but it must not be left to burn. The fumes will relieve the cough and produce sleep.

Or, take 1 pint strongest West Indian rum, 2 oz. anise oil, 1 pint honey and 4 oz. lemon-juice.

To ease soreness in the chest, rub with the following: Half-an-ounce oil of amber; half-an-ounce oil of cloves; an ounce of olive oil; two teaspoonsful of laudanum. Diet should consist principally of barley-water and whey.

God cures: the doctor gets the credit

It is easy for a man in health to preach patience to the sick

Causing a symptom to disappear is very seldom the cure of any human infirmity. The true course is to prevent the symptom

Sickness is a sort of old age; it teaches us a difference in our earthly state, and inspires us with thoughts of a future, better than a thousand volumes of philosophers and divines

The wise for cure on exercise depend, God never made His work for man to mend

Fond of lawsuits, little wealth
Fond of doctors, little health

Who goes to bed supperless, all night tumbles and tosses

8

Grannie's Cosmetics

RANNIE was not only a competent healer. She was, in her lighter moments, something of a beauty specialist, and her home-made lotions, balms and salves enjoyed a high reputation among the young women of the village and surrounding farms. Here are some of her favourites:

Complexion Cream

Take 1 oz. oil of sweet almonds; $\frac{1}{2}$-dr. each of white wax and spermaceti, with a little balm. Melt in a glazed jar and pour into a mortar.Stir until it becomes smooth and cold. Add gradually 1 oz. of rose or orange flower water. Stir until well mixed and creamy. This makes the skin supple and smooth.

Complexion Hints

Cucumbers cut in slices and soaked in rum are great

complexion-improvers. Or, pare and cut small cucumbers and bring to the boil in water, then allow to cool. Strain and bottle for use.

Oatmeal made into a poultice, strained, and the liquid mixed with bay rum, is a great softener and whitener.

Boiling milk poured over violets is said to keep the skin white, soft, and free from wrinkles.

Freckles

Use an ounce of fresh cream; 8oz. milk; lemon-juice. brandy, and an ounce of Eau de Cologne, sugar, 1 dr. Boil and skim.

Another way is to apply 4 times daily a lotion made of ½ dr. of muriate of ammonia, 2 drs. of lavender water, and ½ pint of distilled water.

To make a freckle paste, take a teacupful of sour milk; scrape into it a quantity of horse radish; let it stand for several hours; strain well, and apply with a camel-hair brush 2 or 3 times daily.

The following recipes are also said to remove either freckles, tan, or sunburn, and are harmless.

Dip a bunch of green grapes in a basin of water; sprinkle with powdered alum and salt mixed; wrap the grapes in paper and bake them; then squeeze out the juice. Wash face with the liquid, which will usually remove either freckles, tan or sunburn.

Or, put 2 spoonsful of sweet cream into half-a-pint of milk. Squeeze in the juice of a lemon, add half-a-glass of brandy, a little alum and sugar; boil the whole, skim well, and when cool, it is ready for use.

Glycerin and lemon juice removes tan and subdues freckles, and freckles can be made dim by rubbing them daily with water in which a tablespoonful of powdered alum has been dissolved. Use a large glass.

Hair

Take 1 oz. of palma christi oil and perfume with some bergamot or lavender, and brush it well into the hair wherever it is getting thin.

Hair Tonic

Glycerin	4 oz.
Alcohol	2 oz.
Water of ammonia	2 oz.
Tincture of cantharides	2 dr.
Rosewater	4 oz.
Water	4 oz.

Don't use any other pomade or wash with this.

Hair Falling

Wet the head occasionally in salt and water. This is often most effective when hair is falling out.

When hair falling results after illness, frequent application of sage tea is first-class. Sponge the hair with it.

Hair Lotion

To strengthen the roots, simmer dock roots in water and rub in the strained liquid daily on the head.

For a good stimulating lotion take 10 gr. of sulphate of quinine, 1 oz. bay rum, ½ oz. glycerine, 2 drs. tincture of cantharides, and 6 oz. of rosewater. Mix well and shake before using. Brush it gently into the scalp every morning.

A cleansing and restorative hair wash is made with the froth of a hard soap beaten with the yolk of an egg and a dessert spoonful of spirits of rosemary.

Hair Restorer

Make a wash of 45 gr. of sulphur, 20 gr. of acetate of lead, ½ oz. of glycerin, and 10 oz. of water well mixed.

An ointment for thin hair partings is made by mixing 2 drs. of balsam of tolu, 20 minims of oil of rosemary, 1 dr. of tincture of cantharides, ½ oz .castor oil, and 1½ oz. of prepared lard. Rub into the thin spots every night.

Superfluous Hairs

A solution of common soda occasionally applied to the upper lip withers hair. The best method of applying is to place a tooth-comb on the upper lip so that the hairs can pass through it, then brush over with the dissolved soda. When the alkali has had time to act the comb should be removed and the lip sponged. Smear with pomatum or glycerine to prevent redness. Don't apply too often or you may irritate the skin. A strong solution of potash can also be used similarly. Get some peroxide of hydrogen and apply to superfluous hairs with a small camel-hair brush; or rub petrol jelly over them, then rub gently at night with a piece of pumice-stone. Rinse afterwards with warm water.

Stains

For hand stains, clean with salt and lemon juice rubbed over the stains until they disappear. Wash with clean water; but the best thing to use is the little india-rubber brush and pumice-stone soap. Silver or sea sand soap and very warm water, using a stiff nail brush, make hands white, but they must not be exposed to the air for several hours after. Linseed oil is good for rough hands.

Lime Cream for the Hair

Mix 1 drachm of oil of bergamot with 16 oz. of melted

marrow; beat well, add 8 oz. of lime water and 1 oz. of
tincture of cantharides. Mix well and bottle.

Lip Salve

Take 8 oz. of sweet almond oil, 4 oz. prepared mutton
suet, 1½ oz. of white wax, 2 oz. of spermaceti and 20
drops of otto of roses. Steep a little alkanet root in the
oil and strain before using. Melt the suet, wax and spermaceti together, then add the oil and otto of roses.

Tanning

To prevent skin tanning, dissolve 2 drs. of chloride of
ammonia in 1 pint of rose water, and 10 drops of otto of
roses in 1 oz. of spirits of wine. Mix the two solutions and
add 1 oz. of powdered Venetian talc. Sponge on the skin
in the morning after bathing.

Tobacco

To remove tobacco odour from the breath, take 1 teaspoonful of tincture of myrrh, ½-teaspoonful of spirits of
camphor, and add a pint of hot water in which some
borax has been dissolved. Use a wine-glassful of this
mixture to half-a-tumbler of water when brushing the
teeth.

Tooth Powder

Two drs. Castile soap, ½-oz. powdered orris root, 2 drs.
borax, 2 oz. precipitated chalk, 30 minims carbolic acid,
40 minims oil of eucalyptus. Mix well and brush the
teeth with it, using tepid water.

To remove blackness from teeth, mix 1 oz. of muriatic
acid, 1 oz. of water, and 2 oz. of honey. Wet a brush freely
with the preparation and briskly rub the teeth. Immediately wash out the mouth with water to prevent the
acid affecting the teeth enamel. Only use when the teeth
are stained again.

Wrinkles

To remove wrinkles, mix 2 oz. juice of lily bulbs, 2 oz. Narboone honey, 1 oz. white wax, 3 drs. rosewater. Melt the wax with gentle heat and add the other ingredients. Apply at night and don't wipe off until morning.

Or, smooth the wrinkles by rubbing olive oil into them every night before going to bed.

A good life keeps off wrinkles

A blithe heart makes a blooming visage

'Tis good to walk till the blood appears on the cheek, but not the sweat on the brow

They who would be young when they are old, must be old when they are young

Few believe how far a little health, well managed, may be made to go

The loss of our strength is much oftener occasioned by the vices of our youth than by the ravages of age; it is early intemperance and licentiousness that consign to old age a worn-out constitution

Here is a short prescription for a healthful and happy old age: Short but cheerful meals, music, and a good conscience

The Healing Herb

The herbs which Grannie used in her remedies and recipes—and a great number of others, too—are available today. For the reader's interest and information, here is a list of Herb Simples obtainable from good herbalists. We are grateful to the well-known firm of Heath and Heather Ltd., of St. Albans, for having kindly checked the list

Herb Simples

AGRIMONY: For coughs, simple diarrhoea, relaxed bowels.
ANGELICA: For kidneys and to induce perspiration.
ASH LEAVES: For gouty, arthritic and rheumatic conditions.
AVENS: For diarrhoea.
BALM: Cooling for fevers; to induce mild perspiration.
BLACKBERRY: An excellent tonic; useful in cases of diarrhoea, etc.
BLADDERWRACK: For kidneys, and in bath for rheumatic conditions.
BLUE MALLOW: For coughs and colds.
BORAGE: For chest and fevers.
BROOM: For bladder complaints.
BUCHU: For urinary affections, gravel, inflammation of the bladder.
BUCKBEAN: For liver troubles, some skin diseases, rheumatism.
BUGLOSS: For fevers and inflammatory pains.
BURDOCK: For blood purifying. Seeds used for kidney affections.
BURNET (*Greater*): Useful for bleeding piles.
BURR MARIGOLD: Used in gouty and kidney complaints.
CALAMINT: For coughs, bronchitis, etc.
CARROT, WILD: For coughs, bronchitis, etc.
CELANDINE: For jaundice.
CENTURY: For dyspepsia; with other herbs for jaundice.
CLIVERS: For gravel and other urinary disorders. Also as a tonic.
COLTSFOOT: For coughs and in herbal smoking mixtures.

COMFREY: For chest troubles, for reducing inflammatory swelling; as poultice for healing superficial wounds.

CRANESBILL: For diarrhoea, incontinence of urine. Root to stop bleeding.

DAMIANA: For tonic in nervous and debilitated conditions.

DANDELION: With other herbs used for kidneys and liver. Also as a laxative and tonic. Roots as substitute for coffee.

FUMITORY: Used for stomach and liver derangements and for skin affections.

GERMANDER: Has been used for rheumatic and gouty affections; intermittent fevers.

GOLDEN ROD: For stomach weakness and to promote perspiration.

GROUND IVY: For indigestion and kidneys.

HEARTSEASE: For catarrh and for blood impurity. Also for skin eruptions in children.

HOREHOUND: For coughs, colds and chest complaints as a tonic, and for making Horehound Ale.

HORSETAIL: For gravel and for the kidneys.

HYSSOP: For coughs, colds and the chest.

IRISH MOSS: For chest and bronchial affections and for bladder and kidneys.

LADIES MANTLE: For excessive menstruation.

LILY OF THE VALLEY: Cardiac tonic.

LIVERWORT: For disorders of liver and kidneys.

LOOSESTRIFE: Used to check bleedings from nose, wounds, etc., and as a gargle for relaxed throat.

LUNGWORT: For coughs and chest.

MARJORAM, WILD: Used to promote perspiration and for internal chills.

MARSHMALLOW: For coughs and bronchitis and for bladder complaints. Root is used for reducing inflammation.

MEADOWSWEET: For kidneys and diarrhoea in children.

MISTLETOE: For nervous complaints and circulatory disorders.

MOTHERWORT: For nervous complaints and morning sickness, and as a mild tonic in convalescence.

MOUNTAIN FLAX: Useful for constipation and kidney complaints combined with other herbs.

MOUSEAR: For whooping cough and the chest.

MUGWORT: Used in combination with other herbs.

MULLEIN: For coughs and bronchitis.

NETTLES, STINGING: Very rich in chlorophyll, Used for nettle-rash, rheumatism and blood purifying. Also for making teetotal botanic beer.

PARSLEY PIERT: For gravel, kidney and bladder complaints.

GRANNIES' REMEDIES

PELLITORY OF THE WALL: For correcting suppression of urine and for gravel, etc.

PENNYROYAL: For spasms, flatulence and internal chills.

PEPPERMINT: Used to allay flatulence, stomach sickness and vomiting, and as a cordial.

PERIWINKLE: Astringent and tonic.

PILEWORT: Used for piles, internally as medicine, and externally in the form of ointment.

PLAINTAIN: For diarrhoea, piles and in blood medicines. Fresh leaves relieve insect bites.

RAGWORT: For coughs, colds, influenza, sciatica and rheumatism.

RASPBERRY: Chiefly used as an aid during pregnancy.

RED SAGE: As a gargle for a relaxed throat, laryngitis, quinsy and the tonsils. Also for ulcerated mouth and throat.

ROSEMARY: For headaches, nerves and stomach. As stimulant for the hair.

RUE: Used in small doses for hysteria.

RUPTUREWORT: Especially useful for catarrh of the bladder.

SANICLE: Used with other herbs for blood impurities, dysentery and diarrhoea.

SCABIOUS: Used with other herbs for coughs, fevers and internal inflammation.

SCULLCAP: For hysteria and nervous disorders.

SENNA LEAVES: Laxative. Usually prepared with a little ginger to modify griping effect.

SHEPHERD'S PURSE: For kidneys and diarrhoea.

SILVERWEED: Astringent and has tonic properties.

SOAPWORT: For skin complaints.

SOUTHERNWOOD: Used for worms in children.

SPEEDWELL: For colds, coughs. Also for skin troubles.

ST. JOHN'S WORT: For coughs, bronchitis and the lungs. Also for urinary complaints.

TANSY: For hysteria, morning sickness and for the kidneys. Also for the expulsion of worms in children.

THYME: For coughs, catarrh, sore throat and whooping cough.

UVA URSI: For gravel, kidneys and bladder complaints.

VERVAIN: For nervous disorders.

VIOLET: Antiseptic expectorant.

WOODRUFF: For liver and stomach complaints.

WOOD SAGE: For colds and fevers.

WORMWOOD: For strengthening the digestion; debility and for the expulsion of worms.

YARROW: For promoting perspiration for colds and fevers.

GRANNIES' REMEDIES

Barks

CHERRY: Used with other herbs for catarrhal affections.

POPLAR: Its valuable tonic properties are used in debility, indigestion, etc.

SLIPPERY ELM: Used for its most valuable healing and nutritive properties, as gruel or food, for stomach inflammation.

WILLOW, BLACK: Sedative, tonic.

Flowers

CHAMOMILE: Used in hysterical and nervous conditions, also as a digestive tonic and for debility.

CLOVER (RED): Used for bronchial coughs and whooping cough.

ELDER: A blood purifier; reduces fever and is used in urinary complaints.

HOPS: For sleeplessness and nerves. Also with other herbs for indigestion, debility and worms.

LIME: For headaches, soothing the nerves and for indigestion.

Seeds and Berries

ANISEED: Used in cough medicine and lozenges.

BURDOCK: One of the best blood purifiers. Often used with other herbs for this purpose.

CELERY: For rheumatism.

CORIANDER: Used with other herbs for flatulence. Also used for its flavouring qualities.

FENNEL: Used as a stomach medicine with other herbs.

JUNIPER: Used for kidneys, with other herbs.

LINSEED: Used in cough medicines and for poultices.

MUSTARD SEED: Emetic. Used as poultice for acute local pains in bronchitis, etc. The oil used in Mus-gar ointment.

NETTLE: Useful in chest affections and as a blood medicine.

SENNA PODS: Laxative. Usually taken with ginger to prevent griping.

Roots

BETH: Useful in cases of profuse menstruation.

BURDOCK ROOT: Used universally in herbal practice for blood purifying.

COMFREY ROOT: Used in chest complaints and as a poultice for healing superficial wounds.

COUCHGRASS: Used in bladder complaints, cystitis and for gout and rheumatism.

CRANESBILL ROOT: For infantile diarrhoea and incontinence of urine.

DANDELION ROOT: For kidneys and liver. An excellent coffee is made from the root when roasted and ground.

ECHINACEA: A blood purifier of great power. For boils, etc. Improves digestion.

ELECAMPANE: Used with other herbs for coughs and bronchitis.

GENTIAN: Taken before food it stimulates the appetite. It is a tonic in anaemia and dyspepsia.

GINGER: For colds and flatulence.

GOLDEN SEAL: For liver and disordered digestion, and for gastric trouble, dyspepsia and debility; also especially for catarrhal conditions of the mucous membranes. Used also as an eye lotion.

LIQUORICE: Much used for coughs and chest complaints.

MANDRAKE: Used to stimulate the glands to healthy action; for biliousness and liver disorders. Used in small doses at frequent intervals on account of its potency.

MARSHMALLOW: For relief of asthma, also dysentery and kidney troubles.

ORRIS: Of no remedial value. Used in tooth pastes, powders, etc., for fragrance.

SARSAPARILLA, JAMAICA: Used as blood purifier.

TORMENTIL: For diarrhoea, dysentery, etc. Good for sores and cuts.

Gum Resin

MYRHH: Used as tincture for inflammatory sore throat. Also as a gargle and mouth-wash, especially when ulceration is present.

Herb Simples

EYEBRIGHT: For weak eyes.

FIGWORT: Used for wounds. Applied as a poultice.

INDEX

GRANNIES' REMEDIES

GRANNIES' REMEDIES

GRANNIES' REMEDIES

GRANNIES' REMEDIES

GRANNIES' REMEDIES

GRANNIES' REMEDIES

pretend to like parties, just for tonight," her mother sing-songed in her sweet Southern accent.

"Julia, you know I adore your parties—it's just the people who drive me bonkers," he said to her, placing an arm across her shoulder. He winked at Emily.

Emily observed her parents. Both were still young; in their late fifties, they could pass for a much younger couple. Her mother was as tiny as the day she'd met her dad, her blond hair coiled into a sleek chignon, not a gray hair in sight. Her bright blue eyes sparkled when she smiled at Dad. He towered over her at six three, a head of thick black hair, graying at the sides, his hazel eyes glistening when he looked at her mom. She adored them.

"You are such a party pooper, but I love you anyway. Now, let's see to our guests."

As her mother led Emily's father downstairs, he looked over his shoulder and mouthed the word, *Later*.

She nodded, unsure she wanted to know what was so important he'd sought her out to tell her privately. Tonight of all nights, couldn't it wait? Her parents' retirement party wasn't the ideal time to drop a bad-news bomb.

Taking her empty champagne flute, she whirled downstairs, pasting a smile on her face. Planning to corner her dad at the first opportunity, she spied Mimi and Papaw across the room talking with Bob and Carol Clark, their best friends. Both of her grandparents appeared to be healthy. Mimi's head was thrown back in laughter, as was her norm, her white hair recently cut into the cutest pixie style. Emily thought it suited her quite well. As small as Mom, Mimi had always reminded her of a little sprite. Papaw was tall, though not as tall as her father; his years of skiing had kept him in tiptop shape. She adored her grandparents, too. They'd bought the resort right after they married, working around the clock to make it the success it was today.

When Emily's parents married, they both had worked as hard as Mimi and Papaw, making the lodge a hot spot for locals and tourists. On the day her grandparents decided her parents had been, in their words, "well-groomed," they deeded the resort to them. Yet when needed, they were always there in a pinch. Snowdrift Summit had always been a family operation. The locals flocked to the resort in droves, and tourists from all over the world came to ski the famous slopes, in particular The Plunge.

Other than the six years spent earning her bachelor's and master's degrees at the University of Colorado, Emily had spent her entire life in Loveland, Colorado, living and working at the family resort, which she loved. For a while now, she'd had an itch, an urge to try something different. Not necessarily a new career, but maybe working at a different resort. There were several throughout the state, many of them offering more challenging runs than Snowdrift Summit's. The exception was The Plunge, a massive drop-off on a snow-covered cleft in the rock face where skiers could free fall for almost thirty feet. Then, if you managed to stick the landing on the fifty-degree slope, you had to throw all your weight forward as fast as humanly possible to avoid smashing into the ancient Precambrian rock. From there, The Plunge's upside-down funnel shape opened into an extremely powdery run, challenging even the most expert skiers.

With her experience, Emily knew she could have her pick of jobs at any of the top resorts, though telling this to her family wasn't going to be easy, especially because she knew her parents would be retiring soon. They had fantastic employees—three managers who knew the ropes and the slopes inside and out and would easily take charge. Emily truly hadn't thought about it all in depth.

A waiter passed by with more bubbly. She helped herself to another glass, then meandered through the throngs of guests. Smiling as she crossed the room, nodding at the folks she recognized and giving finger waves to friends she worked with, she managed to weave her way across the large area to the main kitchen without actually speaking to anyone.

Pandemonium filled the commercial-size kitchen. Emily couldn't help but grin. Kathryn, their longtime chef, and her assistants had insisted on catering this event themselves rather than hiring an outside caterer. This had been much to Emily's mother's dismay as she'd wanted all her employees to come as guests, but they'd insisted and she relented.

"You should be out there with your family," Kathryn said as she placed a decorative flower on a plate of hors d'oeuvres.

"I am. I just wanted to see what's happening in the food department. I'm starved." Emily drained her champagne. "I'm already feeling a bit light-headed." She laughed. "From this." She placed her champagne flute on the counter.

Kathryn took a small plate, piling it high with cold shrimp and some kind of cucumber concoction, along with a slice of warm bread with butter. "This should tide you over. No more champagne, young lady," Kathryn said, smiling.

"Thanks," Emily replied, then quickly cleaned her plate. "You're a lifesaver."

"I wish, but no. I just make food," Kathryn told her.

Kathryn was from Spain and had attended the prestigious Le Cordon Bleu cooking school in Paris. She did so much more than "make food."

"What's tonight's main dish?" Emily asked.

"You need to ask? Really?" Kathryn's dark eyes sparkled with amusement.

"No. I thought you might surprise them with one of your delectable gourmet specialties, that's all."

She shook her head. "No way—this is their special day. They must have what they want, even if it's not a gourmet dinner. I cook to please. Always," Kathryn added. "Round of beef and those potatoes they love."

Emily's parents both loved good old-fashioned prime rib with scalloped potatoes and they would have the best, prepared by Kathryn herself, rather than one of her assistants. "Thanks for this," Emily said, waving her hand around.

"It's my pleasure. Now go have fun with the family. I will see you in a while." Kathryn shooed her out of her kitchen.

Unsure if her parents would make their announcement before or after dinner, Emily figured she had best mingle before her mom discovered her in the kitchen.

The lodge's main hall, where guests normally came inside for lunch, a drink, or just to stand by the giant stone fireplace to warm themselves, was packed with folks who'd replaced their ski suits for fancy evening gowns and tuxedos. The main hall held five hundred people comfortably. Emily guessed they were at maximum capacity now. Apparently all who'd been invited accepted, which was perfect given the occasion. She saw the mayor and his wife, along with the chief of police and numerous other folks in positions of power, all good friends of the family's. Probably a good thing in case any of them ever decided to start breaking laws. Emily rolled her eyes at her silly thoughts.

Scanning the room in search of her father, she saw him with a group of skiers from Florida who'd been lifelong members since she was a little girl. Whatever he had to tell her must not be that important, she thought as she watched him laugh and slap one of his pals on the back. He seemed happy, his usual self. Emily had no clue why he'd cornered her earlier. What was so important that he felt it couldn't wait? Deciding it wasn't something life-changing, she saw a group of instructors she worked with. Making her way across the room to join them, against her better judgment, she took another glass of champagne from a waiter passing by with a tray.

"It's about time you joined the party," said Kylie, her best friend. With her long black hair, dark eyes and olive-colored skin, she was stunning. Tiny like her mother, and as muscular as her small frame would allow. Emily adored her. "I was beginning to wonder if you'd make an appearance tonight."

Emily and Kylie Esposito had been best friends since second grade. Their shared loved of skiing bonded them together like boot bindings to skis. They even lived in the same condo complex.

"I've been here, just lurking around. You know how much I love parties," she said. Truly her mother's daughter when it came to entertaining, she'd learned at a very young age how to entertain, loving every party her parents hosted. Mimi and her mother had both insisted she learn the ins and outs of entertaining.

As a child, invitations to Emily's birthday parties were much sought after due to her mom's talent. It made her one of the most popular girls in school, not to mention the fact her birthday was on Christmas Day. All of her friends were on holiday break, so they always attended her party the day after Christmas because her mother didn't think it was polite to intrude on a family's Christmas Day celebration.

Emily made friends easily with her classmates, regardless of their position on the school's social-ranking ladder. In high school she'd never joined the cliques some of her friends had; it wasn't her way. She sailed through high school, then spent the next six years at the University of Colorado in Denver. With a master's degree in business, she graduated at the top of her class. Her parents had been thrilled when she decided to work at the resort. She came home with her new friend, Clarice, a tabby she'd found as a kitten, who still ruled the roost to this very day. Cats aside, Emily didn't ever recall telling her parents the lodge might not be a lifelong career for her as it had been for them. They cared that she was close by. That was what mattered most. Family came first, no matter what.

She was about to put that to the test tonight.

Chapter Two

"There she is," Mimi said loudly. "It's about time you joined us, sweetie. I thought you might've skipped out on tonight's festivities with a hot date."

"I'll see you later," Emily said to Kylie before joining her family.

"Sure," said Kylie, a sly smile on her face. As her best friend and knowing Emily's family as she did, Kylie knew it would be almost impossible for her to have a minute to socialize with her friends for the rest of the evening.

Taking her by the arm and leading her to the opposite side of the lodge, Mimi began to tease Emily about "hot dates," of which she'd had none in months. Yes, she dated, but no one had struck her as "the one," and she refused to settle for second best. Approaching thirty, she'd become sensitive whenever the words "date" or "boyfriend" and the forbidden word "marriage" just so happened to come up in conversation—which was more often than not these days. Most of these conversations were between her mother and Mimi, and always when Emily was within earshot, but never actually directed to her, though Mimi often got a little dig in whenever she could. They weren't hateful in any way, just suggestive hints. She knew they were all counting on her to continue the family line, as she was an only child. Plus, she wasn't getting any younger.

With the upcoming holidays, she knew her family's matchmaking skills would be in full force right after the family celebrated Thanksgiving Day. Then her mother would begin hosting dozens of Christmas parties for her charities, her book club, her yoga class, Mimi's card ladies, and on and on. Though there was never a lack of excuses to throw a party, Emily's distaste for the weekly Christmas parties had gone south the first year after she finished college. That was when her mother had announced Emily's engagement to Harold Wilson. Emily hadn't even liked Harold that much. They were sort of friends; they rode the ski lift together now and then. They had attended the same high school. The downside was that Harold's mother, Lucille Wilson, was her mom's best friend. Apparently, Harold had told his mother he was going to ask Emily to marry him on Christmas Eve. Instead, Emily's mother had announced it herself. Mortified and humiliated, Emily now avoided any and all Christmas activities involving her mother's best friend and her son.

"Emily?" Mimi said.

"Sorry, I was . . ." She paused. "Overwhelmed for a second." She shot Mimi one of her best smiles.

"Look at you. I swear, you could be in an Ultrabrite commercial with that smile," said Mimi.

"Thanks," Emily said. The first time Mimi said that to her, she'd just had her braces removed, clueless what an "Ultrabrite smile" even was. Of course Mimi being Mimi, she found the old commercial on YouTube, thus explaining her comment, and she continued to use it whenever she could.

"Mom, now stop that," Julia said to Mimi. "I think

Emily knows by now she has the prettiest smile this side of the Continental Divide."

Emily said "Thanks" to her mother, then asked, "Where's Dad? I saw him a few minutes ago, but now he's disappeared."

The two older women looked at each other, both with grins as wide as Willie's Way, the most spacious and easiest run on the mountain. It was one of the bunny hills.

They were up to something, Emily could tell. "What? I know something's up—you might as well tell me."

"Nothing that can't wait for the perfect moment, sweetie," Mimi told her. "Relax and enjoy the party. Indulge in a glass of that very expensive champagne your mother ordered."

"I've had three glasses and I'm half-lit, Mimi, so I don't think I'll 'indulge' any more than I have already." She had recovered a bit after eating, but wasn't totally clearheaded.

"Why Emily Nicole Ammerman, you ought to . . . have another glass," Mimi said, tossing her head back and laughing so hard Emily couldn't help but join her. Not one to be a party pooper, her mother started hooting as well, the three of them cackling like a trio of hyenas.

"No more for me, seriously," Emily said, barely able to control her laughter. "I'm teetotaling for the rest of the night."

Mimi shook her head. "You are such a spoilsport. Julia, I thought we raised this girl to party?"

"No, you both taught me how to *throw* a party," Emily added. "Not to be the inebriated gal lying on the floor at the party, wondering how she got there." Memories of that nightmarish Christmas Eve came to mind, but she wouldn't mention it tonight. Her parents deserved this party tonight. The end of one adventure and the beginning of a new one.

"True," her mother agreed.

"Of course not," Mimi reminded them. "Besides, that's not ever going to happen, at least not as long as we're at the same party, right, Julia? I must say it's a miracle you turned out as well as you did. Especially with all the freedom we gave you."

Emily raised her brows. "Freedom?" she said to her mother. "I recall having to ask you and Dad if I could stay up an extra hour just to read. On the weekends!"

Julia looked at her mother. "That's enough, Mom. I can't have my daughter thinking of me in a heathenish way."

"I would never think of you in such a way," Emily told her. "Though I do recall you being somewhat of an anomaly."

"Yes, she was, and still is. She just keeps it well hidden," Mimi said, then winked at Emily.

Julia rolled her eyes. "That's enough, *Mother*," she said, with emphasis.

Emily loved watching her mom and grandmother spar. They reminded her of the characters Sophia and Dorothy from the sitcom *The Golden Girls*, minus the off-color innuendoes they occasionally used.

"We'll finish this discussion later," Mimi said to Emily. "I've loads of stories to tell you."

"*Mother!*" Julia said, loud enough that several of their guests turned to look at them.

"It's true," Mimi said to her daughter, then to Emily, "Later, I'll fill you in on all the sordid details."

"I'll hold you to that," Emily said, adding, "another time."

Mimi chuckled, turning her attention to a group of women heading in their direction. "I'll see you girls in a bit," she called over her shoulder as she joined her friends.

"Aren't they the card ladies?" Emily asked her mother, who remained by her side.

"Some of them. Willowdeen and Mabel are still recovering from their bout with that nasty virus."

"Good to know. Lots of folks got hit with that second round. I'm grateful no one in our family was sick." She knew they'd all been vaccinated, though that wasn't a full-fledged guarantee they wouldn't catch the virus.

"We're from a strong line of folks," her mother said, though Emily had no way of knowing this because the only family she'd ever known were her parents and grandparents on her mother's side. Her father had a brother, William, who he hadn't spoken to in years because of some family feud—one that was never discussed—so as far as Emily knew, her family line wasn't 100 percent confirmed. Her father's parents both had passed away long before Emily was born, so she wasn't sure about her dad's side of the family and their longevity. Someday, when she had a bit of free time, she'd go to one of those websites that searched genetics. Maybe she'd find there were more Ammermans out there, some that her dad didn't even know existed.

"I hope so," Emily replied.

"On my side of the family," her mom added.

She nodded, eyeing the throngs of people, searching for Kylie as she was in need of a break from her mother. "I'm going to mingle," she said before hurrying away. As much as she loved her family, they could be suffocating at times.

Emily slipped out of the party and went upstairs to the private suite of offices her family used. Seeing her dad's office door open, she peered inside to make sure he wasn't there before closing the door behind her. Plopping on the leather sofa opposite the large oak desk he'd had custom-made years ago, she looked out the window. Her mother's decorators had strung white fairy lights throughout the pine trees that led to the top of Ruby's Ride, another one of the bunny hills. Closing her eyes, Emily could imagine the first snow, the soft flakes flittering from above into deep mounds throughout the trails. The first run of the season—the fresh smell of winter pine, her skis edging downhill, the icy air rejuvenating her, her cheeks red from the cold. At the first powder, she never missed getting up at dawn before the slopes were packed with the locals and tourists, and she felt she was queen of the mountain. That was what she lived for. Those few moments alone on the mountain with nature were priceless. Just thinking about it now made her wish for an early snowfall.

She stood up and walked over to the window, gazing outside. She saw a few people gathered around one of the many firepits in front of the lodge's main entrance. It was cool tonight, but not so much so that one needed to stand in front of a fire. She supposed it was all a part of the ski experience for the first-timers, though she also still enjoyed sitting in front of the fire after a long day on the slopes, unwilling to go inside, where the tasks of removing her ski boots and clothing signified the end of the day. Outside in the cold air, with friends and maybe a hot toddy, the day was still hers to do as she pleased.

These thoughts brought her back to the present. She loved being a ski instructor to the intermediates. Two of her students had actually made it to the Olympics, and though they never medaled, she was still extremely proud of them. For a while now she'd longed for something more. A bigger challenge, a change of scene. She wanted to tell all this to her father but couldn't tonight, on his and her mother's big night. Emily would give it a week or so, however long it took for the managers to take over, and then she would tell her parents and grandparents she needed to move on. They were good folks; she knew they would support her as they always did. With them retiring and their plans to travel the world, this would be the perfect time for her to make a change in her life as well. At least she hoped so. Unsure if Mimi and Papaw were going to stay on full time, as their home was built close to the resort, she suspected they'd also travel a bit. But knowing them and how much they loved Snowdrift Summit, they would most likely stay. Either way, she was ready for a change of scenery.

With one last glance out the window, she left her dad's office with thoughts of her future and a tiny trickle of excitement fluttering throughout her. Life was good and about to get even better.

Chapter Three

The sound of laughter, glasses clinking against one another and the voices of all the guests and servers filled the giant room. Emily glanced around before rejoining the party. For a moment she felt sad that this would be her parents' last official duty at the resort, and possibly her grandparents' as well. A part of her already felt the loss of familiarity, what she'd known her entire life, though in her heart she knew it was time for a change. Hadn't she just decided she needed a new challenge?

Cold reality smacked her in the face. Maybe her ordinary, day-to-day life wasn't really all that bad. No, it wasn't bad; it was just the sameness of it all. Yes, she needed and wanted a change; but in all honesty, she would miss this place and the daily contact with her family.

She took a quick glance in the mirror located at the foot of the grand staircase. At five foot ten and with the four-inch heels she wore, she stood over six foot. Tall like her father, yet slim like her mother, Emily had inherited the best of both her parents—or so she was told. With her long, blond hair, her father's hazel eyes, high cheekbones and a full mouth, she knew some thought her a beauty, but she never focused too much on her appearance. Though in

honor of tonight, she'd gone to great lengths to make sure
she looked her best. She wore her hair piled high in a perfect bun, courtesy of Kylie, whose skill with hair was as
good as her skill at skiing. Her silk dress, a deep, emerald-
green sheath, clung to her in all the places it should. She
wore a gold necklace with a pear-shaped emerald with a
round diamond at the top of the emerald, a gift from her
parents for her twenty-first birthday, which she only wore
on special occasions.

"There you are," said Kylie. "Your parents are about to
make the announcement, but they're waiting for you."
Her best friend looked at her. "Is everything okay?"

Emily nodded. "Of course. I was just upstairs, a bit of
'me time' before the party gets too wild. You know my
parents," she said. "This shindig could last all night." She
took Kylie's hand. "Come on, you're in this, too."

Kylie laughed. "Hey, I just work here."

Emily let go of her hand, rolling her eyes. "Sure you do."

"Wait," Kylie said before approaching the group of
folks who'd gathered around Emily's mom and dad. "Do
you have something up your sleeve? You're not yourself."

Friends for most of their life, Emily knew Kylie would
be the one who'd sense she truly wasn't in the mood for
tonight's big announcement. Even though she knew she
and her family needed a change, there was something else
she was unable to put a finger on. "Kylie, have my parents
told you anything about, well, anything?"

Kylie's brown eyes doubled in size. "You mean another
Harold incident?" She grinned. "Exactly how much champagne have you had? Girl, you're sounding strange already!"

"Please, that's the last thing on my mind." Through her
mom's grapevine, Emily knew Harold still had his heart
set on marrying her one day when she "settled down."
She'd die first. "Listen, earlier Dad told me he wanted to

talk to me. He was very serious, like he had bad news. Mom appeared, so then, of course, he clammed up, mouthing *Later*, and walked off. I don't know—I guess that's put me in a weird mood tonight."

"I certainly haven't spoken to your parents about anything I would consider life-altering, other than their retirement. Maybe your dad's feeling, I don't know, *lost* at the thought of leaving. Lots of people who retire later wish they hadn't. At least that's what KiKi tells me." KiKi was Kylie's grandmother, who'd raised her and been their fourth-grade teacher before retiring and moving to Florida after Kylie graduated from college.

"I suppose, but why would he specifically seek me out to tell me?" Emily threw out her hands. "That he had something important to discuss?"

Kylie shook her head. "Maybe he's concerned about the resort. Is there anything going on you don't know about? Possibly—and I hate to bring this up—but are there any financial issues?"

Emily chewed on her bottom lip, a nervous habit. "Not that I'm aware of, but they rarely discuss their finances with me." Could that be what her father wanted to talk to her about? No, if money was an issue, he wouldn't be retiring and throwing expensive parties where Cristal champagne cost three hundred bucks a bottle. It wasn't her parents' way to be frivolous with money in any way. "I don't think they're having financial problems, Kylie. It's more than that, but let's forget I said anything. When my dad is ready to tell me whatever it is, he'll find me. For now, let's enjoy the party."

"Sure, but promise if there's anything you can't handle on your own, you'll share it with me?"

"Of course," Emily said. Kylie was more than her best friend. She was the sister she never had and her mother's bonus daughter, as she was fond of saying.

In the world of skiers the sound of an avalanche alarm was common. C4 was often used to remove massive snow buildup before it became an avalanche. So it came as no surprise when an alarm filled the lodge. A cattle call of sorts, Emily thought. She grinned at Kylie. "Must be time for the big announcement."

"Good thing your parents didn't invite Harold," Kylie teased.

Emily elbowed her in the side.

"Ouch!"

"Shhh—you deserved that," Emily whispered.

The noise in the room came to a hushed silence. Emily's parents stood at the top of the grand staircase landing, both grinning. Her father was the first to speak once the crowd was completely silent. "As most of you know, Julia and I are of a certain age." The guests laughed; Emily rolled her eyes. "Though I know Julia looks like she's barely a day over thirty, I've been lucky enough to marry the gal of my dreams. We've spent our life together at this lodge. It's been our life, life for my in-laws and our daughter, Emily. A family tradition. I'd like to say it's with a heavy heart, but if I did, I wouldn't be telling the truth, so it's with a pure and joyous heart that Julia and I . . ." He paused, focusing his gaze on the crowd, stopping when he saw Emily. "Julia and I had many late-night discussions and we both agreed—tonight we are officially announcing our retirement from Snowdrift Summit. And, as was once given to us, we are now deeding the lodge and all its holdings to our daughter, Emily Nicole Ammerman."

For a few seconds, you could've heard a pin drop, then the room exploded with applause, laughter, champagne flutes clinking in toasts. Emily was surrounded by well-wishers, all congratulating her. She felt as though someone had placed a hand around her neck and squeezed. It was hard to breathe. Her throat felt like a piece of food was lodged in it, preventing her from breathing. She looked at Kylie, who grabbed a glass of something from a passing waiter.

"Here," she said. Emily tossed back the drink, then doubled over in a horrendous coughing fit, not realizing the drink she'd just downed was straight bourbon. Light-headed, she pushed through the throng of well-wishers, heading toward the bright red exit sign. She had to get out; she needed air. Pushing the heavy doors aside, the rush of cool night air helped, but she still had trouble breathing. On her heels, Kylie burst through the same doors. "Emily, what's wrong?" she shouted, not caring that a crowd had gathered behind them.

Emily continued to struggle with her breathing.

"Should we call ski patrol?" Kylie shouted. "An ambulance?"

Emily was able to shake her head from side to side. "Get them out of here," she managed to say.

"Folks, if you all would just return to the festivities, I'll see to Emily. We'll be back in a flash," Kylie said to the group gathered at the door. It took a few moments for her words to sink in, but they eventually left them alone.

"Can you talk now?" Kylie asked her.

"Yes," she said in a hoarse voice. "I need a glass of water."

Kylie ran back inside and grabbed a bottle of water, returning in seconds, giving Emily the bottle. Downing the water as she'd downed the bourbon, minus the coughing fit, she took a minute to gather herself. "Did you hear what he said? My dad?" She plopped down on an Adirondack chair.

"Yeah, I did. Why?"

"Deeding the resort to me? Are you sure that's what he said?" she asked, uncertainty in her voice.

"It's what I heard," Kylie told her.

Emily shook her head. "Did you know about this?"

"Of course not!" Kylie said, her voice a few octaves higher than normal. "If I did, I would've told you. We don't keep secrets from each other. You know that."

"Sorry. I had no idea my parents were planning on giving me the resort when they retired. Maybe when I'm older and settled, but now? I was going to try and find work at another resort. This must be what Dad wanted to tell me before he made his big announcement. Damn, I should've known!"

Kylie searched Emily's face, her own expressing a myriad of emotions. "You're probably right." Her friend paused for a second. "You're serious about searching for another job? And you didn't even tell me your plans? Here I thought we were best friends."

"It's not like that, Kylie. It's something I've sort of . . . had in the back of my mind since they decided they were going to retire this year. I haven't actually looked for work. I don't know; maybe I'm ready for a change, a challenge. Aren't you? We've both been working here since college. And now, without even asking, my parents decide I'm stuck here permanently. They didn't even bother to ask me what I wanted. I don't know what to do at this point." Tears spilled from her eyes.

Kylie sat in the chair beside her. "Look, go back inside, tell your parents you appreciate this grand gesture in front of half the town, but that you're not ready for the responsibility at this stage in your life. They're great people, Em. They'll understand."

Emily wiped at her eyes with the back of her hand. "Maybe, but I can't do it now, with all these folks here. I don't want to embarrass them." She wanted to add, *like they embarrassed me*, but didn't. It had been many years since her mother had publicly humiliated her by announcing the engagement. She knew she needed to move on. But parties always brought back that memory, and another round of humiliation when she also thought of her and Harold's private incident.

Just thinking of it made her cheeks burn.

"Sure, but later, when you're alone, tell them how you feel. You're twenty-nine, unmarried . . . your life, my life . . . heck, we're just a couple of ski bums at this point. I have no clue what my future holds, and I know you don't either." Kylie paused before saying, "Other than you want to work at another resort."

"Come on, Kylie, it's not a big deal. After tonight, I'll probably be stuck here until I retire. Forget exploring the world, having a family and all that goes along with that. Nope, I'll be an old spinster giving ski lessons until I'm so arthritic I'll need some kind of contraption just to get to the lifts."

Kylie laughed. "Maybe, if you don't tell Julia and Mason how you really feel. They adore you and would never do anything to cause you to be unhappy. Just suck it up for the rest of the night, for them and their guests. Then later, you can tell them you aren't ready for the responsibility."

There was a chill in the night air that she hadn't noticed when she ran outside. Her dress was thin, barely enough to keep her warm. "All right. Let's go inside through the back entrance. I'm sure I look awful. I need to fix the mess I've made of myself. I'll let everyone know how I was overcome with such joy, I needed to be alone for a few minutes to absorb the news. Hopefully they'll have had more than enough to drink by now, so they won't give a rat's rear about my behavior."

"You look like a raccoon," Kylie said. "Did you bring your makeup bag with you?"

"Yep. Believe it or not, I did. It's in my locker." She rarely wore makeup, never brought it with her, though tonight she had, just in case. Credit was due to her cat, Clarice, as she always dragged a tube of mascara around, and that was what reminded Emily to bring her kit with her.

"Then let's go," Kylie said.

The front of the lodge faced Snowdrift Summit. Behind, a large parking area was usually filled with hundreds of vehicles. It appeared barren to Emily as she and Kylie skirted around the cars that were parked close to the back of the lodge. Her dad had hired a couple of the part-time chairlift operators to act as valets. They'd parked vehicles close to the building so the guests wouldn't have far to walk in all their finery. Emily wondered if any of them would be too inebriated to drive later tonight, though her dad had chartered a local bus service for that, too, just in case. He always had his bases covered.

The entrance marked EMPLOYEES ONLY was unlocked. Emily opened the door, surprised the lights were turned off, though it didn't matter because she and Kylie could find their way around this place blindfolded. Inside the employee locker room, she took her makeup bag from her locker. "Give me a minute," she said. "Or twenty. I'm a mess." Mascara streaked down her cheeks like two black tributaries. She washed her face using the harsh soap from the dispenser in the ladies' room, then quickly reapplied mascara, blush and lipstick.

"Perfect," Kylie told her. "Now, let's see if we can sneak in without anyone noticing."

Emily took one last glance in the mirror. "Let's go."

They went down three darkened hallways and through three sets of double doors, which brought them to the kitchen. Emily dashed around waiters and waitresses carrying trays high above their heads. As soon as she returned to the party, with Kylie a few steps behind, she spied a group from Florida she'd given lessons to last year. She was surprised they were here, then remembered they were the kids of the Rogers family. All six of them: one set of twins, Ashley and Amber, who were around fifteen, Alan, who was just a year older than the twins if she remembered correctly, and Aidan, who was in his second year of college at Florida State. She couldn't remember the ages of the two oldest, Amy and Adam. Emily smiled when she said, "I can't believe you came all this way to a retirement party. Must be pretty boring for you all."

"We live here now. We left Florida three months ago," Aidan explained. "Mom and Dad love Colorado—the snow and all—so when they said they were moving, we all agreed we were tired of the beach life."

"This must be a huge change for you guys," she said, focusing on all six. "Going from sunshine year-round to cold and snowy, though we do have awesome summers, too. It's a great place to live, so welcome to Colorado." She waited for one of the six to respond. Starting to feel uncomfortable as the group stared at her, she wondered if they'd witnessed her earlier actions. Not wanting to be the object of six sets of eyes staring at her for another minute longer, she excused herself.

Spying Kylie with Jackie, another ski instructor they were good friends with, she joined them before her parents spotted her.

"Jackie, did everyone freak out when I left?" Emily asked, knowing she would be honest with her.

"Not really. Just a few of the older folks, but they were just curious. Your parents gave each other a verbal butt kicking from the looks on their faces, though I didn't hear anything they said. They disappeared right after you, so I'm not sure what happened after that."

"Thanks. I guess they're angry at me for ruining their evening," Emily said to her two friends.

"Oh, they'll get over it," Kylie said. "Stop worrying about them and let's have some fun. We *are* the party girls, remember?"

Emily grinned. "I do, but I can't recall us being surrounded by our parents and grandparents. If they knew some of the messes we got ourselves in to, we'd still be hearing about it."

"True, but we're adults now, and what they don't know won't hurt them. Let's head over to the bar and have a shot of tequila—or two—and get this party started. Jackie, why don't you join us?" Kylie asked. "The more the merrier!"

"Just one drink. I promised Chuck I'd spend the evening with him, though as usual I haven't seen him."

Chuck and Jackie had been dating for two seasons. Whether either of them dated during the off-season remained a mystery, but that seemed to be the way of the world of skiers where many would travel to other countries throughout the year, chasing the snow. Emily had wanted to try that when she was younger, but her parents wouldn't allow it, and by the time she was old enough to make the decision on her own, she'd become a much sought-after instructor, giving up any hope of traveling abroad.

"If he doesn't show, just hang with us. Let him wait for you," Emily suggested to Jackie. "Women shouldn't expect to be at a man's beck and call. I will never allow a man to run my life. No way," she said to her friends as they walked over to the bar.

She'd been burned once. In college she'd been madly and passionately in love with Jonathan Walters, and had been hoping for an engagement ring during the holidays. Instead, he'd ditched her via text message while she was visiting her parents. Then her mom made that mortifying announcement. Committed relationships were not for her.

Emily snuck a glance around the room, searching for her parents, but they were nowhere in sight. So, she'd managed to ruin the big bash they'd planned for months.

Had they told her what their plans were, they might've saved themselves a lot of trouble; she'd suspected they would pass the lodge on to her one day, when she was settled down, married with a family to help her. But no, they had made the decision without her input, so Emily had reacted the only way she could—shocked and unprepared.

Jackie laughed. "You're probably right. I shouldn't wait around for him. What few dates we have are always when it's convenient for him. I'll hang with you guys if you don't mind."

Jackie was a good friend to both Emily and Kylie and she was also one of the resort's top instructors. They'd formed a friendship several years earlier. Jackie, also a born and bred Coloradan, lived in Silverthorne, a short drive from Loveland. They were all the same age, though Jackie hadn't attended the same schools as Emily and Kylie had. At their age, it didn't matter.

"You're always welcome to join us, no matter what we're doing. Don't ever give it a second thought. Now, let's have that shot." Emily told the bartender to set them up with three shots of tequila, slices of limes and salt. They sat at the bar, each licking the salt, tossing back their shots, then sucking the limes. Emily coughed a bit, Kylie wasn't affected at all and Jackie choked.

Kylie slapped Jackie on the back, which did nothing except cause another fit of choking, The three women broke out into raucous laughter.

"Give us three more," Emily said.

The bartender, clad in a white dress shirt, a black vest and a tie, grinned, "You sure about that?" His sky-blue eyes darted over to Jackie.

"Absolutely," she said.

The guests were getting rowdy; laughter could be heard throughout the lodge. Occasional bits of arguments could also be heard, but that wasn't unusual in a crowd this size. Too much alcohol sometimes brought out the true colors in some folks, and it wasn't always pretty.

As soon as the bartender set them up with a second round of shots, Emily decided to make it interesting. "On the count of three, whoever finishes first gets the first weekend of the season off." A super busy time, she'd probably regret this later, but this was a party, and she was going to have fun in spite of the earlier incident.

Jackie and Kylie nodded.

"Okay, on the count of three! One, two, three!" Emily counted. They tossed the shots back, Emily the first to slam her glass down on the bar.

"Figures," Kylie said. "You have the first weekend off, but you'll be our boss now, so this whole charade really didn't mean anything."

Emily, who wasn't much of a drinker despite what Kylie said, felt hurt. If her best friend was going to start viewing her as "the boss," she definitely wasn't ready to take control of the resort.

"That isn't fair, Kylie. I didn't ask for this, you know that. It'll be a long time before you'll be calling me 'boss,' if ever. Like you said, this is a party. Let's have fun while we can. The season is right around the corner. Heck, it could be sooner if we get an early snowfall. Nothing will change, I promise." She hoped she would be able to keep her promise to her friends. She would speak to her mom and dad first thing tomorrow.

"Sorry. I guess I'm a little jealous."

"Don't be. If I ever accept the resort as my own, who do you think is going to be my right hand?" Emily asked her.

"You tell me," Kylie quipped.

"*You*, Kylie. And Jackie, I suspect you'll be in charge of all the ski instructors because you're one of our best and the most organized. But this isn't happening tomorrow, so don't worry. We're going to work this season as usual and nothing is going to change," Emily said to her two friends, though she truly didn't know if she'd be able to keep her word. That bothered her much more than telling her parents she wasn't ready to take over the resort.

Chapter Four

The screeching sound of Emily's alarm jolted her awake. Using her right hand, she reached for the clock's Snooze button, slamming her hand down on it before rolling over to the opposite side of the bed. Emily pulled the down comforter over her head, wishing last night away. An orchestra, a street band and a group of horribly loud rappers performed inside her head, pounding until she thought she would scream. If she screamed, it would only make matters worse. She'd done this to herself. Too many shots of tequila last night. A few beers in between, if memory served correctly. Rarely one to drink more than an occasional glass of wine, she'd outdone herself. Keeping her eyes closed, waiting for the throbbing in her head to calm to a slow and steady beat, she promised herself she would never take another sip of tequila again.

"Meow," Clarice called out from under the bed.

"Haven't you ever had a hangover?" she whispered to her cat.

"Meow, meow, meow."

In people-speak, Emily assumed this meant, *No, I haven't.*

Slowly, Emily lowered her legs onto the floor, her upper body in a semireclining position. Easing her torso into an upright position, she took a deep breath, forcing herself to stand. The room whirled around her like a tornado. Closing her eyes, she stood, placing her hand on the wall, feeling her way across the room to the master bath, with Clarice circling in between her legs as though she were performing in a talent show.

Finally she made it to the shower, reaching inside to turn on the tap. She dropped her sleep shirt on the floor before standing under the icy blast of freezing water. Clarice curled up on the bathroom rug, waiting for her to finish.

"Dang!" Emily cried, the cold water forcing her to open her eyes. Ashamed she'd allowed herself to get in this position, she quickly scrubbed her body and washed her hair. Stepping out of the shower and reaching for her robe, her head still throbbed despite the cold shower.

"Meow." Clarice stretched, her furry back reminding Emily of a camel's hump. Then Clarice placed her paws in front of her, extending the length of her body. Emily thought her cat would be one heck of a yoga instructor.

"Namaste," she muttered. Clarice probably expected her to bow. Not happening this morning.

In the condo's kitchen Emily opened a can of Fancy Feline Salmon Delight, gagging from the strong odor. Emily also kept an automatic feeder filled with dry food in the kitchen, just in case. Clarice's water dish was always full; Emily had purchased a newfangled fountain that constantly circulated the water as long as it was filled. Emily thought of it as Clarice's own personal water park. She scooped the smelly food into Clarice's bowl before she made a pot of coffee and took three Advil. As soon as the coffee finished brewing, she poured a cup for herself. A few sips later, and with help from the Advil, her headache eased up a bit. She sat down at the table for two, sipping at her coffee while her thoughts returned to last night's big announcement.

She'd spent the rest of the evening getting plastered with Kylie and Jackie, never bothering to locate her parents to tell them she wasn't ready for the responsibility they'd bestowed on her, even though she knew their intentions were good. They wanted to keep Snowdrift Summit in the family, she got that, but no way was she ready to take charge. There was so much more than just showing up in time to teach the visitors how to ski. If that weren't the case, of course she would take over. The lodging, the food, the employees, the maintenance . . . on and on it went, and that was the bare bones of running the resort. One also had to allow for contingencies. With this newly added responsibility, how could she possibly be expected to run the show and think about providing her parents with a grandchild? Shaking her head at the sheer impossibility of it all, she poured herself another cup of coffee. She took it to the living area, where she sat on the sofa contemplating her plans for the day. Clarice jumped up, settling on the back of the sofa to watch for birds.

"No birds this morning." She spoke to Clarice like she was human. Clarice was such a good companion, she'd often thought of adopting another cat, or maybe a dog, but hadn't taken a trip to the local shelter because it always made her cry. She made large donations and would continue to do so until she could do more.

At some point Emily had to talk to her mom and dad. It was inevitable. Surprised they hadn't bothered to call or stop over, she guessed she'd really embarrassed them last night. She owed them an apology for her childish behavior but remained firm in her resolve to control her own life.

She went to the bedroom, finding her cell phone at the foot of the bed. Without giving more thought to what she was about to do, she dialed her mother's cell phone, knowing she would be easier to deal with than her father. His disappointment in her would be far worse than her mother's angry words.

"Emily!" Her mother answered in her stern yet familiar you-are-grounded voice.

Here goes, she thought. "Hi, Mom." She cleared her throat. "Listen, I want to apologize for last night." There, she'd said the words she'd been dreading.

"Emily, your father is mortified. I'm not sure he'll ever forgive you for ruining his celebration. You know how important last night was to him, to us." Her mother had a tendency to exaggerate at times. She was sure now was one of them.

She sighed; she had expected this. It was time to tell the truth. "Then you can pass this on to Dad. Tell him he should have given me a heads-up on what he had in mind for *my* future! He has no right to make decisions for me. You both should know that."

"We want to keep the lodge in the family. You've known that your entire life. I guess we both assumed you knew when we decided to retire we would expect you to take our place. He told me he wanted to tell you beforehand, but the timing was off."

"That's all well and good, Mom, but you *didn't* tell me. Your expectations and mine obviously aren't on the same page. You expect me to just take over out of the blue, then find some guy, marry him, give you two a grandchild, all without any input from me? This is beyond ridiculous." She'd never spoken so harshly to her mother before. She felt guilty at her words, but she was not going to back down.

"If that's how you feel, I suppose we'll have to make other arrangements. Though I think we should all talk in person, as a family, before either of us says something we might regret later."

"Sure, I agree. I'll just hop over to the lodge now. You can meet me in Dad's office." Before she changed her mind, she pushed the End button on her cell. She hated being in this position, though she didn't have a choice. Her parents were treating her like a child, not a grown woman. Yes, she loved skiing, loved the lodge almost as much as her parents, but she didn't want to continue to live her life through their dream. Someday, maybe, but not now.

Her headache now nothing more than a dull throb, Emily dressed in jeans, a heavy wool sweater and UGG boots. She grabbed a light jacket and felt around for the keys to her Land Rover in the pocket. She clicked the automatic ignition on her key fob, waiting inside while the car heated up, though it wasn't too cold outside according to the temperature on her cell phone. It came in handy, even more so when temperatures were below freezing.

"I won't be long," she told Clarice, who'd jumped back on the sofa after her phone call She would spend most of the day sleeping. When Emily returned they would horse around a bit, as Clarice was very playful for a nine-year-old cat. Then she would usually hide in the spare bedroom for the rest of the night.

Emily's condominium was only two miles from Snow-drift Summit, but far enough that she maintained her privacy. She parked behind the main lodge, entering through the back as she and Kylie had the previous evening. The buzz from the kitchen wasn't nearly as loud as it'd been last night with the crew preparing dinner for hundreds. Emily hurried through the kitchen without encountering Kathryn or anyone else who'd witnessed her breakdown last night. At least she hoped not too many would be working in the kitchen on a Sunday after last night's big event.

Racing upstairs to her dad's office, she was surprised to see the door closed. She knocked. When she didn't get an answer, she pushed the door open. Her father sat behind his massive desk, her mother in a swivel chair across from him.

"Is not answering the door supposed to be some kind of message?" Emily asked, taking a seat on the leather sofa. She removed her jacket, tossing it on the cushion beside her. Watching her parents as they stared at her, she did not even recognize them. Stiff backed, jaws tightened, both focused on her as if she'd committed a horrific crime. Emily could be stubborn, and she refused to be the first one to bring up the topic at hand. She would sit here all day if that was what it took. She crossed her legs, swinging her foot back and forth while she waited for either parent to start a conversation.

Her father took a deep breath, slowly releasing it, all the while staring at her. "Emily, you have no idea how ashamed I am of your behavior last night."

She said nothing.

"I see you're not going to make this easy for us, so I'll get straight to the point. Your mother and I will remain here at the lodge for the upcoming season. This will give you time to get yourself prepared for the duties ahead. You've always known this was a family operation. I'm disheartened, to say the least, that you had no idea we would be passing the responsibilities on to you."

Taking her coat, Emily stood up, looking at both her parents. Without saying a word, she left the office, hurrying outside to her car. Tears blurred her vision, but she hit the Start button anyway. These people were not the kind, loving parents she had known her whole life. There had to be more to this than what they were telling her. When her father had singled her out last night, it was possible he really had news that was important. Maybe he had planned to tell her he was deeding the lodge to her, or maybe he was ill, or possibly her mother was ill. Shifting into reverse, Emily wanted to talk to her grandparents. If her mom or dad were ill, they would tell her.

Chapter Five

Mimi and Papaw's log home was perched at the top of a small hill a mile from the resort. They could walk to the lodge or, if they chose, use their private chair lift. Emily remembered as a child they would let her ride the lift to the base of the mountain, where she'd catch the main lift to the top of Snowdrift Summit, ski all day, then take the lift back to their house. Those were fun times. She hoped one day she would be able to share her childhood experiences with a child of her own.

She parked next to Papaw's four-wheel drive Ford F-150. She saw Mimi's Subaru was parked in the garage, but the door had been left open. Possibly they were going out, so her timing was perfect.

The cabin was as picturesque as the mountains surrounding it. It was two stories high, with windows in every room, surrounded by a porch that stretched the entire length of the front, plus each bedroom upstairs had a small balcony. She used to sneak out onto the balconies during heavy snowfalls and hold out her tongue to see how many snowflakes she could catch. Smiling at the memory, she tapped on the door.

"Come on in," Mimi called.

She entered the great room, still amazed by the vaulted ceilings. The golden logs created a warmth that even Papaw's handmade rock fireplace couldn't compete with. Dark green leather sofas with red afghans placed casually on the backs reminded her of Christmas, but that was nothing. Mimi had the cabin so well decorated during the holidays that it had been featured in several log home magazines.

"That you, Emily?" Mimi called from the kitchen.

"The one and only," she said. Removing her jacket, she hung it on one of the hooks that were in the shape of a ski. Nothing like keeping the resort theme going, she thought.

"I've coffee if you want," Mimi told Emily when she entered the cheery red-and-white kitchen. This was her favorite room, with the same ski-themed decor. Two old ski lift chairs from the early nineteen sixties that could seat two were on either side of the table that had been made out of old skis. Old photos of the lodge that were framed in bits and pieces of broken skis hung on the walls. Antique maple syrup cans held flowering plants, though Emily knew they were fake as Mimi did not have a green thumb. The most unique bit of decor was the old sled that hung above the kitchen island, which Mimi used to hang pots and pans on. Each piece of vintage ski equipment turned into furniture by her grandparents had a story behind it. Emily knew them all, but now wasn't the time to delve into the past.

"Thanks. I need another cup." Emily sat down at the table, the design never failing to bring a smile to her face. "I love this room," she said to Mimi.

"I know you do. It's my favorite as well." Mimi set two mugs of coffee on the table, then took a seat opposite her. "Your mother just called and said you would show up. You're mad."

Emily took a sip of coffee before answering. "No, I'm not mad. I've been blindsided. I didn't realize Dad was going to . . . hoist the lodge on my back last night. It shocked me."

"Oh Emily, surely you knew this"—Mimi waved her hand in front of her—"was all going to be yours someday? You've lived your entire life here, as we all have. It's a family operation."

"Right. The key word being 'family.' I would like to have the opportunity to live my life, and have a family, too. With this responsibility now, there's no way I could . . ." She paused. "Date, get married, let alone have children. It's too much for me now." There, she'd said it. Maybe now Mimi would inform her mother and she would inform her dad. "I'm not ready for this, and honestly, I'm not even sure I want to."

Mimi's eyes doubled in size. "Emily! Of course this is what you want to do! You're just confused. I admit, you should've been told first to prepare yourself, but it's a gift that you can pass on to your children, and they to their children. Don't you want your children to have the kind of childhood you did?"

Emily drew in a deep breath, slowly letting it out as she tried to stay calm. Mimi was right. Of course she wanted her children, if she had any, to have the kind of childhood she had, but that didn't mean she had to take over the resort at twenty-nine. She needed a life *first*.

"At this stage in my life, I'm just not ready for all this entails. I'm sorry, I'm just being honest."

Mimi cleared her throat, looking away from Emily. "I probably shouldn't tell you this, but I feel it's warranted."

"What? Who's dying?"

"What?" Mimi shouted.

"You heard me! You're scaring me. All this seriousness coming from Mom and Dad, and now you. It's not normal."

"No one is dying. Now, as I said, I shouldn't be the one

telling you this, your dad should, but since he hasn't, I will. Now just think how attractive you are. A great skier, college degrees. Then add 'resort owner' to your dating résumé. Imagine what kind of men you'll attract! You'll be able to catch a sweetheart. That's why your parents want you to have the resort now. They think you need, well . . . I'm not exactly sure what they think, but it is a bonus, owning a resort at such a young age. It might be just the push you need to get that family started. You know Harold has his own law firm now? With three associates. Not a bad fellow, and he skies well."

Emily didn't say anything. All she could do was stare at Mimi. When she saw that the silence was causing her discomfort, she finally spoke. "A dowry to trap Harold?"

Mimi's blue eyes twinkled. "Yes! That's exactly what your mother said."

There was more silence as the shock of this revelation charged through Emily. The concept was absurd, outrageous and insane. She imagined going out with any guy *other* than Harold, and if it was someone she liked, she could explain she had a dowry, so just in case he had feelings for her, she didn't come into the marriage empty-handed.

Back in the day, wasn't a dowry like bringing a pig and a cow into the husband's family? Just thinking about it now made her burst out laughing. Tears streamed down her face. She couldn't help it; this was so far from reality she thought either Mimi or her parents had temporarily lost their minds.

"Why are you laughing?" Papaw asked when he came into the kitchen to refill his cup.

Mimi spoke for her. "She's overtired."

"Mimi! Stop! I'm laughing at this idea that you and Mom think I'll find a husband sooner if I am the sole owner of a ski resort!" She stood, taking her mug to the sink.

"I'm leaving. I have some hunting to do," she said, then burst out in another fit of laughter. Maybe she was still a bit drunk from last night, or maybe she was dreaming. No one in the twenty-first century—at least no one she knew of—had a dowry! She hurried out to her SUV before they followed her or said anything else about a dowry.

Just the thought of it made her crack up laughing. Somewhere along the lines of communication, this had to be a misunderstanding. No way would anyone in their right mind suggest such an absurd idea. Maybe a hundred years ago, but now? As soon as she pulled back onto the main road, she started laughing again, her vision blurring from the tears of laughter. She reached for a tissue in the seat beside her, wiping at her eyes. As soon as she got home, she planned on calling her parents. No, she would go see them now, while the insanity of this suggestion was still fresh in her mind.

She parked in the back parking lot, going through the kitchen to her dad's office. Her mother's voice echoed from the other side of the door. Emily waited a few seconds before knocking.

"It's open," her dad said.

Closing the door behind her, Emily held her hand out in front of her. "Before you say anything, I need to tell you both what Mimi just told me."

Her mother shot a quick glance at her father before speaking. "Your father and I might've been a bit . . . hasty making this decision. We're not sure we want to retire just yet."

"Julia! This is news to me." He looked at her mother, dropping his head into his open palms.

"Sit down, Emily. You're making me nervous," her mother said.

Returning to the sofa, Emily didn't bother taking off her jacket. At this point she wasn't sure how long, or even if, she'd be staying. Unsure if her parents were suffering from some strange delusion or illness, she waited for her dad to offer an explanation.

He seemed to read her mind. When he spoke he said, "I owe you an apology, Emily. I'm sorry about last night. I should've told you when I had the opportunity. Your mom and I, we both thought you would be as excited as we were all those years ago when we were gifted the lodge."

No one said anything for a minute, then Emily couldn't hold back any more. "It's not that I don't want to continue the family business." She paused. "To be honest, it's just too much for me at this stage in my life. I love my job; you guys know that. But I'm not ready to commit to such an enormous responsibility. I want to have a life of my own first, a family without all this." She gestured to the window behind her dad's desk. "And let me be clear—no way in hell I am ever going to date, hook up or be in the same room with Harold Wilson. I wish you and Lucille would move on. I'm serious, Mom. If you continue with this, I'm not sure I'll stay in Colorado. I'm twenty-nine, not that you aren't aware of that. Please, stop trying to manage my life."

Her mother shook her head. "Well, I didn't realize you had such a strong dislike for Harold."

"You do now," Emily said, adding, "not to mention I'm taller than he is." Plus, he was already going bald. She truly disliked the guy. She didn't care to share her free time with him in any way, shape or form.

Emily's mother shook her head, sighing. "Harold is a wonderful young man. You know there is such a thing as shoe lifts, but I've said enough. We realize operating the resort is an enormous responsibility, Emily. You've trained for this since you were old enough to understand the business side of the resort. With your master's degree in business, I assumed, well . . . I thought you would jump at the chance to have complete control. Maybe change a few things around here, liven it up a bit."

"Mom, if Snowdrift Summit gets any livelier, we're going to have to hire more people. We're ranked number one in Colorado for The Plunge alone! We could modernize here and there, but you don't need me to do that." Emily watched her parents. She saw the sadness on their faces and didn't like to disappoint them.

Maybe she was being a brat, or simply wanted things to go her way, as they normally did. Growing up, she'd lacked for nothing, had more than most girls. She expected life to go her way, always, and she'd rarely experienced setbacks of any kind. Maybe now wasn't the time to throw in the towel. Maybe it was time for her to give back, show her parents they hadn't raised a self-centered, immature, selfish brat, which was exactly how she'd acted since last night's big announcement. Yes, it had surprised her. And no, she was not ready for this. But seeing the looks on their faces, she decided she would compromise.

Taking a deep breath to calm herself, she spoke. "I wish you both would've told me before the party, but you didn't, and I'm not going to let either of you get away with that. However, I'll stay this season, if you meant what you said. Maybe I can take on some of the daily operations, do a bit less instructing." That was all she could give them at this point. Who knew? She might end up loving the business side of the resort.

Her dad raked a hand across his face. He hadn't bothered to shave, casting a dark shadow across his face. "Julia, do you want to do this, since apparently we *aren't* retiring?"

"Of course I do, Mason. If I'm honest, I'm not ready to retire. Maybe slow down a little, but that's all. Emily, if this works out, maybe next season we'll retire."

"What about the party? What do plan to tell your friends?" Emily asked.

"That we weren't ready and had second thoughts."

"Okay, though I feel like a spoiled brat right now. I'm sorry I acted so hastily." Emily stood up and leaned over the giant desk, taking her parents' hands. "I'll try this season, I promise. If I don't feel I can successfully keep up with all you've accomplished, I'll tell you. Let me get my feet wet this year, and then I'll make my decision. And no more talk of Harold."

"We can work with that," her dad said.

"I'll call Mom and tell her," Julia said.

"Wait a sec. I need to clarify what Mimi told me. Did you really tell her that giving me the resort would be like offering a dowry to a future husband? That this would increase my value on the dating market?"

Her mother had the grace to look away. Her dad remained silent.

"Well?" Emily prompted.

"I did say something to that effect," her mom admitted. "I know it's a bit . . . dated."

Emily burst out laughing. "Dated? Yes, I'd say so, but just so you know, in the future, my personal life will not interfere with my work here at the resort." She didn't have much of a personal life at this point anyway, and when she did, she planned to keep that part of her life to herself.

"I suppose we can agree to those terms. If you just so happen to meet that special someone, you'll let us know?" her mother asked.

"I will, Mom. I promise," Emily said, knowing there wasn't much hope of that any time soon. If and when she met someone special, they would know. Maybe.

"Then let's put this behind us and get to work," her father said. "I'm expecting a delivery in an hour."

"On a Sunday?" Julia said. "I planned on attending the late church service this morning."

"I'll go with you, Mom," Emily said, feeling she needed a bit of repentance herself.

"Perfect! Do you want to meet there or ride together?"

"I'll meet you there. I need to go back to the condo, change clothes, clean up a bit and check on Clarice."

"Thanks, sweetie. You're the best," her mother said, walking around the desk to give her a hug.

Emily returned the hug and blew her dad a kiss before she left. The last church service of the day started in an hour, which didn't give her a lot of time. Hoping she'd made the right decision, she crossed her fingers.

Chapter Six

"That was a wonderful sermon," Emily said as she and her mother walked to the parking lot together.

"I agree. Very calming. Just what we both needed. Listen, why don't I call your father to see if he wants to meet us for lunch at The Mill? I think the lodge can do without us for a couple more hours."

"Sure, that sounds perfect. If he can't, it'll be just the two of us. A girls' day," Emily said, feeling more like herself with each passing minute. No more tequila for her; it'd made her feel very aggressive. Assuming it was out of her system now, she felt even more ashamed of her actions the night before. She'd still been pretty sober when she'd run out after the big announcement, as she'd only had a few glasses of champagne at that point. It hadn't affected her the way the tequila did later.

After finalizing plans to meet at The Mill, Emily called Kylie when she arrived home, wanting to fill her in on the new arrangement between herself and her parents.

"So you're not going to boss me around any time soon?" Kylie teased.

"Nope. As I said, we've reached a truce. I'll work in the office and cut my lessons down, which may add more work for you and Jackie, and the others, if you all can handle it. I'll see how I like the change. If I do, then next season I'll take over full-time. All of this is a big 'if,' so don't freak out. I'm about to go have lunch with my mom at The Mill. Why don't you pop in and have a bite with us? I saw your car this morning; I know you're home." Kylie lived just one building away from hers.

"Thanks, but the thought of eating makes me sick. I'm never going to drink again," Kylie said. "At least not any liquor."

"Same here, though I didn't get sick, just a massive headache. Okay, gotta run. We'll catch up later." She clicked End on her cell and headed out to lunch.

Once inside the restaurant, she saw it was packed as usual. The hostess said the wait was fifteen minutes even though there were several empty tables. Knowing the restaurant didn't take reservations, maybe there were folks waiting for these tables who were there but hadn't yet taken their seats. Emily didn't really care after the morning she'd had. She appreciated a few moments alone, even if it was in a very popular, noisy local eatery. The Mill had their own brewery, making a different brew once a week. She'd tried pumpkin beer once, and it was like drinking rotting pumpkin. The place was always jammed, though. The food was excellent and the decor had the usual ski theme, with a few deer and bear heads added—which she detested, but it was what it was.

While she waited, Emily watched as a group of at least twenty men and women filled up the empty tables. She could tell they weren't locals by the way they were dressed, decked out in designer jeans, jackets and boots. Her own clothes weren't quite so perfect as they weren't brand-spanking-new. Most folks around Loveland wore their clothes for more than one season. She guessed that they were maybe a bunch of vacationers who'd purchased new clothing for the trip. Emily wondered why they wouldn't wash their clothes a few times before wearing them, but it was none of her business. Maybe they had other reasons for their visit.

Her mother blew in through the door like a fresh breeze. "Sorry I'm late. I couldn't get your grandmother off the phone," she said. "Are we on a waiting list?"

The hostess motioned to Emily. "I'll seat y'all now," she said in a Southern accent.

"Not anymore," Emily said over her shoulder to her mother, following the hostess to a booth by the window, which was across from the large group of recently seated tourists.

As soon as Emily and Julia were settled, their server took their drink order, returning moments later with two large ice teas. Emily could barely focus on the menu, as the large group of people were so loud. She snuck several glances at them, sure that she'd seen at least one of them before but couldn't place where.

"Emily, are you going to order?" her mother asked as their server stood waiting.

"I'm sorry. I'll have a hamburger with sweet potato fries," she said.

"We only have the bison burger. Is that okay?" the server asked.

"Fine," Emily said, though she wasn't a huge fan of bison.

As soon as their server stepped away, her mother spoke up. "You never eat bison."

She nodded. "I'm making an exception, trying something new. Kathryn is always urging me to expand my palate."

"Kathryn is right. I'll make sure she knows you took her suggestion seriously."

"You don't need to do that. Really, Mom. I'm a big girl,

okay?" She raised her brows, a slight smile on her face. She didn't want to remind her of their talk earlier, not wanting to spoil the new truce between them.

"I know, but sometimes it's just hard to remove the mom hat," Julia admitted.

"I hope to experience that myself someday. For now, please remember I'm an adult," Emily said, knowing it might change the tone of the light conversation.

"That group over there," her mother whispered, "I think it's those tacky old movie people."

"What movie people?"

"You didn't hear? Never mind, I can explain. A group of producers, actors, whatever they call themselves are looking for a resort to film some silly CIA action movie."

Emily's eyes widened in recognition. The guy she'd seen and actually thought she knew . . . it was Zach Ryker! Her favorite actor! He starred in the popular CIA movie series she was addicted to, a secret she'd kept to herself for years. Forcing herself to act normal, she replied, "I'm sure it's just talk."

"No, I don't believe so. Wynn Watters over at Diamond Pass is telling all of the resort owners they're going to film at his place. He called your dad last week. I think he was trying to rub his nose in the fact that his place is so ritzy."

And to think I'd thought of applying for a job there, Emily thought. "They get all the celebrities. It shouldn't be too hard for them to accommodate the crew, the actors, whatever staff they have. Dad's too classy to care what Wynn says, right?" Her heart rate sped up just thinking of this missed opportunity.

"Absolutely. He's beyond that superfluous nonsense. If you ask me, we don't need all the hoopla they bring with them. Paparazzi lurking, the added traffic, folks who do nothing but try and get a glimpse of the actors, which is such a silly profession, pretending to be someone you're not."

Good thing she kept her love of Zach Ryker movies to herself. Unsure about the actor himself, she enjoyed the action-packed thrillers, always looking forward to the latest movie. Knowing the actor was practically a few feet away gave her chills.

"I'm sure they believe acting is a job, the same as running the resort," Emily said, hoping she didn't sound as phony as she felt.

"I disagree," her mother replied. "It's too silly to be called a job. I'm so proud you've earned your master's degree and have a stable profession."

Emily laughed. "I'm a ski instructor—not sure that's really a stable job. I'm just lucky you and Dad own the resort."

Their server appeared then, placing their food on the table. "Looks great," Emily said, and it did. It was the taste of the bison she might have issues with. Hoping to change the topic, she took a bite of her burger, surprised by the taste. "This is really good, seriously." Taking another bite, she thought Kathryn was right about trying different foods.

"You really like it?" her mother asked.

"I do."

For the next several minutes, they focused on eating their lunch. When they finished, Emily asked the server for a dessert menu.

"You never have dessert at lunchtime," Julia remarked.

"I'm changing my ways," Emily told her mom as she took the menu from the server. She froze when she saw Zach Ryker staring at her. Quickly focusing her attention on the menu, she ordered a slice of cherry pie. "No ice cream," she told the server.

In her peripheral vision, Emily saw Zach still staring at her. Had she missed something when she'd gone back to her place to change clothes? A zipper? A tag showing?

She'd brushed her long hair straight, not bothering with much else as she hadn't had time. She'd thrown on a red sweater dress she'd purchased from Nordstrom last year along with suede, camel-colored, over-the-knee boots. Pretty fancy for her, but she'd gone to church. Unlike some women, she refused to wear slacks to church. A personal choice, one her mother and grandmother practiced and she'd adopted.

Deciding to give Zach something to see, Emily excused herself to the ladies' room. "Back in a flash, and don't you dare touch my pie," she said to her mom with a grin. As she walked toward the back of the restaurant where the restrooms were located, for a split second there was a hush from the table of noisy movie folks, then bursts of laughter. Feeling her face redden, she hurried inside a stall, standing there and waiting. Had they been laughing at her? If so, she probably deserved it for sashaying her derrière across the room trying to get Zach's attention. She'd been gone long enough for her mother to come searching for her, and that would be the final humiliation. Checking herself in the mirror, front and back, she felt confident enough to waltz back to the table. She saw several guys from the table glance her way, but did nothing to acknowledge them.

"Too much alcohol last night," she said loud enough for those at the table across the way to hear.

"Your pie is cold, Emily. Do you want me to have them reheat it, or take it with you?"

"No, I'll eat it here," she said. In less than five minutes, she'd choked down the pie. "That was delicious."

The server must've been watching her because as soon as she placed her fork down, she came to their table and placed the check on the table. Emily checked the amount, taking three twenties from her purse.

"Keep the change," she told the server.

Once they were outside, she could finally drop the act, though she was sure her mother had no clue she'd been pretending not to notice the guys watching her. "I enjoyed lunch. Let's do it again soon," she told her mom. "I'm going home. Not sure if I'll be back at the resort today, but I'll be in tomorrow so you and Dad can start showing me the ropes."

"That's fine. There isn't too much going on today, other than a few deliveries. See you tomorrow, sweetie." Her mother blew her a kiss before getting into her Lincoln LX. Emily watched until she pulled out of The Mill's parking lot as she wasn't the best driver. Once she saw she'd made it safely onto the main road, she hit the button on her key fob, unlocking the door. As she placed her hand on the door handle, a hand clamped over hers.

"Wait," said a voice she recognized quite well.

Chapter Seven

Emily whirled around to find Zach Ryker standing beside her. He was much taller than he appeared on the big screen, at least six five. His films didn't do justice to his looks. Devilishly handsome, he smiled at her, his teeth strikingly white against his tanned skin, his dark hair much longer than in his movies. Indigo eyes she recognized but had never seen in person were focused on her. For a split second she thought she was imagining him, however the scent of him, piney mixed with some kind of unknown spice, let her know he was very, *very* real.

His hand on hers sent a vague, sensuous feeling throughout her body. Clearing her head, she managed to say, "Yes?" though her throat was as dry as sand in the desert. "Do I know you?" she asked, injecting a trace of annoyance in her voice. His hand remained on hers.

"I don't know, but I know who you are," he said, taking his hand away.

"Sorry, I don't recall you," Emily lied.

"I'm told you're one of the best ski instructors in the state," he finally said. "Is that true?"

Surprised he knew this, she answered, "I'm good, if that's what you want to know." She actually was the best, but modesty prevented her from saying so—plus she didn't care too much for braggarts.

"I'll be in touch." He winked, then started to walk away. He stopped, calling out to her, "I hope it's soon." He winked at her again.

She didn't move. Couldn't move. Emily knew if he turned around he'd find her standing there staring, slack-jawed. How did he know she was an instructor? Was that why he had been staring at her inside the restaurant? Did he assume she knew his name, because he hadn't exactly introduced himself. She heard boisterous laughter coming from the front of The Mill, sure it was the group of movie people leaving. She hurried to get inside her car, pulling away before Zach saw her again. Whatever happened, no way would she let this sexy—and kinda sweet—world-famous movie star know she might be one of his biggest fans.

Once she was on the main road, she focused on her driving, but couldn't get Zach Ryker out of her head. She knew every movie he'd starred in as Gunner West, a CIA operative who didn't always follow the rules, but always managed to save the day. She'd heard he did all of his own stunts, but wasn't sure if this was mere Hollywood gossip. His wide shoulders, which narrowed down to a slim waist, proved he worked out, but not that he actually performed all the outrageous stunts in his equally outrageous films. His world and hers were totally opposite. She didn't like being the center of attention. He apparently did or he wouldn't be in the movie business.

She pulled into the parking garage at her condominium, turning off the ignition. Waiting a few minutes before going inside, she thought about what she would do for the remainder of the day.

Inside her condo, she changed into black leggings and a University of Denver sweatshirt. She made a pot of tea, bringing it into the living room with her. In the coat closet she kept a box that held all of the movies she had on DVD. No one would see them if they just so happened to pop over, and now, more than ever, she had to make sure her mother didn't see the movies. It was her silly little secret.

Planning to watch them in order, she removed *Risk Assessment* from its case, inserting it inside the DVD player. Making sure the front door was locked and her blinds were closed, she sat on the sofa and clicked Play. Clarice slunk out of the spare room to join her.

For the next ninety minutes, she and Clarice watched Zach, aka Gunner West, jump from an airplane into the River Seine, then steal a motorcycle, drive through the streets of Paris, toss his bike aside before kicking down three doors while shooting the enemy, all without a scratch. When he reached his destination, he slid his hand through his thick black hair, and said the words that were now synonymous with all his movies: "Not a scratch." He winked, then turned his back away from the camera. All his movies ended this way. A trademark, not unlike the James Bond character who, when asked what he'd like to drink, famously responded, "A vodka martini. Shaken, not stirred."

Emily followed up with *Foreign Entity*, one of her favorites. It was action-packed, starting with a bomb going off in a fictional version of the White House. There was smoke, fire, people screaming, and then in came Zach via helicopter, searching for the bomber and his gang of terrorists. Emily dozed off, waking in time to see the screen credits rolling. It was late. She wanted to watch another movie, but she had to call it a night.

"Meow." Clarice wanted dinner.

"Come on, girl, I'll feed you, even though I can see you've been eating from your fancy automatic feeder." Long work days meant sometimes she wasn't there to actually open a can of Clarice's favorite wet food.

Once she'd taken care of Clarice's needs, Emily headed to her bedroom, knowing her cat would return to the spare room where her toys would entertain her for the night, or she'd perch on the windowsill, hoping to spot some birds.

Tomorrow was Monday, the beginning of the work-week in this new position Emily found herself in. Who knew what surprises it might bring? If Zach truly needed a ski instructor, he would find her. She smiled as she changed into her pajamas. Monday just might be the best day of her life. Or the worst, if Zach Ryker didn't call.

With dreamy visions of her favorite actor, she fell into a blissful sleep, waking hours later to find the sun streaming in through the slats in the blinds. Emily rolled over to look at the clock on her bedside table. It wasn't there. Tossing the covers aside, she saw the clock on the floor. She remembered throwing it yesterday when she'd been in the midst of a killer hangover. The red numbers on the clock flashing twelve, she went to the kitchen and saw it was after ten.

"Shoot."

She never slept this late. What if the movie people had been to the lodge and she wasn't there? If she missed an opportunity like that, she would never forgive herself. Before she ran out the door, she called her mom.

"Hey, I overslept. Is there anything happening now? Any reason for me to hurry?" she asked her mother while she made a pot of coffee.

Clarice heard her and traipsed to the kitchen for her breakfast. Emily opened a can of food, placing it next to the automatic feeder and water fountain.

"Meow." A thank-you from the cat.

"Nothing we can't do ourselves. We're just paying the monthly bills. If you want to have a look at the vendors and a few other things, just come by when you're ready. No hurry," said her mother, who sounded like her normal self.

"Okay, be there in an hour," Emily replied. Maybe Zach Ryker had been feeding her a line of bull. Wynn Watters always had celebrities at Diamond Pass; there was no reason to believe this would change. Though she wasn't sure any movies had ever been filmed there, she'd never been curious enough to ask. She filled her YETI mug with coffee, taking it with her into the bathroom, where she took a quick shower, then dressed in a pair of jeans with a dark green turtleneck shirt. She brushed her waist-length hair, then added a spritz of hairspray to tame the flyaways around her face. Not wanting to be too obvious, she added one coat of mascara and a bit of blush to her cheeks.

Examining herself in the mirror, Emily decided she looked like she was going out with the girls because these days that was the only time she wore makeup or cared about her appearance. Her mother would be the first one to notice. Emily usually wore ski clothes to work, but now that she was going to actually work in the office it would be the perfect excuse for sprucing up a bit. Today she'd have Jackie or Kylie cover for her, as she'd promised she'd step back from instructing, though she would give anything to get out in the snow because, according to her phone, they'd had half a foot last night. She imagined the edge of her ski cutting into the powder, the spray of snow as she came to a quick stop.

She finished her coffee, pouring another cup to go. Before leaving, she returned all of her Zach Ryker movies to the closet, smiling to herself. So what if she liked fast-paced, larger-than-life characters in movies that were borderline ridiculous? She wasn't the only one; his movies were always big hits.

Hearing Emily's keys jingle, Clarice raced to the door in time to give her a dirty look. "Goodbye to you, too, Queen Clarice."

This was their usual ritual.

Inside her car, Emily hummed the theme song from Zach Ryker's movie *Grave Damage*. As far as she knew, that had been his last major film. After the country had been in lockdown for almost two years, she thought it was about time he made a new movie. Possibly that was why he was in Colorado. Outside and in the open; there wasn't much chance of getting sick here. No one in her family had been ill with the nasty virus, though a couple of the employees who worked in the ski rental department had been sick, eventually returning to work with no harmful side effects, thankfully.

She parked her car and went inside through the back as she always did. It was quiet today. There was a lot of preparation each year. The slopes had to be in perfect condition—with no dead tree stumps or anything that could cause a skier to have an accident. All of the chair lifts had to operate at 100 percent capacity at all times. They needed at least thirty instructors or more, experienced ski patrols, groomers willing to work all night in the freezing cold. Though the Sno-Cats were fully equipped with heating, temperatures were often so cold the heat wasn't enough. They had a large terrain park that needed constant maintenance. Emily guessed they had about three or four hundred employees, half of them seasonal. Maybe more, as they also had the lodge, which served food all day, an aprés lounge that filled up as soon as the slopes closed for the day and would remain busy until closing. There were so many positions to fill to maintain a ski resort. Just thinking of all the responsibilities involved in running it overwhelmed her.

Seeing her dad in his office, she tapped on the door. "Am I interrupting?"

"Hey, kiddo, of course you're not. Your mom went for drinks. You want anything? I can call down to the bar."

"No, not for me. After Saturday night I'm staying away from the stuff for a while," she said.

"Just sodas. No alcohol this early in the day," he said.

"I wasn't thinking. I stayed up too late and slept way too long. I hate starting the week this way. So, what's on the agenda for the day? Kylie and Jackie are taking my classes."

"It's Monday, so not too much on the agenda with all this snow. I'm looking into purchasing another Sno-Cat. The two we have seem to be in and out of maintenance constantly. I need one good machine."

"What about Papaw's old Tucker Sno-Cat? That still runs, doesn't it?" she asked.

"Better than some of the newer ones, for sure. Can't get your hands on them anymore. Folks that have them hang on to them. They're a cult classic now. I doubt that your grandfather is going to give his up anytime soon. He still makes his nighttime crawls up the mountain. Then there are the Tucker Sno-Cat races. He wins every year. I'm beginning to think his Sno-Cat is rigged." He laughed.

Emily laughed as well. "I can't believe he still does that. I went with him a few times when I was a kid. Froze my rear end off even with the heat on high. I enjoy the races, though. They bring in a lot of new people to the resort. Fun times for sure," she said, more to herself than to her father. The Tucker, a true classic, was Papaw's Sno-Cat that he'd purchased in the early seventies, according to her grandfather. He kept it in prime condition, though she hadn't realized he still made his nightly jaunts up the mountain during the season.

Her mother returned with two glasses of soda and a bowl of popcorn, reminding Emily she hadn't eaten since yesterday's lunch. "That smells good," Emily said, reaching into the bowl for a handful. "Dad says there isn't much for me to do today."

"He's right, but it's a good time to go over a few office necessities, things like that. The closer it gets to the holidays, the harder it is to find a minute alone."

"I know. Though I'm on the mountain most of the day, I rarely have time to myself, unless I get up there before we open. Which I still do as often as I can," Emily said. That was always the best part of her day, when she had the mountain to herself.

"You're a true skier," her mother said, passing the popcorn bowl to Emily's dad.

Emily agreed. She didn't understand why her parents thought she'd be happy managing the resort, knowing her love of skiing and being outdoors. It didn't matter at this point. They'd made a deal and she planned on sticking to it, no matter what.

"I am," she said, then changed the subject. "Dad says we need a new corduroy maker," she said, using the locals' term for a Sno-Cat vehicle. "Aren't they super expensive? Is this factored into the budget?"

"Yes," her father answered. "We've planned on purchasing a new Cat for two years. The machines we have now are decent enough, but they get a lot of use. In and out of maintenance, as I said. We need two fully operational at all times. Three is even better."

"Okay, makes sense. Less usage, less time on the mountain," Emily agreed. "What about the terrain area? We can't get a Sno-Cat in there. Who's doing the resurfacing, checking the rails at night?" She was clueless as to who kept the terrain area in tiptop shape for the snowboarders. Much of the area had been updated with new rails and boxes before the first snow, yet she hadn't paid attention to it at the time because she wasn't in a managerial position. Usually they'd start with artificial snow to pack the ice on, then pray for lots of snow before opening day, which they now had plenty of. She could snowboard, but it wasn't nearly as much fun as skiing, so she'd stayed away from the terrains.

"We hire an outside team to design and reconstruct the entire terrain. It doesn't take long. Each year I like to add more challenging rails, and this year the team has really outdone themselves. Or, at least the plans appear to be some of their best work so far. You should have a look. I can drive you up in one of the Cats, or you can go see for yourself."

"Maybe later. I'm not a snowboarder, Dad, though I'm excited to see the changes in the terrain," Emily said.

Emily wanted to ask if either of them had received a phone call inquiring about her giving skiing lessons to Zach Ryker, but there was no way that she would. They didn't appear to have that sneaky parental look she was so familiar with when they were keeping something from her. It had probably just been wishful thinking, she decided. If she brought up the topic, her mother would remind her how tacky those "movie people" were, and weren't they lucky they were going to Diamond Pass instead of Snowdrift Summit. She would agree and move on, as expected. Right now, if she saw Zach Ryker, she would punch him in the face for his far-fetched suggestion. But only *after* she smacked herself upside the head for believing him. How did he even know who she was? Had his producer or assistant asked who was the best ski instructor in the area? Unsure how that stuff worked, she tucked away the thought for later. She needed to focus her attention on her new position, even if it was just a trial run.

"You want to go with me to purchase the new Cat?" her father asked.

"Now?"

"No, maybe tomorrow or Wednesday. It will give you the opportunity to meet the folks we work with. Maybe with my charming daughter tagging along I might get a better deal. Who knows? It's worth a try."

She laughed. "Not gonna happen, but I'll go just because it's part of the job. I'll make sure to look my worst, just in case." Emily laughed again.

"That's impossible, Emily," her mom said to her. "You look exceptionally beautiful today. Sleeping in does one good once in a while."

If she only knew what had kept her up so late. But, what she didn't know wouldn't hurt her. Emily had to stop playing in to her parents' idea of her. She was an adult, though when she spent too much time around them, it was so easy to slide back into the family routine, allowing them to make all the decisions. Not that she didn't enjoy being with them. Of course she did. "Thanks, Mom. I figured I need to look presentable inside the offices."

"I appreciate the effort," she said.

"So what's on today's agenda? For me," Emily questioned.

"I want you to familiarize yourself with all the vendors, starting with the suppliers," her mother answered. "They're our bread and butter, especially when we've had a massive snowstorm. Without them, we can't operate. I usually offer big discounts to them and their family members. I like to barter, too. 'Bring me an extra hundred pounds of flour for Kathryn, I'll give you free lift tickets for the season.' That sort of thing."

"I like that idea, it's not so . . . *corporate*."

"We're all family here," Emily's father said. "Most of the folks we work with are family owned too. When your grandparents bought the resort fifty plus years ago, that's the way business was handled for the most part. When Houston and Ella deeded the resort to your mom and me, the only request they had was that we continue to use family-owned businesses whenever possible."

Emily hadn't really cared too much about the business end of the resort growing up. Even when she received her master's in business, it never occurred to her that she would someday have full control of the resort. Listening to her dad explain their mode of doing business gave her a new outlook. She liked the idea of working with like-minded people. Everything was so high tech, impersonal and competitive; it was nice knowing that her family hadn't joined the rest of the world in the rat race to be the first and the biggest—though she felt they were the best. Their way of doing business appealed to her.

"I think it's worked so far, so why change now?" Emily said. "I wouldn't do anything different, if that's what you need to hear from me. I wasn't planning on making changes, though I do have an idea I'd like to run by you." She knew her idea wasn't original, but it would be new to Snowdrift Summit. "What are your thoughts on a portable vino bar, using the Sno-Cats during the daytime, maybe once or twice a week, at the top of the mountain? A couple of hours before we shut the lifts down?"

Her parents looked at each other, then at her before answering.

"I think it's a terrific idea," her mom said, "though there could be some risk involved." Julia looked back at her husband.

"You mean accidents?" Emily asked. "Anyone who skies risks having an accident. Wouldn't that cover anyone's choice to ride the Sno-Cat, too? It's a possibility for sure but most of our visitors are aware of that."

"True. Let me call Russel Jenson. He's our insurance agent, so he'll know. I've used his company for twenty years. I'll introduce you when I can," her dad said. "I like the idea. I'll check into the pros and cons. If it's feasible, we'll start when I get the new Cat."

"Thanks. I appreciate you both considering it. It's not a new idea. Other resorts have vino cats, too. If all goes well, we can add something unique. I don't have any ideas yet, but I'll come up with one. I'll think on it and let you know as soon as I do."

Her dad's private line rang. Holding up his hand, he mouthed, *Hang on*, then spoke into the phone. "This is Mason." After listening for a beat, he said, "What's going on? I haven't heard from you since last week. Yes, she's here. Actually she's in the office now. Should I put her on? I see. This is not a decision I can make on my own. I'll talk to her, see how she feels. I'm guessing I already know, but as I said, I'll ask." He paused again. "Sure thing, Wynn, I'll let you know." He placed the phone back on the desk.

"You're never going to believe this," he said to Julia. "Wynn is asking me for a favor."

"Then he must be in a bind. He's such an arrogant man," Julia said. "What kind of favor is he asking for?"

He turned to Emily. "He wants *you* to train one of the actors for the new CIA movie they're filming at his place. It seems he can ski, but not well enough to do his own stunts for this particular movie. Yet he insists on doing them for this production. He wants to ski The Plunge."

Speechless, Emily stared at him for a few seconds. Finding her voice she said, "Why?"

"He says his own instructors aren't nearly as capable as you are."

So Zach Ryker hadn't been lying to her when he saw her at The Mill on Sunday. "If I'm working in the office now, how can I train him?" Though they'd had plenty of snow this year. Maybe too much, especially at The Plunge, as it was at the top of the Summit.

"Emily Ammerman! I hope you're not considering this. Those movie people, well, they're beyond silly. I wouldn't want you getting involved with them. It might ruin your reputation," Her mother's voice was laced with irritation.

"Mother, remember what we discussed? I make my own decisions." She took a deep breath, focusing her attention on her dad. "Tell me more."

"They're filming at Diamond Pass right now, the scenes that can be filmed inside. Wynn asked if you'd be willing to train this guy to ski down The Plunge when they finish up. Said they'd be filming here for at least three months."

Truly dumbfounded, Emily didn't know what to say. "How much time do I have?"

"Wynn said they'd give you two weeks, plus a minor part in the film."

"Two weeks! There's no way I can teach someone to ski The Plunge in that amount of time. It took me years to accomplish it myself, and I'm a trained instructor."

"He says his guy is an excellent skier," her dad said, a sly smile on his face.

Emily felt her face grow red.

"They want to film him at The Plunge. You, too, as they need an extra who knows how to ski well," her father continued.

"Mason, that's enough. Don't fill her head with such nonsense. She is not a movie star and doesn't have any desire to become one. Now, pick up that phone, call Wynn Watters and tell him Emily will not instruct his silly actor, and he cannot film his movie on our property."

"Mother, stop! I'm sick of you trying to run my life. I

can decide for myself. Are you getting this? Dad, call Wynn and tell him I'll be happy to instruct his actor, but I'll need one month, maybe longer. If he can't give me that, then no, I won't accept his student." Emily raised her voice. "Don't you remember what we discussed?"

"I do, and you said you'd give up instructing," her mother reminded her.

Yes, she'd agreed, but teaching Zach Ryker to ski The Plunge would be the ultimate addition to her résumé. "Dad? Any input here?"

"Julia, it's a once-in-a-lifetime opportunity for Emily, and it's a short period of time. I think she should do this. Of course, only if she agrees. It's not like we couldn't use the free publicity."

"Mason Ammerman, you know how I feel about this. I strongly dislike all the hoopla they bring to our town. The paparazzi following them like they're royalty. People don't act like themselves when they're around. It's a big no for me. I'm sure Mom and Dad will agree with me, too."

"So I don't have a say in this? You're deeding the resort to me next season, yet I have no say in anything now?" Emily didn't understand why her mother smothered her to death.

Her father spoke up. "Emily, you do have a say. If you want to try this, I'm on your side. I told Wynn I would let him know, so it's up to you. Think on it for a while. You have a few days before you'd have to start."

"You and I are going to have a long talk tonight," Julia said to her husband. "I'm finished for the day. You and your daughter go ahead, make all the plans you want. I'll have nothing to do with this . . . scheme."

She grabbed her purse from a desk drawer, then left Emily and her father staring at her back. After Julia gave the door a good slam, Emily couldn't help but laugh. "Why does this make her so angry?"

"Long story. Maybe someday she'll explain it to you. I

swore I would never reveal her secret, so for now, let's just forget about her anger. Seriously, you don't have to do this. It's a heck of a responsibility, but like I said, great publicity for us." He leaned back in his chair, smiling like the Cheshire cat.

What if she couldn't teach him in the time allotted? Or, what if he hurt himself trying to ski The Plunge? Emily was willing to take the chance, figuring it was time she had a little bit of excitement in her life. If her mom didn't like it, she'd get over it sooner or later. "Call Wynn. Tell him I'll do it with some conditions."

"You want to tell me what they are? Wynn is a deal-maker, so he'll want to know immediately."

"Six weeks, a contract to protect Snowdrift Summit, no liability, that sort of thing. And I want screen credit for the resort when this film hits the theaters. Plus, I want Kylie to be the extra. She would be thrilled. Of course she'll need a contract, with a reasonable payment, and I want a screen credit for the training. I don't need money, but I want a contract to cover my butt in case something goes wrong."

"I'm not sure Wynn will agree to all that, but I'll give him a call. All he can do is say no. You want to hang around while I make the call?"

"Of course," she said. "I'll text Kylie the info while you're on the phone."

"Deal."

Emily typed out a short version of what she and her father had just discussed, while listening to her father's end of his conversation with Wynn. Her phone pinged almost instantly with Kylie's response: **"I'm in!"** She replied with a thumbs-up emoji. Later she would call to let her know if Wynn Watters had agreed to her terms.

"That'll work for us, too. Thanks, Wynn. I'll be seeing you." Mason hung up the phone. "He's agreed to all your conditions."

Emily was surprised because Wynn was known as a tough businessman. He must've really wanted her to train Zach, as she'd figured her conditions might be too much to ask for. Had Zach insisted on lessons from her? Or had Wynn suggested Zach take lessons from her? And why did Wynn have this kind of control over a Zach Ryker film? There had to be a bonus of some kind; otherwise, Wynn wouldn't be involved. Maybe he'd put up a wad of money for the filmmakers to use Diamond Pass? Either way, she knew there was more to the story. For now, she didn't care. When the time was right, she'd do a bit of snooping to see if she came up with anything.

"That was too easy," she said, thinking her father would offer an explanation.

"No, if Wynn wants something, he'll agree to just about anything."

"I guess. You know him much better than I do. I wasn't sure he'd agree to my conditions, so I'll just assume I'm such a good instructor that he'll pay or do whatever it takes."

"Hey, kiddo, remember not to let your head swell. Wynn has his reasons, and I have no doubt they have something to do with making more money. You're the best instructor; I do agree with that. Now I have to deal with your mother. I feel sure I'll be sleeping on the couch tonight," he said, grinning.

"Sorry, Dad."

"Nothing to be sorry about. This is all about you now. A once-in-a-lifetime opportunity," he said before locking his desk drawers. "How about giving the old man a ride home?"

"Absolutely," she said, walking alongside him as they left his office. Emily hoped she was up for the task ahead of her.

Chapter Eight

"**M**eet me at The Eagles Nest for breakfast tomorrow. We'll go take a look at that new Sno-Cat." Emily's dad leaned across the console, gave her a half hug. "Thanks for the ride."

"Okay. Say eight o'clock?"

"Works for me." He got out of her car and tapped the hood as he walked away. Waiting until he was inside, she couldn't help but laugh when she thought of how her mother would tear him a new rear end. She was small but mighty, and used to getting her way with Dad. Emily was glad he had stood up to her. She knew they would have words, then both of them would forget this ever happened. At least she hoped so.

Now she was more curious than ever. She had to know why her mom was so against the "movie people." She could ask Mimi or Papaw, but they probably wouldn't tell her. If they told someone they'd keep a secret, they did. Though Mimi was a little sly now and then, dropping hints when she thought one should know whatever secret she'd promised to keep. Maybe it was time for another visit. Turning her Land Rover in the opposite direction, Emily headed to her grandparents' house. She parked in the same spot as before. Seeing both of their vehicles, she knew they were home, unless they were out with the Clarks. They often went out together, each taking turns driving, though she doubted they were out on a Monday evening.

She tapped on the door. "You all home?" she asked before stepping inside.

"Come on in, Emily," Papaw called. As usual he was sitting in his recliner in front of the fireplace, though there was no fire burning, which surprised her.

"Hey, Papaw, what's up?"

"I'm thinking," he replied.

"That's always a good thing to do. What are you thinking about?" She liked to tease him and he knew it.

"Not sure if it's meant for your ears."

"Oh, one of those thoughts," she played along.

"Yep, it is."

"Then I guess I'd better scoot. Is Mimi here?" she asked.

"No, she's out with Carol. They say they're starting a romance book club, so they're over at Sky High Bookstore. I'm surprised you haven't been asked to join."

That was odd, Emily thought, though knowing Mimi, it would be much more than a romance book club. Another reason to throw a party. "Sounds like fun. I didn't realize she liked to read romance novels."

"There's lots of things you don't know about your grandmother. And your mother. And I am not gonna tell you, so before you try to pry anything out of me, the answer is no."

"Papaw! I would never do such a thing. I respect their privacy. If they have secrets they don't want me to know, that's fine. I have secrets myself, so I understand where they're coming from. Listen, I stopped over to . . ." She paused, trying to come up with a reasonable excuse because Papaw obviously knew what she was up to. News traveled fast in her family. "See if I could borrow Mimi's InstaPot. Kylie and I are having a few friends over later; she has a couple things she wants to try before buying one for herself. Think she'd mind?"

"You two are gonna cook?" Papaw asked.

"Kylie is."

"It's on the kitchen counter. I'm sure your grandmother won't mind. Just make sure to send her a picture of whatever you cook. She's on that InstaPot social media site, so she'll want to share the recipes with all of her followers."

Emily was taken aback, as she'd had no idea Mimi was involved in yet another social media club. "Uh, sure, I'll do that, but only if it turns out as good as Kylie says."

He nodded. "Then get the silly thing and get on with it," he said with a smile.

Emily knew that Papaw knew she was feeding him a big bite of bologna. "Thanks, Paps. I owe you one." She went to the kitchen, took the InstaPot, then headed out without another word. Now she had to ask Kylie over to cover her lie. She normally wasn't a big liar, but she needed to know why her mother was so against "movie people." Without Mimi being here, she'd have to save this for another time. If anything, she and Kylie would have a fun evening messing around with this InstaPot thing. Or rather Kylie would.

Before starting her car, Emily dialed Kylie's number, then clicked on the Bluetooth so she could talk while keeping both hands on the steering wheel. "I need a humongous favor."

"I can only imagine, but whatever it is, yes."

Emily laughed. "This must have something to do with our little arrangement, I'm guessing."

"Duh! It's not every day my best friend offers me a part in a *movie*. A *Zach Ryker* movie. I've never told you this, it's stupid, but I've had the biggest crush on him since his first movie," Kylie confessed, "I'm in love with the guy if I'm being honest. Emily?"

"Uh, yes, sorry I was distracted. I'm driving."

"I hope you're on Speaker," Kylie said.

"Bluetooth. Aren't you going to ask me what the favor is?"

"No, because you wouldn't ask me to do anything that you wouldn't do," Kylie said, which was true.

"I borrowed Mimi's InstaPot. I need you to come over tonight and make something, so I can share it with Mimi's cooking club. It's another one of her social media things."

"Emily Ammerman, I know you're up to something! It's okay, you don't have to tell me what it is. But a cooking club? This is off the charts, even for you. Say no more—I'll give it a shot."

"Thanks. Just come over when you can," Emily said. Kylie was a fantastic cook, but she didn't have a clue if she had a recipe for this InstaPot thing that Mimi constantly bragged about.

"Half an hour work for you?"

"Perfect," Emily said, grinning. "You're the best."

"I wouldn't say that just yet," Kylie joked.

She laughed out loud. "Okay, see you soon." Emily clicked End, turning off the Bluetooth.

She'd purchased the Land Rover last year. The second-hand, nine-year-old Ford Bronco she'd purchased when she'd left for college had served its purpose. Nothing fancy, but it had four-wheel drive, a must when driving in the Colorado mountains. She'd felt sad when she'd donated the old vehicle to charity, but knew someone would benefit from her generosity. It'd taken her a few weeks to get used to all the fancy upgrades in her new SUV, but once she had, she knew she'd never have another vehicle without them. She pulled into her parking garage, grabbed the InstaPot from the passenger seat and hurried inside to make sure there were no lingering signs of her movie madness two nights before. Clarice greeted her at the door.

"I think you're a spy, you know that?"

"Meow, meow." The cat rubbed against her legs. Emily picked her up, snuggling Clarice against her cheek. "You are a stinker, but I'll get your special dinner," she said, placing the cat on the back of the sofa. She checked the closet where she hid all of her Zach Ryker movies. Once she was assured they were as she'd left them, she went to her office in the spare bedroom, booted up her computer and began her search for Mimi's cooking club. Emily clicked through the recipes the members posted. If she wanted to make sure she wasn't caught in her lie, she needed to find what the club had already posted. Kylie needed to make something new, unusual and, more than anything, delicious.

She clicked out of the site, then Googled recipes for the InstaPot. She chose five and printed them out before realizing that whatever Kylie picked, they'd need to make a trip to the grocery store. Emily took the recipes with her, placing them on the kitchen table, thinking each one sounded delicious.

The doorbell rang and a muffled voice sounded from behind the door. "It's just me. Could you hide the cat, please?"

Clarice zipped out of the kitchen, returning to the spare room. She didn't like Kylie much.

Emily let Kylie inside. "Clarice recognizes your voice. She doesn't like you, so she hides on her own. It's not like I was expecting anyone else. Did you lose your key?"

They'd traded condo keys a couple of years ago, a "just in case" kind of thing. "I forgot I had one," Kylie said.

"It's on your key ring, remember?"

Kylie rifled through her keys, "Yes, here it is. I don't know what half of these belong to anymore."

"Just don't lose mine. I'd hate for some weirdo to pop in unannounced," Emily joked.

"That's not going to happen. Now, let's see what this InstaPot is all about." Kylie used her cell phone to scope out information on the contraption. "I may have to get one of these for myself." She noticed the recipes on the table and scanned through them. "Any one in particular you'd like me to try?" she asked.

"No, just whatever looks best. Or if you have any ideas of your own, go for it."

"And you're going to the grocery store, right?"

"Yes, and you too. I'm a terrible cook *and* shopper. You know that."

"You are," Kylie agreed as she thumbed through the recipes, picking one. "This looks delicious. Should be fairly easy, plus it's quick, and who doesn't like a pot roast?"

"You're right. Let's get this started. I'll drive," Emily said, grabbing her keys. On the drive Emily explained to Kylie the real reason she'd stopped by her grandparents' house, necessitating a quick excuse when she learned Mimi wasn't there.

"So you thought she'd spill the beans on your mom's dislike of all those 'movie people'?"

"Maybe. It was worth a try, anyway. It will keep for another time," Emily said as she made the turn onto Trout Drive.

Not a fan of the big chain supermarkets, she pulled into the parking lot at Benny's, a local grocer that had been around long before she was born. They had everything the big stores had and more, as their bakery had the best peanut butter cookies in town. Occasionally Kathryn would order from them when they were slammed during the holiday season.

Benny's was more crowded than usual, especially for a Monday. "Must have a special," Emily said to Kylie.

"I guess so," Kylie told her as she removed a shopping cart from the nest of others. "Give me the recipe."

Emily took a folded piece of paper out of her pocket and gave it to her. All of a sudden she felt like she was in a glass bubble, with only herself and *him* inside. Or maybe their eyes were magnets pulling toward each other. She could not move, could not take her eyes off him.

"Emily!" Kylie shouted so loudly that several customers stared at her.

Still she didn't move. Kylie stood beside her, following her gaze. "Oh," was all she said.

Emily's heart pounded. She felt sweat bead across her forehead, a sure sign she was nervous. Taking the deepest breath humanly possible, then slowly releasing it without blowing her breath out in pregnancy labor gasps, she repeated the process before saying, "Let's go, Kylie."

"But—"

"Now!"

"Wait!" Zach called.

Emily stopped, turning around to face him. "Yes?"

"I thought I'd say hi, that's all. Hey, you don't look too hot. Are you all right?"

Zach Ryker. Right in front of her. And he said she didn't look too hot. Was she all right? Of course she was not all right!

"Why wouldn't I be?" she managed to ask. Her throat was dry, causing her voice to sound scratchy.

"You tell me," he said, grinning at her.

Kylie stuck out her hand. "I'm Kylie. I'm going to be an extra in your new film. I have to say, I am truly one of your biggest fans. It's such an honor to meet you." Kylie's hand was still hanging out in front of her, as Zach didn't offer his own hand as expected. Kylie dropped her hand. Emily hoped no one noticed them. As Kylie's best friend, she'd never make fun of her, especially now that she'd told her about the crush she had on Zach. Now she could never reveal that she also liked him. But she didn't have a crush on Zach; Emily simply enjoyed his movies. Nothing more. He was just a character from those movies.

"Kylie, we need to go," Emily said, her voice sounding stronger.

"Why? We haven't bought what we came for," Kylie said, her dark eyes flashing toward the cart.

"Well, I . . . forgot the list," she said, knowing she'd just given it to Kylie. Another lie to add to an ever-growing list.

"I remember what we need, no worries."

Zach watched the two of them. "Am I missing something here?" he asked.

"What?" Emily shouted.

Again, a few of the customers looked at her like she was crazy.

"I'm sorry," Emily said to Zach, then to Kylie. Time for the truth. "I wasn't expecting to see you in a grocery store."

He tossed back his head and laughed. "So where were you expecting to see me?" he asked her, smiling. His gorgeous eyes twinkled in what appeared to be amusement.

"On the big screen?" Kylie answered for her friend.

"No, I thought . . ." Emily stopped herself. "Never mind. Let's get the stuff we need so we can go home. We're making dinner at home tonight," she explained to Zach.

"I see. Okay, then, have a great evening. Enjoy your dinner. Together." He gave a half-hearted salute, then walked away.

"Emily," Kylie whispered harshly, "do you realize what you've just done?"

"Yes. I fawned over that guy and made an idiot out of myself," she said while pushing the cart so fast Kylie had to jog just to keep up with her.

"Not that. He thinks we're together!"

"We are, Kylie." Emily rolled her eyes while continuing to push the cart at breakneck speed.

Kylie stepped in front of the cart, forcing Emily to stop. "Look at me—and don't move this dang cart, okay?"

Emily nodded.

"He thinks we're together *together*." Kylie annunciated the last word.

"Oh. That's just great. That is not the impression I wanted to give the guy. I need to find him and explain. I'll be right back." She pushed away from the empty cart and started running up and down the aisles, searching for Zach. She saw him standing in line at the bakery with locals who didn't seem to know who he was or, if they did, certainly didn't care. She thought of her mother and the "movie people." There weren't any googly-eyes in Benny's. Except for her and Kylie.

There were two people in front of him and three behind. "Excuse me," Emily said to those behind him. "I need to speak to this guy." She wouldn't say his name for fear of causing more of a scene than she had already. When she touched his arm, he turned to her. Their eyes were as magnetized now as they had been a few minutes earlier. "I need to speak to you."

"Can it wait a couple minutes? I have an order to pick up," he said. "I like their cookies."

She nodded, smiling. "Sure."

Unsure how she planned to tell him that she and Kylie were just friends, she couldn't believe how duncelike her behavior was when she was around him. If this continued, she wouldn't be able to instruct him on The Plunge. She would be a failure, and maybe his film would be as well.

Chapter Nine

Emily waited while Zach picked up his order and paid for it. She thought it odd that no one other than she and Kylie had recognized him. It certainly wasn't the reaction her mother told her to expect. No hawkeyes here just waiting to follow the "movie people." No one with cameras following him around, trying to catch a picture of him eating a cookie.

When he stepped away from the register Emily walked alongside him. "Listen, I need to explain about my friend."

"That's not my business. No worries," he said. "I'm not one to judge." He had to be at the minimum six five. She was taller than most guys she'd dated and could never wear heels, but Zach towered over her.

She smelled his spicy cologne, loving the scent. "I know, but it's not what you think," she added hastily, wanting to make sure he understood their relationship before they left Benny's. "Kylie and I, we're just friends. Since elementary school."

"That's cool," he said, "I've got a few long-term pals, too."

"We aren't girlfriends in the sense I might've implied. Kylie has a boyfriend. And I'm in a relationship with Harold Wilson." Yet another lie. "I couldn't let you leave without explaining." *Keep digging*, she thought. If word got out that she'd even uttered Harold Wilson's name, their mothers would start planning a wedding. Again.

"That's good to know, since we'll be working together in a few weeks. Maybe you and your friend could bring your guys to The Mill and we can all have a beer together sometime. I'd like that." Zach glanced at the watch on his wrist. "Look, I've got an early shoot. I hope I'll see you later," he said, then walked through the electronic doors. After giving her a two-fingered wave he disappeared into the night like an apparition.

"There you are," Kylie said. "What's going on with Mr. Movie Star?"

Like she knew, but Emily wasn't going to tell this to Kylie, who had a major crush on Zach. "He has an early shoot so he had to go." She said this as though it had been told to her in a private conversation between friends. Rather than an excuse to get away from her.

"So you're on friendly terms already?" Kylie asked.

"A little. I just met him a few days ago." Emily couldn't help but smile when she saw the look of surprise on Kylie's face.

"So how come I'm just now hearing about this?" Kylie shoved the cart down the produce aisle, grabbing a bunch of organic carrots. Emily followed her, remembering the lie she'd told Papaw.

"Actually, I forgot about it until Wynn Watters called Dad." Another lie, and to her best friend. Later she would explain to everyone why she lied, but really, there was no reason for her to lie in the first place. Emily was simply lying to herself, and to admit why to others would feel shameful.

"So spill it," Kylie asked while Emily took over pushing the shopping cart.

"There isn't anything to spill. I met Zach once. At The Mill, a couple of days ago, when Mom and I were having lunch. He approached me, asked if I would help with his training." Emily said it as nonchalantly as possible.

"This happened before your dad spoke with Mr. Watters?"

"Yes, though I'm pretty sure Wynn knew I'd accept his offer. He always gets what he wants, according to Dad."

"I'm missing a piece of the puzzle. So Mr. Watters calls your father earlier today, but Zach asked you Sunday if you could train him?"

Emily took a bag of potatoes, placing them in the cart. "Yes, that's exactly how we met."

"Then how did Zach Ryker know who you were?" Kylie asked.

Emily had expected this question. "I have no idea. Probably one of the locals at The Mill? Truly, I'm not sure." For once she told the truth.

"Don't you think it's odd?" Kylie asked.

Emily stopped pushing the shopping cart. "What I think is you're making a big deal out of nothing. Who cares? For now, it's just another job. We both give private lessons. It's not a big deal." She was tired of the subject. "Look let's get the pot roast, have a nice dinner and forget about Zach Ryker for the night, okay?"

Kylie nodded. "I suppose, though I know you're not telling me everything." She held her hands out in front of her. "Not that it matters. I know you can be very secretive when it suits you. Now is one of those times. I get it. When you're ready to spill the beans you'll tell me. Meanwhile, I am going to do everything in my power to make sure Zach Ryker notices me while he's in town. Maybe he'll ask me out on a date once we start filming. I'm going to get this trimmed." She flipped her waist-length braid. "First thing tomorrow. Then I'll get my eyebrows waxed, something you've been trying to get me to do since high school. Maybe a facial, a manicure and a pedicure. Some new winter clothes. As I said, everything in my power." She smiled at her, and Emily wanted to tell her Zach was not available because she'd seen him first. However, they were no longer in high school. They were grown women, free to do as they pleased. If Kylie had the courage to go after a guy like Zach Ryker, more power to her.

"I'm not sure you need to go to such lengths, Kylie. You're gorgeous just as you are," she told her. It was the truth—though she *could* use a little work on her eyebrows.

"You've been after me for years to wax my eyebrows, don't say you haven't," Kylie teased.

"True, but you have to do what makes you happy. Not what makes me or any guy happy. If Zach Ryker asks you to go out with him, his first impression of you is what will resonate with him. At least that's what some girl told me when her best friend was dying to get asked to senior prom by Bryan Roderick," Emily reminded her.

"I'm much older now. I've put a few miles on this face. Nothing wrong with a little bit of upkeep. Maybe I'll try Botox. It's supposed to prevent wrinkles if you start using it early. Or that's what all the YouTubers claim."

"Yeah, and most of them are barely out of their teens. Look, let's get all the stuff we need for dinner, otherwise we'll be eating at midnight."

"You're right. I'm getting hungry." Kylie picked out a sirloin tip roast along with a few spices, all they would need for their InstaPot dinner.

"Me too," Emily said. She'd actually been hungry thirty minutes ago. When she saw Zach, or rather when Kylie told her she had a crush on Zach, her appetite had gone down the tubes.

Once they were back at her condo, Emily peeled potatoes while Kylie seared the roast according to the recipe. "Smells good," Emily said. "Need the potatoes now?"

"No, we'll put them in last. They cook fast, especially in this InstaPot. I have a couple more steps, then I'll add them in."

Emily was a bit embarrassed that she'd never learned to cook, though she'd never had to. In college she had her own apartment with a fully equipped kitchen, which she only used to brew coffee or heat leftovers in the microwave.

"You want a glass of Cabernet Sauvignon? I've had this forever," Emily said. "Looks like it's decent stuff."

"Sure, I'll have one glass. Remember, I only have to walk across the parking lot."

"I refuse more than one glass after last Saturday. I can't believe I let myself get wasted like that." Emily took two wineglasses out of the cabinet, uncorked the bottle, then waited a few minutes before pouring a small amount of wine in both glasses.

"Same here. I'm off the hard stuff," Kylie said. "I'm ready for those potatoes." Kylie took the bowl from her, then put the potatoes inside the pot. "Really, this is just a pressure cooker, just a bit safer than the old-fashioned ones that explode."

"I'll take your word for it," Emily said.

"Dinner will be ready in ninety minutes," Kylie said, accepting the wineglass Emily offered. "I might have to buy one of these for myself. I wonder what Zach's favorite food is?" She took her cell phone out of her pocket. "He has a fan club, maybe I can find out."

Emily watched as her best friend searched the Web. If Zach did have a fan club, it was doubtful any of the stuff was true, though she wouldn't say that to Kylie; she didn't want to hurt her feelings.

"Look," Kylie said, showing Emily her cell phone. "It says he loves lobster with lots of lemon."

"Okay, so we're kinda landlocked here, but I suppose you could order lobster online if your plans work out. Are there any restaurants around here that actually serve lobster?"

Kylie looked up from her phone. "I don't know. I'm not a huge fan of seafood, you know that. But, if Zach likes lobster, I'll give it a try. Let me check Google." She used her thumbs to type on the small screen. "Nothing here in Loveland, but Frisco has a seafood place that opened during the summer called The Lobster Lady."

"Then it's settled. When you and Zach have your first date, you can take him to this lobster house, get to know him and then who knows? You could end up in a serious relationship, give up this ski bum life and head to Hollywood." Emily heard a trace of sarcasm in her words.

Kylie laughed, her eyes sparkling. "Now that would be the ultimate ending, but I think he lives in Wyoming."

"You found this out how?"

"It's right here." Kylie handed Emily her cell phone.

She scanned the small print. "If this fan club is legit, you wouldn't have far to travel."

"True, and it's not like I can't drive. Long-distance dating isn't a big deal with the Internet. We can FaceTime, Zoom, chat online . . . there are all kinds of ways to stay in contact. I can't wait to see what role I'll have in this movie. I should try to lose a few pounds. They say the camera adds ten pounds. I wouldn't want to look like a giant snowball."

Emily shook her head. "Are you listening to what's coming out of your mouth? You sound exactly like you did in seventh grade. Remember the new kid, Manny Lopez? You were going to marry him, have five kids and live off the land."

"Ugh, that was pretty bad, huh?" Kylie crinkled her nose.

"This is worse. You're an adult now."

"Nothing wrong with fantasizing. You've said that to me a zillion times."

Emily wanted to say there were limits but didn't dare give herself away. If she even hinted that *she* was Zach Ryker's biggest fan, sparks could fly. Her best friend was not worth losing over a fly-by-night actor. Amused, she thought she sounded exactly like her mother. "Fantasizing is fine." She cleared her throat. "As long as it's within reason."

Kylie tucked her phone in her back pocket. "So you think Zach isn't a reasonable fantasy? For someone else, maybe?"

"Oh come on, I didn't say that. You know what I meant. We're different—his lifestyle isn't like ours. I'd bet my last nickel he's full of himself. Probably carries a mirror in his back pocket."

Kylie smiled. "It is a little unrealistic, I agree, but who says I can't have him? He's not married or engaged."

"Does this fan club page mention if he's dating any-one?" Emily had to ask even though she seriously doubted anything they read was true.

"Nope, he's a free agent. There is hope for me and I am not going to let this once-in-a-lifetime chance pass by without at least trying to make myself available to him— in the dating sense, before you think otherwise. I've seen all of his movies. He even does his own stunts. I know all the lines he's famous for. That's enough to impress him."

Emily rolled her eyes. "If you think so, but half the world has seen those movies and all the cliché lines he tosses out there for his audience."

"You've seen his movies?" Kylie asked.

To lie or not to lie? Undecided, she went with a half lie. "I've seen the trailers. Who hasn't?"

"It doesn't matter. I've made up my mind. I'm going to focus on myself for the next few weeks. I want to look my best, feel my best, ski my best. When Zach Ryker lays those sexy blue eyes on me, he will never regret it."

Emily was stunned at the passion in Kylie's words. Her friend truly believed she had a chance with this guy, who could have any woman in the world. Why would he choose Kylie? Yes, she was extremely pretty, smart and any guy would be lucky to have her . . . but Zach Ryker? She didn't want to be the one to tell Kylie he was out of her league. Let her dig her claws in; then she'd find out for herself. In the meantime, she couldn't let on that she was also interested in him, other than training him to ski The Plunge. If she told Kylie how she truly felt, their friendship could be permanently damaged, and she valued that more than Zach Ryker.

The alarm on Kylie's phone pinged. "Okay, let's see if this InstaPot lives up to all the hype. I'm starved."

Emily followed her to the kitchen, making sure to take pictures of the pot roast before removing it from the Insta-Pot. "Mimi's social media club seems to believe this contraption is the best thing since sliced bread. Let's see for ourselves." She watched Kylie plate the food, arranging it just so. She took a few pictures, then dug in. After a few bites, Emily said "This is delicious. Mimi and her online club know what they're talking about." She finished the food on her plate, then had seconds.

"I'm going to order one of these myself," Kylie told her. "I wonder if Zach ever has a home-cooked meal?"

Emily had to laugh, "I'm sure there are plenty of folks out there who are more than happy to see that Mr. Ryker is well-fed."

"Yes, but homemade is from the heart, you know. Not a fancy catering service. You really don't get it because you're not into cooking. It's okay, really. If you ever want a lesson, let me know. Though you'd have to promise you wouldn't make a meal for Zach."

Emily took her plate to the sink, rinsed it off, then put it in the dishwasher. "Never going to happen. Cooking isn't my thing."

"True, you're not the type. You've always been a tomboy. Heck, I couldn't believe my eyes when I saw you had makeup on at your parents' party, though I thought I did an awesome job on your hair," Kylie informed her while she emptied the leftovers into a plastic container. "You want to give this to your grandmother so she can have a taste?"

"You won't mind?" Emily asked, given Kylie prepared the roast.

"Not at all. I'm going to order one of these as soon as I get home, or drive to town, whichever is the fastest. I like the idea of making an all-day meal in practically no time."

"Thanks. You're a good friend, you know that?"

"Of course, and you are yourself. Now, l need to get going. Let me know what Mimi thinks of the roast. If you hear anything from Zach, you'll let me know?"

"I doubt I will, but who knows? Walk safely," she said to Kylie as she gave her a hug. "I'll see you at the lodge."

Closing the door behind her, Emily returned to the kitchen and cleaned the dishes and the InstaPot, her thoughts all over the place. Having had no clue up until now that Kylie had a crush on Zach Ryker, she felt weirdly betrayed. Even though Kylie didn't have a clue about her own crush, if you could even call it that.

Could she train this guy without revealing herself? While she certainly didn't have the kind of starstruck feelings Kylie did, she had to admit it wouldn't be hard to fall for this star.

Chapter Ten

The locals flocked to The Eagles Nest Café daily. The parking area was jam-packed, as usual, when Emily squeezed the Land Rover between a small Honda and a motorcycle.

Inside she saw her dad seated in the back at a table for two and offered him a wave. There wasn't an empty table in the place. The scent of coffee permeated throughout, along with the smell of fried bacon. Emily took a seat across from her father.

"I ordered for you," he said, sliding a cup of coffee in front of her. "The usual."

"Thanks," she said, then took a sip of coffee. Her usual was an avocado omelet, a side of fruit and an English muffin. "You and Mom work things out?"

Her father laughed. "Your mother never works things out, but we've come to an agreement that each of us can live with."

Emily smiled. "So who won?"

"I did, but don't you dare tell your mother. She believes she's controlling this 'movie madness,' her exact words. She realizes this is a great opportunity for you and the lodge, and she's a smart businesswoman. It's sad that she doesn't care too much for all those 'movie people.' I didn't tell her you were training Zach Ryker."

"So she thinks it's just a run-of-the-mill 'movie star'?" Emily grinned.

"Something like that," he told her.

The waitress brought their food then, and they both dug in while it was hot. As usual, Emily could only eat half of the giant omelet. She finished her coffee and asked for a refill before she spoke. "Dad, I know you're not going to tell me, but did Mom ever have an interest in the movies? Maybe she wanted to be an actress? Or a dancer?" Her mother was an excellent dancer.

He pushed his plate to the side and took another drink of coffee before answering. "It's not my place to tell you, Emily, though you could say she's had other interests besides skiing. Remember, back in the day your mother was considered to be quite the catch. She was gorgeous. Heck, every guy in town wanted a date with her."

"She's still beautiful," Emily said.

"Of course she is. I'm the luckiest man alive."

"If you're not going to tell me—which is okay, I get it—then I'm going to assume she wanted to become an actress and wasn't successful. And that's why she has such a grudge against movies. I won't mention this conversation to a soul. Now, what about the Sno-Cat? Are we going to buy a new one today or just have a look? If you're truly interested in my vino idea, and if it's in the budget, maybe we should look at a Cat with a passenger cab."

Her dad stood, removed a few bills from his wallet and left them on the table. "I thought about that. One of the models I'm considering holds up to twelve passengers—six front seaters. We're buying. I've narrowed my search down to a couple of models. I'd like your opinion before making the final decision."

They walked outside together. "You realize I know

nothing about this type of machinery, other than what it's made for? I would think Papaw should be here, too."

"Houston knows what models I'm looking in to. He's with me on this one hundred percent."

"Good, because I would hate to shoulder this responsibility alone when I'm clueless. You want me to follow you or ride together?"

"Just follow me. I've a couple of errands to run when I finish."

"Sure, I'll meet you there." After she left, she remembered she had Mimi's InstaPot to return, along with Kylie's leftover roast for her to try. She'd make a quick stop at Mimi's, because it was on her way, before heading to Carter's Mechanical.

Parking behind Papaw's Ford, she assumed Mimi was there as well, even though the garage door was closed. As was normal, she tapped on the front door and called, "Anyone home?"

"Yes," Mimi replied. "We're in the kitchen."

Emily had the container of leftovers stacked on top of the InstaPot. "I'm just returning this—plus I want your opinion on the roast Kylie made." She tapped on the container. "I'll email a few pictures for your social media group later. Dad's waiting on me at Carter's now." She set the pot and leftover roast on the countertop. "I'll touch base with you two later." She blew them a kiss, then hurried out before they started asking her a zillion questions. Plus, she didn't want to be too late meeting her dad.

Parking beside her father's new Ford truck, she saw him talking to a guy in the back lot where the pre-owned Cats were parked. Her dad saw her and motioned for her to join him.

"Sorry I'm late. I had to make a pit stop at Mimi's," Emily explained.

Her dad nodded. "Frank, this is my daughter, Emily,"

her father said. "You'll be dealing with her in the future."
Frank had to be close to her father's age. He wore the
usual Colorado attire: denim jeans, a plaid flannel shirt
with heavy-duty boots and a heavy jacket. Emily did notice that the morning air had a bite to it as they shook
hands. He was a plain but pleasant-looking man.

"Nice to meet you. You're one famous gal around here,
the way you've mastered The Plunge."

Emily couldn't help but laugh. "Thanks, but it's just
part of my job."

Frank smiled, then simply nodded his head. Emily liked
him already.

"Mason, you want to have a look-see at those Cats?"
Frank asked. "And Miss Emily, too? I've kept them inside.
Didn't want 'em to get scratched up, being they're worth a
small fortune these days."

"Let's get to it. I've saved a long time for this; I can't
wait," Mason told Frank. "Emily thinks we ought to start
a vino bar. You know anything about those?"

Frank chuckled. "Oh, I know a lot about a vino bar, but
it's not fit for a lady's ears."

Emily couldn't help but grin. "Frank, I'm almost thirty;
I've probably heard and done more in a vino bar than either of you would care to hear. Most of the large resorts
have them. I told Dad it might be a good idea, one or two
days a week, a couple of hours before closing."

Frank held the glass door open for her. Dad followed,
then Frank turned to her. "That's an excellent idea. Most
of the lodges have them running all day. Which people
seem to like. The downside is that quite a few folks are so
danged inebriated when they reach the bottom of the
mountain it takes a handful of extra employees to assist
them and make sure they return safely to wherever they're
staying. Too much expense, I think. Couple hours, maybe
a drink limit. That could work."

Emily agreed. "I think if we were to go that route, we could manage. Maybe charge less, though we wouldn't have the aggravation or the liability of dealing with folks who have one too many."

"Let's get the machines first," her dad said.

For the next two hours Emily listened to her dad and Frank explain the basic functions of the different vehicles. There was so much to learn that it would take a while, plus, when it came to anything mechanical, Emily was a hands-on kind of learner. She'd ride and learn, but also knew her limits.

"So which is it going to be?" Frank asked both of them.

Emily didn't speak as this was not her decision. Yes, she'd been involved, but only so she could learn how to wheel and deal. At least that's what she assumed.

"Frank, you got me and you know it. Emily, you too. I like the idea of the vino Cat, so I'm going with the twelve-seater. Your mom is going to have a hissy fit, but we can deal with that later. So, how long before I can expect delivery?"

Frank shoved his hands in his pockets and squinted at a large calendar on the wall behind his desk. "Four weeks, but I can push it if need be."

Her father shook his head. "You looked at the almanac?"

"Of course," Frank said. "I'll push it. A couple of days less is the best I can do."

Her father held out his hand to Frank, giving him a good handshake to seal the deal. "That's perfect for us. I'll have my bank send a direct wire as soon as I leave here."

Frank took a card from his desk, wrote something on it, then gave it to her dad. "This is all my information. Good doing business with you, Mason. You, too, Miss Emily. You need the other Cats checked out, I'll send Glen over to help your guys out."

"Thanks, they're good, but who knows what might come up? I'll let you know if I do." They had their own mechanics, but Mason knew not to burn bridges, as one never knew.

"Nice to meet you, Frank." Emily smiled and shook his hand.

"Good day to you, too," he replied.

Emily walked alongside her dad. "Would it be nosy if I asked how much that cost you?"

"No," he said. "It would be smart. Six figures, leaning toward the number four," he said, grinning at her. "You'll see the paperwork soon enough. I'm having the bank transactions copied to you, and if I don't get to the bank, Frank's going to think I'm trying to cheat him." He gave her a kiss on the cheek. "See you later, kiddo."

"Yep," she said. Inside her vehicle, she realized her parents and grandparents were very rich. Having always known they were very well off, she'd never given their finances a lot of thought because she had plenty of money herself, having invested wisely. If what she thought her dad implied was correct, he'd just spent close to half a million bucks on the Cat. She needed to brush up on business and common sense if she planned to take over for her family next season, she thought as she cranked over the engine. Her personal finances she could manage just fine. But she hoped she would be able to maintain the family fortune when it was time for her to take over.

Chapter Eleven

Emily woke to the hushed silence of what she'd expected was coming, according to last night's weather report: Loveland's first massive blizzard of the season. It never failed to excite her, no matter how many times she experienced it. She hurried to the kitchen to make a pot of coffee, then went to the living room to open the blinds. A total whiteout.

"Awesome," she said to herself.

Clarice emerged from the spare room. "Meow."

"It's snowing, sweet girl, but I know you're more interested in breakfast, right?" She emptied a can of Fancy Feline Delight into Clarice's dish, then took her cup of coffee to the living room. Two minutes later Clarice joined her, finding her usual spot on the back of the sofa.

Looking out the window, Emily imagined herself inside a giant snow globe as lacy patterned flakes of snow blew against her condo's window, forming a giant snowbank against the brick walls. Knowing it was possible she would be snowed in for a while, she didn't mind. The snowplows would be here after they cleared the main roads. It would be the perfect time to watch a Zach Ryker movie, but she didn't want to risk being caught. Kylie could pop over anytime, regardless of the weather, because she lived in the next building. On a whim, she dialed her best friend's number. Kylie answered immediately.

"Have you looked outside?" Emily asked, not bothering with formalities.

She heard Kylie yawn. "No, I was sleeping. What's going on?"

"A three-foot snowbank against my window," she said, "We've had a major winter storm."

"Hang on," Kylie said.

Emily could hear her fumbling out of bed, a few stumbles, then the sound of her blinds opening. "Dang! I didn't listen to the weather report last night. Does this mean what I think it means?"

Knowing Kylie would ask this, Emily honestly didn't have an answer. "I'm clueless. I know Wynn Watters and the movie folks wanted to start as soon as we had the first big snow, but it needs to settle, plus the groomers need to do their jobs before anyone can go up the mountain."

This year they'd had plenty of snow, but nothing like this. They wouldn't be able to open the lodge under these conditions. Personally, December was their lucky month, given what she saw outside.

"You have any coffee?" Kylie asked.

"That's a silly question. Come on over; bring food." Emily clicked the End button, laughing to herself. They were like two old ladies the past few weeks. With neither doing as much instructing as they were used to, they'd started this coffee klatch because she didn't have to be in the office until nine and Kylie's classes were down. Emily had started looking forward to the mornings. She dressed and ran a brush through her hair before returning to the kitchen.

There was a tap on the door and she knew Kylie had forgotten her keys again. Opening the door, she was surprised to see her best friend with her hands full. "Let me help you." Emily took a large plastic container from her, Kylie followed her to the kitchen with three more containers stacked on top of one another.

Clarice pounced off the sofa, but not before giving Kylie one of her famous dirty looks.

"I can't believe you like that cat," Kylie said. "Take these; I was bored last night," she said, placing the containers on the counter.

"I guess so! Smells yummy," Emily said, opening up one of the containers. "Blueberry muffins! My favorite. You didn't have to make these, but I'm glad you did." She removed the paper wrapping from the muffin, sinking her teeth into the warmth. "You're just ticked because you don't have a pet."

"I'm going to get a dog when the time is right. It's not the right time now. I couldn't sleep last night, so I made these around four o'clock this morning, so they're fresh."

Emily used her tongue to lick crumbs from her mouth. "They're still warm."

"I don't know how you can eat all the time and never gain a pound," Kylie said as she poured herself a cup of coffee. "I can have one or two and gain five pounds, I kid you not."

"I'm tall, Kylie. You, my friend, are a gorgeous, petite, muscle-bound little . . . I don't know, I want to say a curse word, but I won't, so I'll call you an elf. You're perfect, and you never gain weight." She gave her friend the once-over. She wore black leggings with a red sweatshirt and Doc Martens that she hadn't bothered to tie. Her hair was piled on top of her head and most likely hadn't seen a brush in a day or two, yet she still managed to look like a

Vogue model. Kylie didn't realize how striking she was. Emily knew she hated being short, but that was part of her beauty. Emily was always telling her this.

"Thanks, but I know I look like crap right now. I haven't washed my hair in three days," Kylie told her. "Gross, huh?"

"It isn't as though either of us has been out and about. I can't wait to get back to work. I don't see how people can sit around all the time," she told Kylie. "I'm going nuts."

"Going?" Kylie teased.

"Seriously, I'd welcome some filing, anything to do right now."

"I've kept busy. Cleaned out all of my kitchen cabinets, tossed out all of my spices, ordered more online. Threw out last year's leggings—well, except for these." She looked down at her legs. "A girl has to have at least one pair of worn-out leggings, right? I've read three books this week, too. Romance novels. I fell in love with all the male characters, which made me give serious thought to this thing I have for Zach. If I can fall in love with men in novels, are my feelings for Zach simply infatuation?"

Emily took another muffin, slowly peeling the paper away. "I suppose you're just a little captivated by guys. Remember in elementary school, you fell in love at least once a week. In high school you were a little more finicky. It's just part of who you are."

Kylie nodded. "It really scares me. I'm not being silly either."

Emily sat down, Kylie seated across from her. "I'm sorry, I didn't realize you were serious about this kinda stuff. I know you had a serious relationship with Paul, but I didn't know you had any lingering issues from the breakup."

Kylie shook her head, "It's not him. We broke up on good terms; we were better as friends. I think I'm in love with all these fictional characters. The books, the movies, and the way I acted at Benny's the other day. I embarrassed myself. I know you heard me, so don't act like you don't know what I'm talking about."

"Okay, so what? You and a ton of other women like Zach Ryker and fall in love with fictional people in books. Isn't that what entertainment is all about? Making one fall just a little bit in love with the characters they've created? Then I believe the author has succeeded at his or her job. Personally, I don't see where this is a problem." She really didn't because she felt the same way herself, only she kept her feelings for Zach hidden.

"You really don't think I'm a little over the edge? When it comes to guys? What if the right guy comes along, and I'm too . . . crazy to know what real love is? That's what worries me."

Emily stood up, taking their mugs and refilling them. When she sat back down, she took her best friend's hand. "Look, Kylie, you're like a sister to me, you know that. I've spent most of my life around you. You are not crazy in any way, okay? I think all women our age might have feelings like this. I know I do, especially when Mom and Mimi continue to remind me I'm not getting any younger and that they want a grandchild. You've heard them. As much as I would like to make them happy, I refuse to settle for just anyone because I'm getting older. If it's meant to be, it'll happen. If not, so be it."

Grinning, Kylie asked, "What about Harold? He's still waiting for you."

Emily burst out laughing. "If it's a choice between Harold and spinsterhood, I'll choose the latter."

"So you think I'm okay?"

"I do. And I think you worry too much about meeting the perfect guy. I don't know if there is a perfect guy out there, but I am not going to obsess over it. As I said, when the time is right for both of us, we'll know."

"Thanks, Em. You're the best friend in the world." Tears filled Kylie's eyes.

"Don't go getting all mushy on me, or else." Emily stood and walked to the other side of the table to give Kylie a hug. "I've an idea. Since we're not working, and I've just eaten two of the best blueberry muffins in the world, why don't we put on some warm clothes, go outside and have a snowball fight? Or, we could build a snowman in the parking lot?" Emily teased, knowing Kylie would be game for this. "I need to burn off a few calories."

"That sounds like fun. I'll meet you out front in fifteen minutes," Kylie said, back to her normal, cheery self.

"Sounds like a plan. Meet you in the middle."

"Okay," Kylie agreed.

After she left, Emily cleared away their cups before heading to the bedroom to change clothes. She found an older ski jacket and pants, grabbed a pair of gloves from a drawer and a warm hat. Once her boots were on, she stuffed her house keys in her pocket, then stepped outside, unprepared for the icy blast of air that slammed her back against the door. She hadn't realized it was this windy. Maybe this wasn't such a good idea. She was about to go back inside when she saw Kylie digging her way through the deep snow, barely making any headway. *What the heck*, she thought; there wouldn't be too many days such as this, so she might as well have fun before all the tourists came to the mountain.

"You didn't tell me the wind was going to blow me over," Kylie shouted, the gust of wind muffling her words.

Emily could barely drag her legs through the deep snow as she crossed the parking lot. "Stay put," she called out. "It's easier for me to come over to your side." Her long legs did offer a few advantages.

The snow reached the top of Kylie's legs, preventing her from moving more than a few inches at a time. "You sure you want to do this?" Emily asked as she used her boots to scrape a path in the deepest areas of the snow so Kylie could follow her to the center of the empty parking area.

"Of course," Kylie shouted at her. "It's not like this is something I haven't been through before. I'm behind you."

Once they were in position, ready to toss snowballs at each other or build a snowman, Emily shook her head. "It's too deep to enjoy." Which often was the case on the mountains until the Sno-Cats did their job. "We're closer to my condo. Let's go inside and rethink this."

Kylie nodded, following the carved-out path in front of her. When they reached Emily's condo, they stomped their feet before going inside, removing their boots and tilting them on the boot rack Emily had installed when she purchased the condo.

"So now what? We sit here and watch TV all day?" Kylie plopped down on the sofa.

"When the snowplows clear the parking lot, we'll go out for lunch."

"Is food all you ever think about?"

If she only knew, Emily thought. "Most of the time. That and of course skiing the mountain. I think those are my favorite things to do, at least at this stage in life."

"Let's make it a late lunch. I made myself a peanut butter and jelly sandwich while I was changing clothes. Figured I needed the protein."

"Works for me," Emily said. She really wasn't the least bit hungry. However, it being Friday, she figured The Mill would be packed and maybe she would run into Zach. She hadn't seen him since that night at Benny's, when she'd acted like a starstruck teenager. No wonder he hadn't contacted her. Seriously, there was no reason for him to in the first place. She would train him for a few weeks, nothing more. They had agreed to start after the first heavy snow-fall, which they'd now had, but she and Wynn Watters also knew there wouldn't be any action until the mountains were cleared. So maybe the movie people were as bored as she and Kylie.

"You look serious. What's going on in that head of yours?" Kylie asked.

"Just bored. Thinking of all the things we could be doing with our free time. Fun things, not work-related," Emily said.

"Me too, only my thoughts are too racy to share." Kylie laughed. "Want to know what they are?"

"Absolutely not! You need to quit reading romance novels. Try reading a historical novel, or one of those new domestic thrillers. That'll clean up your dirty mind," Emily said, then burst out laughing. "Or, you could try going on a date."

"Right, like Zach is going to ask me. After humiliating myself at the store, I don't think so."

"There's always Harold. I'm sure he'd be fine with you, and you're so tiny, he'll tower over you." More laughter; Harold was at the very least three inches shorter than Emily. Not that she cared all that much; she just didn't care about Harold. His lack of height had bothered her a little, but he was just definitely not her type.

"I'd rather date you," Kylie quipped.

"Please, whatever you do, don't say that in public! I love you to pieces, just not in the romantic sense. So, seriously, about you and Harold . . ." Emily tossed her head back, laughing so hard tears streamed down her face. Using the hem of her shirt to wipe her tears, she kept laughing until she felt a pinch in her side. She slid onto the floor, exhausted from laughing. She looked up at Kylie, still sitting on the sofa, staring at her as though she belonged in a mental institution. This brought about another round of laughter. Emily managed to control her giggling, but each time she looked up at Kylie from her position on the floor, her thoughts returned to Harold. Then back to Kylie. Then both of them as a couple. Hysterical laughter spewed out of her mouth, and she just let it go. She couldn't stop. Imagining her best friend with Harold and his nosy mother running their life was too much.

Kylie got down on the floor beside her. "If you don't shut up, I will personally call Harold myself and tell him you want to sleep with him. Like today."

"I would choke the life out of you if you did that," Emily said, still laughing, though she had more control now. "I visualized you and Harold married, his mother guiding you through life. Can you imagine?"

Kylie pushed herself off the floor. "I'm going home. We've been hanging together too much." She put her boots back on, then went to the kitchen for her containers. "I purposely left all the muffins. I hope you get fat and break your leg." Kylie chuckled as she let herself out.

"Some best friend you are. My cat hates you, too," Emily said to the door. They could say anything to each other and never get angry. She couldn't imagine not having Kylie in her life. Even if she did marry Harold, she supposed she would act as maid of honor, and she thought of all that would entail. Standing up, she spoke aloud. "Emily Ammerman, you are truly losing your mind."

Several hours later, the parking area cleared, Emily decided to get out of the house, regardless of the weather. She took a shower and then spent extra time blow-drying her hair because she could. She put on soft brown eye shadow, mascara and a little blush, though she didn't need it. Her face was still flushed from laughing. In her bedroom, she dressed in jeans and a heavy, black wool sweater. Knowing how windy it was, she added a beanie that tied under her chin, a scarf, leather gloves and a black down jacket. All dressed up with no place to go, she thought as she searched for her cell phone and purse.

"Get over it and go," she said to the room. Maybe this was what cabin fever did to a person. "I'm going out for a while," she said to Clarice, who'd been hiding since Kylie's departure. While Emily loved her privacy, too much was definitely not a good thing.

Chapter Twelve

The Mill was packed, just as Emily had thought it would be. The laughter coming from the giant, U-shaped bar was loud enough to deafen a person, along with the sound of utensils tinkling against plates and conversations humming in the background. Emily waited for the hostess to return to the stand. Feeling silly for going out alone, she regretted not asking Kylie to join her. She scanned the room, searching for a friend, someone she could have a drink with, but she didn't see anyone she knew.

Except *him*.

Walking toward her with a grin as wide as Willie's Way, she wished she could melt into the floor like snow on a warm boot. With just seconds to get her act together, she managed a smile.

"So, what brings you out on one of the snowiest days I've seen since I arrived in Colorado?" Zach asked.

To lie or not to lie. Again, she wondered if she was turning into a habitual liar. Or maybe a pathological liar? Or both; it didn't matter. She didn't know the difference anyway. "Honestly," she said, almost choking on the words, "I was bored." *Hot damn*, she thought. She was telling the truth for a change. Up until now she had only told lies about him and to him.

"Same here. You want to have a drink with me? I have a table." He nodded toward a table at the very back of the restaurant.

She wanted to ask if he was alone or if his friends were with him but couldn't form the words, so she said, "Sure." Following him to the table, she cast side-glances to see if anyone was watching them. Most folks were minding their own business. A couple of glances here and there, but nothing to get all riled up over. If she were being truthful, she didn't want Kylie knowing she was here with Zach.

He pulled out the chair for her, then pushed it in before sitting down himself. "I'm having a Coke. I'm not a big drinker, but get whatever you like. It's on me."

Did that mean this was a date? Not planned, but in her world when a guy paid the tab, it was considered a date. When the check was split, it wasn't a date.

"Sure, of course." She suddenly wondered if she had on too much blush. Did she look like a clown? One of those creepy ones from a horror movie? Or the goofy type from the circus? She brushed her hand against her cheek, wishing she had a mirror.

"Emily?" Zach called her by name. Had she actually introduced herself? She couldn't even recall. "Your drink?" he asked.

"Oh, I'm sorry. I'll have a Coke, too. I'm driving."

He ordered another for himself.

"Emily, please don't feel you need to get all flustered around me, okay? I'm a regular guy despite what the tabloids say."

Emily chewed on her lip. "I don't read the tabloids."

"Good, then we're off to a fresh start. So, tell me something about yourself."

"You're serious? You want to know about me?" Her throat was dry. She wished their waitress would hurry up with the Cokes.

"I do," he said.

Suddenly she thought of Harold and Kylie. As in "I do accept you as my dearly beloved husband." Before she could control herself she started laughing. Like a lunatic. Their waitress set their drinks on the table. Emily guzzled hers. Hearing the gulping sound in her throat, she knew Zach must think she was a pig or, at the very least, extremely ill-mannered. An unexpected burp flew out of her mouth.

She prayed for the building to cave in. "Excuse me," she managed to say. Never in her life had she been in a more humiliating situation. Taking another sip of her drink, praying she didn't belch, she finished the Coke, pushing the glass to the side. "I am so sorry. I don't drink soda very often." She truly didn't as the carbonation bothered her.

"I could hear that," Zach said, a smile on his face.

"I'll just go, uh . . . I'll see you when you're ready to train." Pushing out her chair, Zach reached for her hand before she could stand. She could feel her face turning red with embarrassment.

"Emily, please don't go."

Zach Ryker was asking her to stay after she'd just humiliated herself? Did he plan on teasing her? Taking a deep breath, she nodded. "Okay." Not usually one at a loss for words, Emily couldn't think of anything to say. This guy had her tongue-tied.

"Like I said, I'm just a regular guy whose job just so happens to be actor. I'm a little smitten, and you're not making this easy for me." Zach waved his hand for the waitress. "May we get a couple of cranberry juices, please?"

I'm a little smitten.

Of course she knew what that meant, but she didn't

dare believe him. "Thank you. As I said, sodas aren't my drink of choice." She sounded almost normal.

"That's a start, so I know to never order a soda when we're together. Okay, now tell me something else about yourself."

Emily waited for the waitress to bring their second round of drinks before she answered him. As soon as she placed the drinks on the table, Emily spoke up. "I like to ski." She smiled, knowing he already knew this.

He laughed so loud, he drew the attention of the table of eight across from them. They stared at him for a few seconds before returning to their own conversation.

"That's obvious, otherwise I wouldn't be here. You're the best in this part of the country."

So he was here only because of her skiing ability? How could he be smitten with that?

"There are others who are just as well trained as I am. Kylie, my best friend, is an excellent instructor. I could name half a dozen others." She took a sip of her juice, grateful she could tolerate this.

"I met a couple before you. I didn't click with any of them, plus they were guys trying too hard to impress me. When my producer pointed you out, I knew you were the one I wanted to train me. Of course, after being face-to-face with you, I couldn't stop thinking about you. It's been a tough few days."

Her heart pounded like a drummer in a marching band. Was he telling her what she thought? He was attracted to her? Risking another round of humiliation, she had to ask, "Could you explain that to me? I'm not sure where you're going with this." She hoped she knew, but it was unbelievable, like something she'd seen in one of his movies.

"When I put my hand on yours that day in the parking lot, I felt . . . a spark of something, and I thought maybe you did, too," He paused. "Let's just say I'm smitten. You know what that means; I don't need to explain it to you. Though the more I talk, the more I'm beginning to think I've overstepped a boundary I wasn't aware existed. Your guy—I think you said his name was Harold? I asked around about him. What I heard wasn't what you told me in the grocery store. Am I wrong? If so, tell me and I'll back off."

Caught in her lie, she had no choice but to tell the truth. No way did she want Zach to believe she was involved with anyone, especially Harold. "I wasn't telling the truth. I was worried you thought Kylie and I were a couple, so I found you in the bakery and said the first thing that popped into my head. I'm not—" She was about to say dating, but caught herself. "I'm not proud of telling you that earlier. I didn't want you to think . . ." She took a sip of her drink to steady herself. "I don't need to draw you a picture, do I?"

"No, I'm old-fashioned, but not so much that I'm clueless as to what goes on in today's world. May I ask you a question?"

Mopping up the water from the condensation on her glass with a napkin, she said, "Of course. I'm not that standoffish." Besides being ill-mannered, maybe she'd presented herself that way, but under normal conditions, she was very easygoing.

"Did you feel anything at all that day?" Zach's extraordinary, indigo-colored eyes were as magnetic now as they were that day in the parking lot and at Benny's. If Emily told him the truth, she'd hurt Kylie, but if she lied, she wasn't being completely honest with herself. "Maybe," she said, figuring that was safe as it could go either way.

He shook his head, then reached for her hands. Removing the wet napkin, he tossed it aside. "Now, tell me."

She closed her eyes, yet couldn't ignore the tingling sensation in the pit of her stomach, the rapid beating in her chest. Opening her eyes once more, she nodded. "I would be lying if I told you I didn't feel a jolt or two." She felt a little embarrassed admitting this to him, but for once where he was concerned, she would tell the truth.

"Same here." He gently squeezed her hands in his. "So where do we go from here?"

While Emily was beyond flattered, maybe a little bit starstruck, this was not what she'd expected to hear. Did he want to have a winter romance? A fling while he worked on his movie? She had no way of knowing any of this. She only knew him as the character he portrayed in his movies. "I don't know. I suppose we get to know each other? The normal way?"

He released her hands and she felt empty. This was not good. Knowing he would only be in town for a few more weeks, it probably wasn't in her best interest to get involved with him. There were so many reasons why she should get up and walk out the door. Go home and focus on how she would train him on The Plunge.

"I agree," he said. "If I tell you something, will you give me your word you'll keep it between us?"

"Yes, of course." She hoped it wasn't anything life-altering because she wasn't at that juncture in their . . . she hesitated to think of it as a relationship yet.

"My dad has a place in Wyoming. He trains horses for handicapped kids. It's a big deal, but I like to keep that part of my life private. I'm supposed to spend a few weeks helping him and Levi when I finish up here. I thought you might like to come along—though don't feel obligated. I realize we barely know each other."

"You live in Wyoming?" She remembered Kylie telling her this. And, who was Levi? she wondered.

"My family does. I stay there as much as I can, but work takes me all over the world, so I spend a lot of my time traveling."

Emily wanted to pinch herself. Was she being pranked? It was possible. Wynn Watters wasn't the nicest guy in the world, though she truly didn't believe he'd be so childish as to stoop to this. "Are you teasing me?"

Zach appeared to be hurt, his eyes showing his emotions. "Why would I do that? You think I'm like Gunner West, don't you?"

In truth, she did think that, but she didn't want to admit it. "I don't know you other than the fact you're very famous and Hollywood's most eligible bachelor. Just what's known to the public."

"If you're willing to give me a chance, I'll show you I'm not Gunner West. He's a character created by a team of writers, nothing like me. I'd like you to get to know *me*."

She nodded. But she knew she couldn't travel with him, so she said instead, "I heard you do all of your own stunts."

"A few, but not all. I don't have a death wish."

"That's good to know. You might have a change of heart when you see The Plunge. It's quite the challenge, even for someone as physical as you. Maybe you shouldn't ... never mind. I got ahead of myself. Forget I said that." She'd wanted to say that The Plunge would be the perfect time for his stuntman to step in, but she'd caught herself just in time.

"It's forgotten. Let's have dinner tonight and we can talk more about the training I'll need. I'm a decent enough skier. I can handle a black diamond once in a while, but for The Plunge, you'll have your work cut out for you. I watched the resort's video; it was quite the eye-opener. I'm assuming it's you in the video?"

She'd forgotten all about the video. They'd filmed it four or five years ago, when they'd updated the website. "It is, but it's a few years old. Still, it's a tough challenge, even for me, and I've been skiing since I was two years old." She grinned. When she said that to folks who'd never lived the ski life, they thought she was crazy. But it was normal for most Coloradans.

"We skied in Jackson Hole in the winter, so it was about the same there as it is here. Lots of tourists, but you already know about that. So, let's get out of here and plan where we're going to have dinner tonight." He stopped. "I'm being too pushy, right?"

She smiled at him, her first true smile that wasn't plagued by doubt. "Maybe. I don't know if pushy is the word I'd use. It's fine. I'm normally a very direct person myself, so this doesn't offend me, just surprises me." She was talking normally now, as though she spoke to Zach like this all the time.

"Because of who I am?"

"Yes. It's not every day a famous Hollywood actor invites me to have dinner."

"Pretend I'm not an actor. That might help," he suggested.

Emily saw the crowd at The Mill was beginning to thin out. "I'll try, but I'm not making any promises. Look, about dinner—everyone in this town knows me. If you're serious, let's meet in Dillon or Silverthorne. It's just a few miles away." As she stood to leave, he removed cash from his wallet, laying it on the table before following her out.

The temperatures were dropping. Emily shivered, knowing the weather was going to get worse by the hour. She should stay home. No one in their right mind should be driving in this weather unless it was an emergency. But right now, she wasn't in her right mind.

"Already ashamed to be seen with me? I get it. It's not a problem. Any suggestions on where to go?" Zach asked.

She offered a few places and let him decide. He chose Fiesta Jalisco in Silverthorne.

"You're sure you like Mexican food? I don't want to be responsible for another tummy upset," Zach teased.

She laughed. "It's my favorite food." Which was true; she'd grown up on Mexican food of all kinds. "We're gonna have more snow later this evening. It might be a tricky drive."

"Should I send a car for you?"

"No!"

"Are you sure you want to do this?" he asked.

"Sure, it's just that I'm a nervous passenger. A backseat driver."

"Okay, then you can pick me up. I'm good with that. Do you know where I'm staying?"

"Diamond Pass?"

He shook his head. "No way. I've rented a house. I don't need all the extra excitement." He took a card from his pocket. "You have something to write with?"

She dug through her purse, finding a pen with Snowdrift Summit's logo of The Plunge on it. Emily gave Zach the pen and he scribbled on the card, returning it to her, along with the pen.

She read the address. "I think I know this place," she told him, tucking the card in her purse. "So seven, eight o'clock?"

"Seven thirty?" he suggested.

"Perfect," she said, still in a semistate of shock that she was actually standing in the parking lot making dinner plans with Zach Ryker. "I'll see you then." Taking her keys from her jacket pocket, she clicked the Land Rover's start button.

"Pretty fancy ride," Zach said.

"Thanks. I like it; it does the job." As soon as she put her hand on the door, just as he'd done before, he placed his hand on hers.

"Wait a sec," he said, gently pulling her hand away from the door. He leaned close to her, pulling her against him, holding her against his chest before dipping his head so that his mouth reached hers. He planted a light kiss on her lips. Before she could respond, he stepped back a few inches, the warmth of his body against hers brief, yet she felt an intense yearning for something she had yet to experience.

For the first time in her adult life, she understood what full-fledged physical attraction was. Zach's soft kiss melted her inside and out. She stared at him, and he at her. "Take me back to my place," he said.

Cold reality slapped her in the face. She took a step away from him. "Are you kidding me?"

"No, I'm serious."

"You think one little kiss and I'm going to hop in the sack with you? Forget it. I don't play that way. Go back to Hollywood to your little starlets. I'm sure they'll be thrilled with the attention." Her hands shook as she hit the key fob, accidentally shutting off the engine.

"Emily, I didn't mean it that way."

She whirled around. "Do you think I'm stupid? I know guys like you. I've been around quite a few. I'm sorry, but you'll have to find someone else to train you. I don't work with your kind." She opened the driver's door, and he reached for her arm.

"I took an Uber here. I don't have a ride," he said. "I thought you could come back to my place, then we'd go to dinner."

She stared at him. Was he serious? Was he acting? She had nothing to compare his actions to. "You're telling the truth?"

"Yeah," he said, stuffing his hands in his pockets. "It's fine; I'll call for another ride."

"Okay, then." She didn't want to leave him stranded. "Get in," she said. Despite what he'd just said, she couldn't leave him standing alone in the cold.

"Only if you're sure. I don't want you to think I'm going to attack you or anything. Seriously, Emily, I am not the man you see in the movies. Come with me to Wyoming and I'll show you who I really am." He walked around to the passenger side, giving her a few seconds to think about it. She hadn't even had a real date with him, and already they were fighting. She didn't see a good outcome, but she would give him a ride to his rental house. Hitting the Start button again, then adjusting the heat, she turned on both front seat warmers. "I'll take you to your place." She backed out of the parking lot, then onto the main road.

"Emily, I'm sorry you misunderstood me. Let me walk you through my day," Zach said in a serious tone, one she hadn't heard before.

"If you want," she said, focusing her attention on driving.

"Like you, I was bored. I had a meeting with the crew at the house, then everyone went their separate ways. I had cabin fever, so I called an Uber, had lunch at The Mill, and just hung around for a while. When I saw you walk through the door . . ." He stopped speaking for a moment before resuming. "I felt like destiny had taken over because I'd been thinking about you."

"Sounds pretty cheesy to me," she said, but part of her believed him. He didn't need her; he could have any woman he wanted, so why lie to get her attention?

"It does, I agree. It's the truth, though, so make of it what you will," he said. "I'm as surprised as you are, trust me."

"Famous last words," she countered.

She took the Snowmass exit, carefully navigating through the narrow pass. Not a big fan of driving in this area in bad weather, she gripped the steering wheel with both hands, easing off the accelerator. There were no guardrails along this stretch of mountainous road. The locals would stop, allowing oncoming vehicles to pass; however, there were tourists who weren't aware of the dangers, and Emily knew there were plenty of them in town right now.

"You really don't like to drive, do you?" Zach asked. "If you're not comfortable, pull over and I'll drive. I'm used to these narrow roads."

"Thanks, but I'm okay. It's the lack of guardrails, that's all," she said without taking her attention from the road. The snow was falling more heavily the higher she drove up the mountain. Worried she'd have trouble on her way home, she brushed the negative thoughts aside to focus on the present.

"Why doesn't the county add a guardrail?" Zach asked her.

"I'm sure it's a financial thing. You'd have to ask your buddy Wynn Waters. He's a member of the city council."

"I'll do that next time I see him."

"Don't mention my name," Emily said.

"Of course not," Zach answered, "I take it you and Wynn aren't on good terms?"

Now was not the time to discuss their biggest competitor. "He's just another lodge owner," she said. "Can this wait?"

"Sorry," Zach said and sounded like he truly meant it. "We need a restart, you and I."

Emily smirked. "Right." She made a sharp turn, finally off the treacherous Snowmass pass. When she saw the sign for Old Taggart Road, she knew where Zach was staying. "You've rented the Taggart farm?" she asked.

"You're familiar with the place?"

"It's been around since the early eighteenth century. The place with the silo built into the house. Everyone around here knows about the farm."

"That's it—it's very unique and private, which is why I rented the place."

That seemed reasonable enough, but she kept the thought to herself. Emily had never been inside the old farmhouse, but according to those who had, it had been remodeled- with the silo incorporated into one of the rooms. Plenty of acreage, she knew. Some said the stables were top-of-the- line, with built-in heating and the indoor trough providing a continuous supply of fresh water from a well on the property. "Do you have horses there?"

"Actually, that's another reason I wanted to rent the place, to check out the stables. Who knows? If the place is ever put up for sale, I might be interested. I have three horses I keep at Dad's ranch."

This surprised her. Where did he find the time to care for horses while he trotted around the globe? "I assume your father takes care of them for you?"

"Levi does most of the work. Dad's getting up there in years, so I wouldn't expect him to take care of my horses, plus all of his other duties. He spends most of his time training the horses with the kids. He's got that magical touch with both."

Unsure what to say, she kept quiet. Zach continued to prove her wrong. She pulled up the drive that led to the farmhouse. Two red barns, both in need of a fresh coat of paint, situated at the back of the property were quite pic- turesque with the fresh snowfall on the roofs. The large brick house with the tip of the old silo peeking out from behind was before them. Emily had to admit she would love to see the inside of the place.

The snow was getting heavier by the minute and she felt anxious about the drive down the mountain. "Here you go, home sweet home," she said in what she hoped was a neutral tone.

Zach unbuckled his seat belt, but didn't open his door. "Emily, it's too dangerous for you to travel down the mountain. I noticed you don't have chains on your tires."

As if she'd been punched in the gut, she couldn't believe she'd forgotten about this very important aspect of driving in the mountains this time of year. Her brain was fried and she knew why: Zach Ryker. But she could never tell him. "Shit," she said. "Sorry, I simply forgot. I don't know how I could've let that go. I have the chains put on in late October every year."

Zach gave a half laugh. "Could be you were just too busy, or—and I hope this is why—you were too busy thinking about me."

She had to laugh as well. If she didn't know better, she'd swear he could read her mind. "I've been busy at the lodge. Working in the office," she added because he knew she hadn't been on the slopes.

"You're a busy woman, but don't be a ditzy one, Emily. It's too dangerous to drive down the mountain tonight. You can stay in one of the spare rooms. I think there's at least four to choose from. I promise I'll lock myself up and won't bother you."

He was right, though she hated to admit it. What if Kylie popped over and she wasn't at home? Would she call and ask where she was? Then she'd have to lie to her. Even worse, what if her mother called? She was not one to be put off easily. However, Emily was an adult, and she could make decisions for herself.

"You're right, though it kills me to admit it," she told Zach.

"Good. Let's go inside, I can make a fire, whip up something for dinner, then we'll call it a night. Sound good to you?"

She was spending the night with Zach Ryker.

"Yeah, I . . . uh, I'm sorry about what I said earlier." She was ashamed that she hadn't given him the benefit of the doubt, of how quickly she'd judged him because of who he was. She promised herself she would do her best to treat him like she would any of her male friends.

It would be very, very tough.

Chapter Thirteen

"Apology accepted," Zach said. "I don't know about you, but I'm freezing out here."

She'd automatically shut the engine down, as she was used to doing. She hadn't planned on staying in her vehicle talking with Zach. "Me too. I guess I should stay . . . common sense and all."

"Of course it's certainly not the company," Zach teased as he opened his door.

Emily laughed. "I didn't say that."

He opened her door before she had the chance. A gentlemen, she thought, rarely seen these days. She remembered to bring her purse, and she was glad she always kept a mini toothbrush kit inside. She'd been a fanatic about her teeth for years, as she was constantly reminded by Mimi that she had that Ultrabrite smile. She did her part to maintain Mimi's view of her.

She felt like a schoolgirl at her first prom as Zach held the door open for her. He closed it, then said, "Make sure to lock the doors. There's all kinds of wild animals out here."

"You think they're going to drive off in my car?" She laughed.

"One can never be too sure of anything," he told her. Without her realizing it, he'd taken her hand. It felt normal. Opting not to comment or pull her hand away, she walked beside him up the steps to a large, wraparound porch. Rockers with side tables and what she thought were kerosene lamps hung from the beams. Tall electric heaters—the kind they used outside at the lodge—were at either end of the porch.

He let go of her hand, punched in a code, then pushed open the giant double doors. Emily wasn't sure what to expect—after all, a bunch of "movie people" had been hanging out here, so it could be a disaster.

"Let's go to the main room, I'll get a fire going, then we can talk about food."

"Sure," she said, taking note of her surroundings as she trailed behind him. Nothing was out of place: no beer cans lying around or dirty ashtrays, nothing you would expect from a bunch of guys.

The main room almost took her breath away, but she didn't want Zach to see she was so easily impressed. She'd grown up in a beautiful home, but nothing quite like this one. Floor-to-ceiling windows gave a view of the Great Rocky Mountains. Hewn log walls throughout the room gave off a warm, golden glow. As soon as Zach had a fire going, she relaxed.

"Is the fireplace part of the original home?" she asked.

"Yes, and the walls are, too. The floors have been refinished a few times, but they're original. Have a seat, Emily. Warm up. I'll make us a hot drink. What would you like? I have tea, coffee or hot chocolate."

"Hot chocolate sounds divine," she said, then realized how silly that sounded. When had she started using the word "divine"?

"Just what I wanted. Be right back, or you can come with me and see the kitchen."

"I'd love to see the kitchen," she said, adding, "I've always wanted to see the inside of this place." Emily followed Zach to the kitchen, surprised when she saw how large it was.

"Impressive, huh?" Zach said.

"Beyond."

"That's the bar area." He nodded to a space where an actual U-shaped bar made out of rough-hewn, oak barstools matched the log walls in the main room. The barstool cushions were some kind of well-worn leather, probably from an animal Emily didn't want to acknowledge. Behind the bar were more shelves made out of rough wood, stocked with every kind of liquor one could imagine.

"The real estate agent tells me those stools were made from an old barn they tore down on the property. The shelves behind me, too," Zach explained.

"Is the oak from a tree felled on the property?"

He took two mugs from the cupboard, nodding. "You know quite a bit about this place, don't you?"

"I've heard bits and pieces, just never had the opportunity to see for myself. It's so fitting for this part of the country," Emily commented, seated on a tall chair at the island in the center of the massive kitchen, watching Zach prepare their drinks. He took a pot, then a gallon of organic milk out of the refrigerator and a can of Hershey's Cocoa powder from the cupboard. He whisked them together.

"How sweet do you like yours?"

"However it comes. I don't know." Weird, she thought, but the way he made hot chocolate was odd to her. She bought little packets, nuked water in the microwave, then dumped the chocolate powder in a cup.

"I like mine sweet, so I'll make it the way I'm used to. If it's too sweet for you, I can fix that."

Emily nodded, clueless as to what he was talking about. She continued to watch him, his back to her. She admired his wide shoulders, then, daringly, she scanned him all the way down. Slim hips, nice butt. Though she'd seen plenty of his body in his movies, actually having the goods in front of her was a fantasy come true.

He stirred his concoction, then filled their mugs, setting them on the countertop before taking a seat beside her. "You'll like this, though I forgot to ask if you want marshmallows."

"No, this is fine." She blew on her hot chocolate, then took a sip. "This is delicious! Best hot chocolate I've ever had. I'm impressed. If your cooking skills are anything even close to this, I'll be doubly impressed."

"Never judge a man by his movies," he said, then winked at her. "The secret is a little vanilla extract. For dinner, I have two filets I can prepare, or there's tons of frozen stuff in the freezer."

Should she tell him she didn't know how to cook? "Your place, your choice." She figured that was the safest answer.

"Then we're having filets. How do you like yours prepared?"

"Medium rare," she said.

"A woman after my heart." Zach took a sip of chocolate. "My mom taught me how to make this. I never could drink that powdery stuff with water."

"Your mom must be a very good hot chocolate maker," Emily said, knowing how lame that must sound.

"She was," Zach said, a faraway look in his eyes.

She touched his arm. "I'm sorry, Zach. I didn't know."

"Most people don't. We try to keep out of the public eye. You're okay keeping this between us?"

"Absolutely. I would never repeat what isn't mine to share." She wanted to ask what happened, but if Zach wanted her to know, he'd tell her.

"It was a long time ago, before I started working in the movie industry. I was fifteen, Levi fourteen," he said.

"Levi is your brother?" she asked.

"And my best friend. We're so close in age, we've been best friends as far back as I can remember. When we lost Mom, we became even closer. Dad, too, though we'd always been a close-knit bunch. Mom kept us all in line, made sure her boys—that's what she referred to us as— could take care of themselves. One night a week, she'd have Levi and me make dinner, with her help. After a while, I really enjoyed piddling around in the kitchen. Levi not so much. He's the outdoorsy one, spends most of his time with the horses. I'm sure this is more than you wanted to hear."

"No, no, I want to hear about your life," she said. "You have my word I won't repeat anything you tell me."

"I know I can trust you; I feel it in my gut. Plus a few other places." He took another drink of chocolate. "Let's get these filets going. We can chitchat while we make dinner."

"Zach, I am totally useless in the kitchen."

"Do you know how to chop vegetables? Tomatoes, cucumbers?"

"Of course."

"Then you're not useless. You can make the salad." He opened the massive, subzero refrigerator and took out several vegetables, placing them in the sink. "Wash these, then put them in . . ." He looked through a couple of cabinets before finding what he was searching for. "This colander. I'll walk you through the rest of it."

She chuckled. "Hey, I'm not *that* useless."

Zach gave her a paring knife, a cutting board and a vegetable peeler. "I think you know what to do from here," he teased her.

The Taggart farm had been updated with every modern feature there was. Next to the stovetop was a built-in grill. Zach put the steaks on a dinner plate, seasoning them on both sides before seating himself at the island. Emily felt a little anxious with him watching her. She washed the tomatoes and cucumbers, then peeled a Bermuda onion, which she wouldn't dare eat. She used the peeler to remove the skin from the carrots, then chopped each into bite-size pieces. "You have the lettuce?"

"It's already cleaned and shredded. Did that myself when I was bored out of my mind this afternoon. We can mix everything together before the steaks are finished. I was going to toss a couple of potatoes in the fireplace, if you want."

"What?"

"You never made hobo packs as a kid?" Zach asked.

"I've never even heard of them," she said as she put the vegetables in the colander so they could drain.

"Wrap a potato in foil, some ground beef, chicken, whatever you like, toss it in the wood fire, gives it the best flavor. I'll have to microwave them a little bit first, otherwise we'll be waiting all night. It takes a while for them to roast. Tonight we're just doing the potatoes."

"Sounds good. I don't know why Kathryn hasn't tried that. I'll mention it to her."

"Who's Kathryn?" Zach asked as he put three large potatoes in the microwave.

"She's our chef at the lodge. She's from Spain, but went to a fancy cooking school in Paris."

"That explains why she doesn't make hobo packs. I doubt a fancy chef has this in their repertoire." He seemed so comfortable in this setting, Emily had to remind herself this was only temporary. If the groomers did their job, it was highly possible she and Zach would begin training tomorrow. She didn't want to get too comfortable around him.

"No, I'm sure she doesn't. With her Paris lifestyle, I'm sure French onion soup and baguettes were her mainstays." Emily didn't know if that was true or not, but she felt hurt, knowing tonight might be the last night they'd be alone this way, so her reply was snappy.

"Hey, Emily, I didn't mean to offend you."

He could already pick up on her moods and they barely knew each other.

"No, I'm fine, it's just . . . I don't know. I'm enjoying this, and I didn't want to." That was the truth.

"Then we'll do it again," Zach said. "Maybe next time I can teach you how to make Mom's hot chocolate."

"Really? I'd like that."

"Good. Then let me get these potatoes wrapped in foil and I'll show you where to place them so they don't burn."

"Sure," she said, knowing she would agree to almost anything he suggested at this point. *Almost* anything.

In the main room, after starting a fire in the fireplace, Zach positioned her in front, then stood behind her. "Right here." His hand on her shoulder, he eased her closer to the fire. "Under the logs, even though the heat rises, is where the smoky taste comes from. The skin will be crispy. You'll like them, Em." He stepped to the side, placing the potatoes in the fireplace.

No one called her Em except Kylie. Her dad called her "Nick" occasionally, but to have Zach use the endearment meant more than he probably intended. "I'm sure I will. I love to eat."

"You're the woman who's gonna capture my heart if you keep talking that way."

She turned to face him. "Admit it—that's just another line from one of your movies." She laughed.

"If you'd ever seen any, you'd know it's not. I meant what I said, Emily. I don't joke around at my age."

It occurred to her she didn't even know how old he was. Would it be uncouth to ask? She decided she didn't care if it was; she wanted to know. "So how old are you?"

He busted out laughing. "I am thirty-nine, soon to be forty."

Dang, she had no idea he was ten years older than her. "I wasn't sure."

"Now that you know my age, you have to tell me yours."

"Is it a cliché that a woman should never tell her age? Or something to that effect?"

"Maybe, but it doesn't matter. You owe me one."

"Almost thirty," she said.

"Then we're both 'almost.' When's your big day?" Zach asked.

"Believe it or not, Christmas Day."

"Tell me you're joking?" He used the fire poker to move the potatoes around before standing up.

"No, there's no reason to joke about my birthday, other than the fact my mother threw me the grandest birthday parties because I was born on Christmas. Every kid in school wanted an invitation. It was the highlight of my younger years. I always received tons of presents. It's a huge deal in my family, though at my age I've asked them to tone it down."

"Let's get those steaks on," he said.

She followed him to the kitchen. "So, aren't you going to tell me your big date?"

"I'm not sure. It's almost laughable."

She sat down in the chair he'd sat in earlier and watched

as he put the steaks on the grill. She heard them sizzle and the smell reminded her how hungry she was. All she'd had to eat were Kylie's muffins that morning.

"Okay, I hope I won't need to produce my birth certificate, but my birthday is on Christmas Day, too."

Emily started laughing and couldn't stop. "Come on! Don't tease me like that! We're adults, and I don't believe in coincidences."

"I'll show you my driver's license." Grinning, he turned to face her. "We have a lot in common, wouldn't you agree?"

She couldn't wait to tell Kylie. No, wait—she couldn't do that. Kylie had a huge crush on Zach; she couldn't forget that. Though, what if she and Zach really did have more than a winter fling? Kylie would get hurt. Emily didn't know if she could do that to her best friend.

"If you're telling me the truth, it appears we do," she told him. "It's odd having the same birthdays, though, you have to admit."

"It isn't odd, it's perfect," Zach said, turning around to grin at her.

Butterflies were dancing in her stomach, a dance she both loved and hated. At her age she knew better, but with each word Zach spoke, she knew she could get used to having him around. More than casual dating, more than a buddy, definitely more emotions than she could put in words.

"I'm going to get the potatoes. You want to put the salad together? The lettuce is in the crisper," Zach said, reaching for a bowl in the cupboard above him. "You can put all the good stuff in here."

"Sure, I'm starving," she told him, glossing over his "it's perfect" remark. Emily opened the massive refrigerator and took the bag of lettuce from the crisper drawer. She added the salad ingredients to the bowl but didn't have anything to mix it with, so she started opening drawers until she found a set of salad tongs.

Zach jostled the hot potatoes in his hands before dropping them onto the counter. "Ouch, forgot the pot holders."

"You okay?" she asked, though she could clearly see that he was.

"Nah, better call 911," he teased. "I'm tough. Seriously, I'm fine, just forgetful."

"I can splint a broken bone in an emergency, but when it comes to burns, I'm clueless."

Zach removed plates and utensils from the cupboards. "You want to sit here or in the dining room?"

"Here is fine with me," Emily said. She liked this giant yet homey kitchen. Too bad she didn't know how to cook; she'd never be able to appreciate all the gadgets and gizmos it came equipped with. Not that she expected to spend any more time here. The snowstorm was why she was here, she reminded herself, nothing more. She would be wise to remember that.

"Good, I usually eat here," Zach told her.

Within minutes, he'd plated the steaks and split the potatoes while Emily filled their bowls with salad. He'd placed butter, sour cream and a few varieties of bottled salad dressing on the counter. "You mind if I take a minute?"

This surprised her more than anything. She bowed her head as Zach gave thanks for the meal and his new friend.

"Dig in," he said once he was done with the blessing. "Look at the skin on these potatoes! See how crispy?"

For the next half hour they enjoyed dinner, stopping only to comment on the snow outside. The serene snowflakes gently swirled against the windows. It was amazing how something so beguiling could cause the world to stop.

"You love this?" Zach asked her, nodding toward the window.

Distracted for a moment, Emily answered, "It never gets old. The first snow, second, any snow day . . . I suppose you could say I was born for this. I love where I live and my job. I'm very fortunate." She turned to face him. "What about you?"

He raked a hand through his tousled hair, the dark stubble on his angular jaw making him even more attractive. "I've been fortunate, too, in a variety of ways. Losing Mom was the worst tragedy I've had in my life so far. I have an unusual job, certainly a career I never expected, but I have Dad, Levi, the horse farm. I think it's enough to say I'm lucky."

Emily finished her water before asking, "You didn't want to be an actor?"

He laughed. "No, it wasn't my first choice, but the time I was first offered a job as an extra on a farm near where they were filming, my family needed the money, so I took it. A director spotted me and within a year I was cast as Gunner West. I'm sure you know the rest."

"But you keep making the movies. How many?" She knew the answer, but she didn't want him to know she was a fan.

"The film we're working on now will be the tenth."

Spot-on, she thought. "So when Gunner West is killed off, what's next?"

"Hey, don't bury me yet." He took their plates to the sink, rinsing them and adding them to the dishwasher.

"I didn't mean it that way. What I meant was what's your next film? Or, do you plan that far ahead?"

He turned around to face her, leaning against the counter. "I'm not planning that far ahead. I may take a sabbatical for a while. Old Gunner isn't getting any younger. I'm not so sure the character hasn't become tiresome for audiences. Too much of a good thing can go sour."

Emily didn't know what to say; that wasn't what she wanted to hear. Not having his movies to look forward to would be a bummer, but she did have a closet full of them on DVD. She thought of his invitation to go to Wyoming with him. Had he been serious when he asked, or was he just making conversation?

"You're too quiet," Zach said. "Tell me your thoughts, if you want to."

She did want to, so very much, but couldn't. He'd think she was a nutjob. Emily wanted to pinch herself because never in a zillion years could she have imagined she would be where she was right now. So far, no one had called her. A good sign, she hoped. Getting off this mountain and back to her condo before anyone found out she'd spent the night here should be fairly easy provided the roads were cleared. "They're scattered, all over the place," she said, which was true.

Returning her focus to the present, she said, "Zach, that was an awesome meal, and I can't thank you enough for letting me hang out here tonight. I was a little anxious about driving down the mountain. I don't like the Snowmass pass. It's so dangerous, though honestly, I don't drive in this neck of the woods very often."

"I'll drive you down in the morning. Remember, I'm a Wyoming guy, so I've driven through a few snowstorms in my day. I'll worry if you won't let me."

Wouldn't that cause tongues to wag? Kylie would never speak to her again. Emily weighed the pros and cons, deciding the cons were too many. "I should be fine. As long as the roads are clear."

"And if they aren't?"

"Zach, I don't think even you would drive down Snowmass pass if the roads aren't cleared. It's treacherous—

makes The Plunge look like the bunny hill. There's been quite a few deadly accidents throughout the years. I don't want to be responsible for yours."

"Or, I yours," he countered.

"We're getting ahead of ourselves. Let's see what tomorrow looks like before making a decision. Deal?" she asked, trying to stifle a yawn.

"I'm sorry, Em, you're tired. I could sit here and talk to you all night, but we'll have more time once we're working together, right?" he asked, as though he needed assurance.

"Absolutely. We'll be up at the crack of dawn working until sunset. I have six weeks to train you, and that's it. Wynn Watters's orders."

"What?" Zach asked her, looking stunned. "Six weeks? I was told at a minimum we'd have a couple of months. Wynn Watters might be overstepping the line. He is not the executive producer, or the director. There's a lot more to this than a guy investing money. That doesn't automatically give him the right to order time limits on anything. Don't worry about this. I'll take care of Wynn Watters first thing in the morning."

Emily didn't understand the movie business, so she'd let Zach take care of his business, his way. "Sure. It's not my area of expertise, though, I'd appreciate it if you wouldn't repeat this. Watters is known for making business deals to benefit himself and Diamond Pass. He's known to get down and dirty if he needs to."

Zach raked his hand through his hair again. Emily watched him quietly, as she didn't want to intrude on his thoughts. She waited for him to speak.

"I don't know all of the details of Watters's investment, but I do know an investor doesn't control a filming schedule, especially given what I'm expected to learn in this time frame. I will take care of this, Emily, don't worry. In this business you learn to expect the unexpected. Now, let's find a room for you so you can get some rest. I'm a bit tired myself."

"I really do appreciate you going to all this trouble. I've acted like a child," she said, knowing it was true.

"Today has been my best day since I arrived." He smiled at her. "You're the real thing. Nothing pretentious about you, Em. I like that."

He wouldn't say that if he knew what a big liar she was. Would it be so horrible if he knew she'd been a fan since the very first Gunner West movie? What would he think if he saw her box of DVDs hidden in her closet? Maybe he'd call her a closet fan? She smiled.

"What?" Zach asked. "Am I missing something?"

She put the barstool in place before she spoke. "No, just happy I had such an excellent meal."

He chuckled. "I don't believe that for a minute, but that's okay. You'll tell me all your little secrets one day. I can feel it in my gut."

"Overconfident," she said, grinning. She wanted to say so much more, yet now was not the time. She would re-main focused on his training for his upcoming film. If—and this was a very big *if*—they became more than friends, she would let her guard down.

"Let's get you settled in. We'll finish this conversation later. So, you want to sleep in a king-size bed or a bunk bed?" he teased.

She placed her index finger against her cheek as though she were contemplating her options. "King-size."

"I didn't think you were the bunk-bed type," he told her. "Levi and I, we had bunks when we were small. I think we must've been nine and ten when Mom put us in regular beds. Both of us were tall even then. Now, let's stop talking about my childhood and find a room you like."

Emily could've stayed up all night listening to him talk, but she didn't want him under the impression she was in awe of his fame or that she wouldn't trade these past few hours for anything.

Instead, she gave an exaggerated yawn and said, "I am tired." But Emily doubted she would be able to sleep for several reasons, Zach Ryker being at the top of the list.

Chapter Fourteen

Once she was alone in the guest bedroom, for a moment Emily wanted to jump up and down like she had as a child. The room had a living area that contained a small beige leather sofa, a tiny kitchen with everything a guest could need, a mini refrigerator, a microwave, a fancy coffee maker, and built-in shelves filled with books. The eye-catcher was the small, winding staircase that led to the loft bedroom. There was a large bed with cream-colored bedding and decorative pillows in pale green, a small chair and table in one corner, then another door that led to the en suite.

"Wow," she said upon first seeing the room. She didn't care that she let that slip; anyone would have that response. "This is the silo room?"

"It is," Zach said, watching her as she explored the room.

The old silo contained a shower, the roundness of the silo wall untouched, yet modernized with a rainfall shower. Built-in nooks and crannies on the opposite side held soap, shampoo and washcloths. A soaker tub centered below a giant window invited one to soak off the worries of the day. She turned to Zach. "This is the most awesome room . . . *rooms*. I've always wondered how the silo was used."

"A big shower, as you can see. I was impressed, but I took the master suite because the bed fits me better." He laughed. "It's tough sometimes when you're tall."

"I know. I always had trouble finding jeans that were long enough when I was younger," she said.

"If you need anything during the night, my room is downstairs. There's a door at the back of the main room," Zach told her.

Emily couldn't imagine needing anything more, given her situation. "No, I'm good. I'll just . . ." She looked at the tub. "Maybe soak a bit, if you don't mind."

"Do what makes you comfortable." He scanned her from top to bottom. Emily normally felt uncomfortable when a guy looked at her that way, but with Zach she only felt excitement.

"I have a T-shirt you can sleep in," Zach told her. "Give me a minute." He whirled out of the room so fast, she felt a slight gust of air. She didn't want to familiarize herself with the rooms until Zach returned. Emily wasn't normally too nosy—well, she really was when she needed to be—but she was more than curious how the inside of the silo wall had been incorporated into a shower, let alone into the farmhouse.

She could hear Zach on the stairs. He had a funny look on his face when he returned, almost as if he were embarrassed. "Look, I'm not good at this, so I brought you three of my shirts. I wasn't sure what you like to wear to bed."

If Zach continued to talk about the bed and what she slept in, who knows what might happen?

"I'm sure they're all fine. Thanks. I appreciate everything, Zach. I . . ." She wanted to apologize again for her earlier assumptions, her horrid manners at The Mill, but didn't. Mimi told her overapologizing wasn't proper etiquette. If anyone knew of these things, Mimi did. Suddenly Emily's mouth felt like she'd gargled sand. Her heart thudded noisily in her chest. His closeness, the spicy smell of him, the sheer virility of him almost took her breath away. Truly, she couldn't think of a word to say, she was so struck by his intensity. Those indigo eyes looking into hers spoke volumes.

Before she fumbled and said something she'd later regret, she turned away from him, then felt his presence as he stood behind her. Placing his hand on her shoulder, he gently turned her so she faced him. He tilted her chin up so that she had no choice but to look up at him as he lowered his mouth to hers. Without overthinking the situation, Emily welcomed Zach's kiss, his touch gentle as he loosely wrapped her in his arms. Their breath became undistinguished from each other's as Emily wrapped her arms around his waist, allowing herself to enjoy the pure sweetness, the fiery passion his kiss evoked, a mix she'd never experienced before. He tenderly eased his lips away from hers, then kissed her cheeks, the tip of her nose, her forehead. Beyond it being the most romantic kiss of her life, she wanted more of his kisses, his touch, *him*. For a few seconds neither spoke, the atmosphere thick with sensuality.

A seductive flame sparked in Zach's dark blue eyes as his mouth curved into the sexy smile he was so well known for. For a second she wondered if he was acting, but no, she realized this wasn't an act.

"You always have such deep thoughts?" he asked, his arms still draped loosely around her. She saw no reason to remove hers from his waist because she'd never felt more alive and in the moment than now. Even flying down The Plunge didn't give her the intense rush of pleasure she felt now, though skiing and being held in Zach Ryker's arms weren't quite the same.

"I'm not thinking right now." She wanted to explain she could only feel while wrapped in his arms, but it was too soon.

He took a deep breath, yet still held her before speaking. "I believe we are both incapable of thinking too much right now. True?"

Sighing, she couldn't help herself. She nodded.

"I take it that's a yes?"

Another nod.

"Okay. As much as I'm going to regret this, I'm going to let you get some sleep. We can talk in the morning," he said before releasing her from his arms. She dropped her arms to her sides. Bereft, Emily felt empty. She guessed he planned to ask her to forget this ever happened.

"Of course," she replied, sounding like an old spinster whose chances of love were slim to none.

"Hey." He tipped her chin up once again so she could see him. "Are you sorry this happened?"

What to say? The truth or a lie? Because she'd been honest with him after she'd admitted lying about Harold, she decided she owed him the truth. "No, I'm not."

He smiled at her. Emily thought his smile was almost as seductive as his kiss. "Me either. One more question, then I promise to leave you alone."

Glowing inwardly like a ball of fire, at that moment Emily decided she would answer any question he asked. Personal or professional. "Okay, what do you want to ask me?"

"How do you like your eggs?"

Emily burst out laughing. "You're serious?"

"I make a mean breakfast, specializing in sausage gravy topped with eggs."

Could he be more perfect? "Over easy," she said, conscious of her use of the word "easy" and hoping he didn't read anything into it.

"Same here," he said. "Now I'm walking down those steps to my room. Good night, Em." He turned and left the loft, closing the door to the living area downstairs.

"Night," she whispered to herself.

Taking the shirts Zach brought for her to sleep in, she held them close to her face, breathing in the scent of fabric softener and his spicy cologne. Out of the three shirts, she chose a soft, well-worn chambray. She glanced at the time on her cell phone. After ten; not too late for a soak in the tub, as she'd never bathed and watched a snowstorm at the same time. Checking her phone for messages, she was relieved when she didn't find any. Hopefully, Kylie was busy baking, or maybe she'd gone into town and purchased an InstaPot to stay busy. When Kylie was idle, her cell phone pinged constantly with text messages. Poor Kylie, Emily thought as she figured out how to use the faucet on the tub. She would kill her if she knew where she was spending the night. But the kiss—that was hers alone; she would not share that experience ever. As soon as she adjusted the water temperature, Emily returned to the silo shower, where she retrieved a bar of gardenia-scented bath soap, a washcloth and a towel. Stripping down to her birthday suit, she lowered herself in the tub, sighing as she leaned her head against the back of the tub.

"This is heaven," she said to herself. The warm water relaxed her as she stared out the window. Large snowflakes blew against the window, heavier now than they were two hours earlier. If this continued, she doubted the Snowmass pass would be cleared early enough for her to get home without Kylie noticing. She would be in a pickle, big-time, if the weather worsened. Forcing herself to forget about what might happen, she relaxed. Tomorrow would be here soon enough.

Emily dozed off, then startled awake when she realized she was still in the tub. She quickly washed, then drained the water. Wrapped in the luxurious bath towel, she found her toothbrush kit in her purse and brushed her teeth before wrapping herself up in Zach's shirt. It was as close as having him cradle her in his arms without him actually being there. Pulling the bedding aside, she crawled beneath the covers, amazed at how comfortable the bed was.

Her thoughts were all over the place. Kylie, her family, but mostly she thought of Zach. He appeared to be totally the opposite of the character he portrayed in his movies. He was an actor; she couldn't forget that. And, a good one, so all of his words, actions and those sexy smiles could be just that—part of his job. Would he feel differently once they began his training? Even worse, could she work with him without revealing her feelings? To him and to the rest of the world? Unsure, she rolled onto her side. Within a few minutes, she drifted off into a dreamless sleep.

Hours later, Emily awakened to the smell of coffee. Pushing herself into an upright position, it took a minute for her to gather her thoughts and remember where she was. The snow, she thought, and tossing the covers aside, she hurried to the window to check outside.

She peeked out the window in the bathroom. The world outside was totally white. The land surrounding the farm looked as if the clouds had dropped to the earth, their shapes reminding her of white sand dunes, each one shaped differently. Snowbanks several feet deep surrounded the faded red barns she'd seen yesterday. There was no way Snowmass pass would be cleared in time for her to return to her condo before anyone noticed she was gone. Emily brushed her teeth, dressing in the same clothes she'd worn the day before. She searched in her purse for a tie, then twisted her long hair in a low bun.

"Emily, this is as good as it gets," she mumbled to herself.

Spying her cell phone beside the bed, she checked the time. It was almost seven o'clock. Unbelievable; she'd slept like a baby, never once waking up to check her phone or go to the bathroom. Emily glanced at the battery and saw she only had 20 percent power left. Unsure what she was going to do, she quickly straightened the bedcovers, making sure she left the room neat.

Downstairs in the main room, Zach was in the midst of building a fire. The woodsy smoke, the scent of coffee lingering in the air, snowbound . . . what a perfect scenario to wake up to. "Hey," she said to Zach, who hadn't yet noticed her.

"Good morning, Em. You have a good sleep?" He poked a few logs, put the fire poker aside, then walked toward her as though this was something he'd been doing for years. "I've got coffee in the kitchen." He placed his hand at the base of her back, gently guiding her to the kitchen.

"I smelled it as soon as I woke up," she told him. "It's great waking up with the coffee already made," she added, then wished she hadn't. She was sure in his normal life, Zach didn't get up this early just to make coffee for an overnight guest.

"It is. When I'm home, I set the pot to brew before I go to bed just so I can wake up knowing my caffeine fix is waiting for me."

Okay, so she was wrong. In the kitchen, Emily sat on the same barstool she'd sat on last night. Zach took a Christmas mug with Santa's chubby belly forming the handle from the cupboard, filling it with coffee. "Black, right?"

As she watched him, Emily couldn't recall any situation where they'd shared a cup of coffee. It had to be a lucky guess on his part. "Black is perfect," she answered. "What's with the Christmas mugs?" Emily saw his mug matched hers.

"It's about that time of year. I saw these in the cupboard and decided we might as well start celebrating the holidays."

We? As in us?

Taking a sip of coffee, Emily tried to focus on her current dilemma—not Zach's muscular arms, his very messy, yet sexy hair and gray T-shirt with letters so faded she couldn't make out what they said. Faded jeans clung to his thighs, emphasizing his legs, which she knew were the epitome of perfection. *Focus on your dilemma, Emily.* She had to leave as soon as the roads were clear or she would have to make a couple of calls. She didn't want to lie to Kylie, but right now she couldn't think of her friend's feelings for Zach because her own were scary in their intensity, unlike anything she'd ever experienced She'd had a couple of serious relationships, knew what love felt like— or thought she had—until now.

"Are you always this quiet in the morning?" Zach asked her.

She was determined to give him the honest-to-goodness truth. "I live alone. I admit there are times in the morning when I talk to myself and Clarice, my cat. I yell at the coffee maker because it takes too long to brew. I talk to the news anchors if I'm listening to a weather report, which in my business is essential. I can't cook so I don't have lavish breakfasts—a bagel or a muffin is good. I go to work, I eat lunch at the lodge and that about sums me up." Pretty boring life, she thought, but at least she was being truthful.

"So I take it when you have a bit of downtime, you what? Go to The Mill? Shop at Benny's?"

"Hey, that's not fair—you've only seen me at those places because you were there, too."

Zach tilted back his head, roaring with laughter. "I'm teasing you, Emily. I like you."

"That's nice," she replied, then added, "I like you, too.

So now that we've decided we like each other, have you heard the weather report this morning? I'm sure the roads are horrid."

"I haven't listened to any news, but let's check." He went to the bar and opened a cabinet, turning on the TV inside. "Weather channel?"

"No, they're always wrong," she told him. "Could you switch to channel nine?"

He used the remote to change the channel. They both listened as Denver's finest meteorologist reported the forecast for the next two days. Upset, Emily walked around the island to refill her mug. She was definitely making herself comfortable here with Zach. This was fantasy, and the real world—her world—was blanketed in snow.

"I need to go, seriously. If I stick around any longer, I'll be stuck here for who knows how long. I appreciate your hospitality, Zach. You're a great host, but I truly need to leave." She felt tears welling up in her eyes. What the heck was wrong with her? She'd drive slow, use the four-wheel drive, plus she would be on the safe side of the mountain, not the opposite side, where the guardrails were null and void. She took a few breaths until she could control her emotions, then finished her coffee. "If I can't make it to town, I'll . . ." She was going to say she would call, but she didn't have his phone number and refused to ask for it. "I'll call a tow truck."

It was unlike her to get so emotional. She thought maybe she was on the verge of a crying jag. "Thanks for all this." She gestured with her hand to the kitchen, the coffee. Before she totally lost it, she slipped into her jacket, then headed to the main room and the double doors.

"Wait," Zach called. "Emily, you can't drive in this. You said so yourself."

She turned around, practically knocking Zach squarely

on the chin. "I'll be just fine. I have to get to work. No one knows I'm here, Zach." She let those words hang in the air, hoping he understood her underlying meaning.

"Is there a reason why no one knows you're here? Or, I don't know, are you ashamed of what's happening between us?"

Unsure, she shook her head. "No, it's nothing like that. I'm an adult. I don't have anyone to answer to. It's just . . ." She paused, needing a minute to think if she should tell him about Kylie's feelings for him. "I might be hurting someone if they knew I spent the night here. They'll read into it, and this person is close to me." There—she'd said what she needed to say without revealing Kylie's crush.

"So you and Harold really are an item?"

Her eyes widened; then she shook her head so hard, her hair tie fell to the floor, her uncombed tangles draping down her back. "No! Never!"

"Then there's someone else?" Zach took a couple of steps back.

Taking a deep breath, Emily opted for the semitruth. "Zach, trust me when I say I'm not involved with anyone. I haven't had a date in months, and there isn't anyone special in my life, except for my parents, my grandparents, and my best friend. My life is pretty boring. I know a person who is very fond of you, and your movies. When they found out you were filming at my family's lodge, they revealed their true feelings about you to me."

"That's all?" he said, his features softening, a smile lifting the edge of his sexy lips.

"Yes, and I don't want them to find out about this." She waved her hand around. "It will be incredibly hurtful if they do."

"Let's have another cup of coffee. We need to talk. Seriously." Zach raised his brows in question.

"Sure," she said, removing her jacket as she followed him back to the kitchen. Emily sat down and let Zach refill her mug.

"I promised you breakfast. While I cook, tell me about this person, your friend."

"You don't have to make breakfast for me," she said. "Coffee is enough."

"Okay, I'll make it for myself, then. So, tell me about your friend." Zach had his back to her as he took a carton of eggs, a white package of some kind of meat—she recognized the familiar Benny's label—and a carton of milk from the refrigerator, along with a small bag of flour. Why flour, she had no clue.

"There isn't much to tell. I know a person who likes you and your movies so much, they would give anything to trade places with me."

"If they knew you were here with me, I assume?" he asked, still with his back to her.

"Yeah," she said, realizing how childish this all was. "I know it's silly."

"Emily." He turned around to face her. He held a spatula in one hand and the package of meat in the other. "I've had experience with crazy fans for a while now. Never once have I dated one, taken them seriously or behaved in a condescending way to those that I've met. As I said, I work very hard to keep my private life private. It's one of the reasons I don't live in California. It's a hot spot for gossip and not an atmosphere I care to be a part of. The acting is for the money. Nothing more, nothing less. I continue to help Dad and Levi at our farm. The horses are my true passion. So, knowing this, please tell this person that I am not interested, but I appreciate that they enjoy my movies. That's the whole truth, which you would know if you would go to Wyoming with me." He turned around, his back to her once again.

Taking a sip of coffee, she contemplated what he'd said. If he knew she was a crazy fan, he wouldn't have anything to do with her. She was sure of that. Would it be fair to pretend she hadn't seen his movies, that her interest in him was purely . . . physical? Not in a skiing-down-the-mountain sense either. She was undecided if that mattered at this point in their friendship—for that was all it was. She would remain silent and see how this all played out.

"I don't know you well enough, Zach. I've never done this kind of thing before," she said, which was true.

He dropped whatever kind of meat he had into the skillet. A sizzling sound came from the stove as he used the edge of the spatula to break the meat apart.

"Is that sausage?" she asked, feeling stupid.

"It is. Straight from Benny's. Good stuff," he said. "What is it you haven't done before? I can't think of anything we've done that's in any way wrong or deceitful. We're not committed to anyone. We're two adults who just so happen to be attracted to each other. We can date. We can have a long date in Wyoming. You could meet Dad and Levi. I'm not asking you to hop into the sack and call it a night, Em. I am not that guy, despite Gunner West's reputation. You have the two of us mixed up. He's not real. I, Zachary William Ryker, am a real person who likes you, Emily. Tell me what's wrong with that?"

Chewing her bottom lip, she debated with herself before she answered. "Nothing is wrong with us, Zach. I just don't . . . well, honestly, I don't see why you're attracted to me. I don't want to be a winter romance, a notch in your belt, though, I'm not looking for a serious relationship at this stage in my life either. You're an actor. How can I be sure you're not acting? That whatever we have going on between us isn't, well . . . just an act?"

He turned around so fast he knocked the skillet off the burner, sausage flying across the counter. He righted the skillet, then used the spatula to scoop the sausage back into it before he swiveled around to face her. "Is that what you believe? Truly?"

Feeling insecure, she just nodded.

"Have I done anything to make you feel like you're just another 'notch in my belt' as you put it?"

"You're right, Zach. You've been nothing but a gentle-men. My hesitancy is my own, and yes, it does have a little to do with who you are. What woman wouldn't be intim-idated by you? I'm ashamed to say I'm beyond flattered by your interest in me. I won't lie—I'm attracted to you. I don't know what else to say."

"If that's how you feel, there isn't anything else you need to say. We should date, get to know each other. Wy-oming isn't that far. Tell your friend I'm spoken for."

Emily visualized telling Kylie that she and Zach were dating. Foot stomping, cussing and maybe something thrown at her was sure to be the result. Then what? Kylie would accept this and they'd continue to be best friends as they'd been most of their lives? Kylie was strong-willed. When she wanted something, she went after it with a vengeance. Kylie aside, Emily adored Zach's old-fashioned term, "spoken for." Her mother would have a heart attack if she knew she was falling for an actor, one of those "movie people." When the time was right, she would ask her mother why she felt so strongly about them. Maybe if her mother met Zach while they were training, she would have a change of heart.

"Over easy, right?" Zach said.

"Yes."

"I'm using canned biscuits. You okay with that?"

"Zach! I can't cook anything. A canned biscuit is fine by me. I eat Pop-Tarts, okay? And I don't even bother to toast them."

"Cherry or Brown Sugar Cinnamon?" he asked.

"Cherry."

"See? We're learning about each other. This is a breakfast date. I like the sugar cinnamon on occasion, so there isn't anything wrong with liking Pop-Tarts. I freeze mine sometimes, then crush them up and toss them in a bowl of vanilla ice cream. It's delicious."

"I'll try that sometime. I think I can manage to toss a couple of Pop-Tarts in the freezer. So, how do I get down the mountain?" She knew she could call her dad or Papaw. They would send one of the Sno-Cats over, yet she wasn't ready to leave. Seriously considering what Zach said, she had every right in the world to date him. If Kylie found out, she'd have to deal with it.

For now, Emily planned to enjoy this time alone with him.

Chapter Fifteen

Zach set a plate in front of Emily. "Eat this and give me your honest opinion."

Emily loved food. If she ate like this every day, she would have to ski from sunup to sundown daily just to burn the calories. "It looks delicious." She dug into the sausage gravy topped with an egg. It melted in her mouth. Could breakfast actually melt in one's mouth? She closed her eyes, swallowing. "Who taught you how to make this?" she asked, continuing to talk around half a mouthful of food.

"Me," Zach said. He sat beside her with a plate piled high. "I told you, I like to cook."

"This stuff—is there a recipe I could give to Kathryn? This would sell like hotcakes at the lodge." She kept eating while she talked.

"No recipe, just a little of this and that. I go by the smell, the consistency. So no recipe from me, though, I'm sure you can find one out there. It's not like I have the exclusive on this." He used his fork to point to the gravy. "It's better when I make the biscuits from scratch, but I don't have the ingredients here."

"Does Benny's have biscuit stuff?" She knew she

sounded like a total ditz, but she wanted to know so she could purchase the items he needed. For another time, if she were to have another chance to have a breakfast date with Zach.

He looked at her, amusement flickering in his eyes. "I'm sure they do, Em. You want me to teach you how to bake, too? I'll be happy to, since you're going to train me how not to break my neck or legs."

Liking the humorous sparring between them, she continued to banter. "You forgot about the arms. Most people, if they break anything, it's usually the arms. Odd—you would think it would be the legs," she teased.

"That's comforting. Em, I can't wait now. Seriously, have you ever hurt yourself on The Plunge?" He'd finished his breakfast, taking his plate to the sink, where he rinsed it as he had the night before.

She took her empty plate, following him. "Fortunately, I haven't. I did fall once when I was eight or nine, but I was trying to ski backward on one leg. I had a concussion and broke my arm."

"Ouch."

"What about you when you're filming? Some of those stunts you're known for, it's a miracle you haven't broken every bone in your body." As soon as the words were out of her mouth, she once again wished she hadn't said them.

"I thought you'd never seen my movies," Zach said, his lighthearted tone gone.

Once again, to lie or tell the truth? He didn't date fans. He had made that clear. "I've seen bits and pieces on television," she said, which wasn't really a lie.

"Luckily, I've only had a sprained ankle. Nothing broken, though there isn't a spot on my body that hasn't been bruised."

The humorous wordplay from moments ago was gone. Had Zach picked up on her half lie? Should she tell him she enjoyed the action-packed movies, but wasn't an obsessed fan? Which made her wonder if Kylie *was* obsessed with Zach. That would be an entirely different story if she were. She did have a temper when she didn't get her way. No, Emily thought to herself, no way would Kylie do anything . . . stalkerish.

Wanting to change the topic, she said, "I've had my share of falls, but you said you could ski a black diamond. You'll do fine on The Plunge. It's really a matter of positioning, and you'll need skis that will enable you to edge. New Frontier Skis has a great model out this year in their new Genesis series. I was one of the testers last year. I'll get you properly fitted, then before we even think about The Plunge, I'll want to watch you ski in a practice area that's off-limits to the public. Then, if you're comfortable, I'll have you ski Maximum Vault, a tough black run. I think both of us will enjoy playing in the snow." She hoped this would return Zach to his jovial self.

He'd cleaned the stove and counters, then handwashed the skillet he'd used as he listened. "I'm excited we get to work together, which means we'll probably have to have dinner together, rehash the day's work. You can give me pointers if I need them, which I'm sure I will."

"Absolutely," she said quickly. "I'll be giving you plenty of pointers." She didn't want to appear like an overzealous fan. She would have to watch what she said in the future. She'd kept her little secret to herself for many years—now wasn't the time to focus on his movies, just the man.

The ringtone coming from her cell in her purse interrupted their conversation. "Hello?" she said in a low voice into the phone. "I can't hear you—we have a bad connection. I'll call you back," she said before hanging up. Kylie was the last person she wanted to speak to, given her situation.

Grinning, Zach said, "I take it you didn't want to talk to whoever that was."

"No, I didn't, though I really need to get back to my condo. I like this place, Zach. It's a shame it's not for sale. I'd consider purchasing the place myself if it were. I'm going to call my dad and see if he can take the Sno-Cat this far. I'll just leave my car here if that's okay. You can use it as long as you need to. I can borrow a car from my family."

She dialed her dad's cell. "Dad, it's me. Can you hear me okay? Great. I need a favor. A ride from the old Taggart farm. The plows haven't cleared Snowmass pass, so can you drive the Sno-Cat that far? Okay, that's perfect. Thanks, I appreciate this." She clicked the End button on her phone.

"So you're leaving me?" Zach stated, making a silly face by turning his lips downward like a pouting child.

Unsure how to answer, she laughed. "I have some work to do at the lodge. I want to take the lift to Maximum Vault this afternoon. As I said, it's one of the toughest black runs, plus it's tough to maintain. A good challenge before taking the plunge, pun intended."

"I promise I'll give it my best shot. So this Sno-Cat— how long will it take before it arrives? Would I be able to hitch a ride? I don't want to stay here all day with nothing to do."

Emily liked the idea, but wasn't sure about sharing a ride with him, even though they were going be working together. "They're not very fast, so a couple of hours, maybe. Of course Dad will give you a lift to wherever you're going." She said this hoping he would tell her where he planned to go.

"You okay if I tag along with you?" he asked. "I don't have anything on my schedule today."

There wasn't a reason to tell him no. They might as well start working now, despite the heavy snow. "Not at all. You can ride up the mountain with me. We'll get your skis first. Do you have ski clothes?"

"I'm sure the costume designer has taken care of what I'll wear on set, but no, I don't have my own ski clothes with me."

Emily nodded. "We can take care of that. I'll make sure to have a new suit ready for you. I don't think you'd want to wear a rental, even though they're cleaned after every use."

"I'm not a snob, Em, but I'll take whatever you think is best."

She wasn't a snob either, but she didn't want Zach Ryker to wear a rental even though they were in top-notch condition. "You're tall, so I'll take care of this. I'll call Max Jorgensen. He'll have your size at his shop if we don't."

"Wasn't he in the Olympics?"

"A few years ago. I believe he's married with a couple of kids now. He owns Exhilaration, a ski shop in town. They specialize in big and tall sizes. We'll go there if we need to, when the weather permits. I can't see driving around town in the Sno-Cat." She snickered. "We'd be a laughing-stock."

A huge grin overtook his handsome features. "I've been a laughingstock so many times I've lost count. On set, there's been all sorts of mishaps. I've busted my butt in front of hundreds and always got a good laugh out of it."

"So you're not one of those actors who storms off the set when things aren't going your way?"

"Never! It's unprofessional. I've worked with a couple of actors—I won't say their names out of respect—but let's just say they can hold up production for days if they aren't given a specific type of bottled water."

Emily sometimes scanned the tabloids while waiting in line at Benny's. She didn't have to think too hard to know who he referred to. "Fame has gone to their heads, I guess."

"It does to a lot of actors and actresses. For the life of me, I don't feel any different now than I did when I was an extra in my first film. My bank account has increased, I'm recognized, but I'm not special. I would never ask for a specific drink in my contract. That's just bull, but they know they'll get whatever they want if the director really wants them in their film. It's ridiculous."

"I'm glad you aren't that way," she said, then felt her cheeks turn red.

"Why is that?" Zach asked her.

Emily believed it spoke to his character. "It helps me believe you really are who you claim to be," she told him.

He gazed at her, his eyes as sensuous as she'd experienced last night. "Just wait until you get to know all of me."

Chapter Sixteen

As soon as Emily heard the Sno-Cat, she went outside to wait, Zach beside her. Her dad wouldn't ask why she was here, and she didn't feel the need to offer an explanation.

"You sure you're okay having me tag along? I don't want to cause any trouble," Zach said.

"It's fine, really. It'll be a slow ride back, but you can get to know my father. He's a decent guy most of the time." She laughed.

As soon as she spied the giant machine grinding its way up the long drive more than two hours after she called, she realized this was the new Sno-Cat. "Frank must've delivered early," she said, more to herself than Zach.

"Frank?"

"Dad purchased this new Cat from Frank. He's the local guy you deal with when you need one of these giant machines. He said it would take a few weeks to deliver, but apparently cash speeds things up."

"That a brand-new corduroy maker?" Zach asked.

"With seating for twelve. I want to start a mobile vino bar," she told him while they watched the Cat maneuver its way as close to the farmhouse as possible.

"Fancy."

"It's nothing new, just new to us," she said. "We'll see how it works out." Emily could swear she saw someone in the back of the Cat, but her dad wouldn't dare bring her mother. She didn't like being closed inside where she had no control; she always said it made her claustrophobic. Could it be Papaw? But he wouldn't sit in the passenger area. The front had seating for six.

As soon as the engine stopped, her dad pushed the door aside, jumped out, then reached up to help *Kylie* from the Sno-Cat.

Emily's thoughts were racing. What was Kylie doing here? Did she know Zach was staying here? Even worse, did she know that Emily and Zach had spent the night together?

"Who's the girl?" Zach asked, apparently not recognizing her after their brief encounter at Benny's.

No way could she tell him Kylie was the woman who claimed she'd secretly been his biggest fan forever. "She works at the lodge with me. Another instructor." Emily was ashamed she didn't tell Zach that Kylie was her very best friend. But she didn't want to reveal Kylie and her secret. Hopefully her friend wouldn't gush all over Zach—if so, he might suspect who she was.

As soon as Kylie's feet hit the deep snow, Mason caught her before she face-planted into the white powder. Emily couldn't help but laugh, knowing her friend would be mortified if she knew who was watching her, though she wasn't entirely sure what Kylie knew at this stage. It was extremely odd that she had accompanied Emily's dad.

Kylie trudged toward the front porch, Mason following behind. "Where have you been? I've been out of my mind with worry! I thought you were dead. No one knew where you were. You cannot do this, Emily. People worry about—"

"I'm fine, okay?" Emily interjected hastily.

"You should have called me. Like I said, I was sick with worry. You should be glad I called Mason or my next call would've been to the police." Kylie hadn't focused on Zach yet.

"I thought she was going to bite my head off," Mason said. "When I told her where I was headed, she insisted on coming." He stepped toward Zach, holding out his hand. "I'm Mason Ammerman, Emily's dad."

Zach shook her father's hand. "Zach Ryker; nice to meet you, Mr. Ammerman. It looks like we're going to be seeing a lot of each other."

"Emily!" Kylie's eyes practically bulged out of her head. She walked closer to her, staring up at Zach. "It's you— Zach Ryker?" She actually grabbed his arm and tugged him closer to her. "Oh my gosh, you are real!"

"Kylie, stop it! You're acting like a doofus." Emily grabbed her hand. "Seriously," she added, her tone cold as the snow.

Kylie wouldn't stop staring at Zach as he gently removed his arm from her grip. Emily was humiliated for her and for Zach. Finally her father spoke up. "Kylie, why don't you help Emily with her things, maybe see if she's left anything in her car?" He raised his eyebrows, nodding at Emily. She knew the look. He wanted to distract Kylie and have a moment alone with Zach.

"Of course. Come on, you can help me." Emily yanked her friend's arm harder than normal, but she didn't have a choice. Later Kylie would thank her for stepping in and preventing her from embarrassing herself more than she had already.

"Hey, is brutal force necessary, Emily?" Kylie whispered.

"In this case, yes."

Emily dug through her purse for her keys, unlocking her car. She opened the driver's side door, leaning across the seat and pretending to search for an item she had allegedly forgot. Opening the middle glove compartment, she spied an extra phone charger. She actually needed that. "Here it is," she told Kylie. "I thought I lost this." At least that was true.

Kylie watched her, but remained silent. Emily closed the car door, hitting the key fob and locking the doors. "You ready?" Emily asked.

"No, I want an explanation. Why are you here with him? You'd better tell me what's going on, Em. You do know he's off-limits, right?" Her face deepened, red as a beet. Emily wasn't sure if it was from the cold or anger. It was definitely not normal behavior and it frightened her.

Using a calm tone, she asked, "Are you listening to yourself?" Emily shivered as she spoke. The temperature was below freezing and they weren't dressed properly for this. "Let's get back to the lodge. We can talk then."

Kylie shook her head. "No, Emily. We aren't leaving until you tell me how you wound up here. With Zach. I think it's the least you can do, considering you know I have feelings for him."

Emily stood as close to her as possible. She lowered herself a few inches so she could look Kylie directly in the eye. "Are you serious? Zach Ryker doesn't even know you, Kylie. I think we should leave; then we can discuss this later. I'm not going to stand out here and freeze my ass off, so let's just go." She walked away from her, tears stinging her eyes. Fear for Kylie's mental state dominated her thoughts. When she reached her father, she whispered, "Dad, see if you can drag her to the Cat. She won't listen to me."

"No prob, kiddo. Let me crank the engine over and turn

the heat up. It's too cold to stand out here." He jumped inside the Cat, leaving the door open for her and Zach.

Without thinking, Emily allowed Zach to lift her into the Cat even though she was tall enough to climb inside with no assistance. He closed the door and motioned to her dad. Maybe he decided he didn't want to tag along with them after all. She didn't blame him. Or, he'd figured out Kylie was his biggest—and seemingly craziest—fan and wanted nothing to do with her. Emily felt sad for Zach herself, but mostly for her friend. She was unsure if she'd suffered a breakdown or possibly was in a delusional state. Mental health wasn't her area of expertise, but she knew Kylie. This wasn't her best friend. Usually this time of year, Kylie spent her free time baking for the upcoming holidays or, when she wasn't working, helped them decorate all the Christmas trees throughout the lodge. Her mother loved having "her two best girls" help out. Emily enjoyed it almost as much as her mother. Except for the Harold incident. That had turned her off the holidays for a while, but all had been forgiven. Mom would know what to do to help. And, if she didn't, she would know who would.

Feeling guilty, she watched her dad and Zach speak to Kylie. Apparently one of them talked a bit of sense into her because they were all now heading to the Cat. Her father gave Kylie a boost, then stepped aside as Zach lowered his head to get inside. He sat next to Emily, while Kylie inserted herself in the farthest seat away in the passenger section. Mason took over the controls, turning the giant beast around.

"This is a slow crawl back to Loveland. Your mother asked Kathryn to make a few snacks to bring along, so there will be enough to eat if any of you are hungry."

"Zach made breakfast," Emily said.

Kylie gave Emily such a vile look, she knew there had to be something seriously wrong. Maybe she had fallen and injured her head? Or eaten a bad piece of meat? Emily knew these were stupid guesses, but what would cause such a dramatic change? In all the years they'd known each other, Kylie hadn't ever acted so mean and hateful. Yes, she did have a temper; she'd always blamed it on her passionate nature. As soon as they returned, Emily would call her mother to see if she had any insights. If Kylie's behavior continued, Emily wasn't sure if she would be able to continue working as an instructor.

The drive down the pass took an hour. No one spoke, which Emily thought was for the best; she didn't want to distract her father. The Cat was as wide as the narrow pass. He needed to focus on keeping them safe. Once they were off that treacherous stretch of road, the rest of the ride should be uneventful.

"Em, would you mind reaching into the cooler and getting one of those sandwiches for me? I missed breakfast this morning," Mason said.

Emily stooped low as she peered at the contents of the large YETI cooler in the back. "Jeez Louise, did Kathryn think you were leaving for a week?" She took out four sandwiches wrapped in plastic along with four bottles of water. Kylie refused to even look at her. Emily placed a sandwich and water bottle beside her, whispering, "You need help, Ky." No response, but she hadn't expected one.

Once back in her seat, Emily unwrapped another sandwich and handed it to her father. This new Cat had holders for all of their drinks, so she opened his water for him and placed it in one of them.

"Thanks," Mason said without taking his attention away from driving.

"This is good." Zach *finally* spoke. Emily thought he may be regretting his decision to come along, but he seemed to be relaxed. "Prime rib sandwiches, riding in a Cat during a blizzard. Doesn't get much better."

Emily had a mouthful of sandwich, so she simply nodded. Kathryn didn't know what a ham and cheese on rye from a deli was. Most likely the bread had been freshly baked this morning, too. Nothing premade or artificial came out of her kitchen.

"Mr. Ammerman, before we start filming, would it be possible for you to give me a tour of the mountain in this rig? I'd like to see the entire summit before I start jumping off cliffs," Zach said and laughed.

"Sure thing, I can take you up tonight. The runs need to be groomed, and I want to try this Cat out myself before I hand if off to Rob."

Rob was their lead groomer and had been with them as long as Emily could remember. He lived to ride the mountain. Getting this top-of-the-line piece of heavy-duty machinery would be the highlight of the season for him.

"Great. I'll find a place to stay in town," Zach said.

Emily spoke up. "You won't, not this late in the season."

Kylie jerked her head in their direction, but remained silent.

"We have plenty of room at our house. You're welcome to stay with us," Mason said. "Or Em's place. She has a spare room, too."

Did Emily just hear her dad inviting Zach to spend the night at *her condo*? "I think Zach will be more comfortable with you and Mom. You have all those extra rooms. My spare room is full of Clarice's toys. She's been hiding under the bed for days, so I doubt she'd welcome a visitor."

Emily told Zach the story of Clarice, how she'd found

her as a kitten, abandoned in a laundromat in Denver. Emily adored her cat, and Clarice adored only Emily. She'd been so traumatized that the poor cat still had trust issues, even after all these years.

"Clarice, huh?" Zach teased.

"Yes. It's a strong name, I think. Clarice had a rough beginning, like the character in *The Silence of the Lambs*. She's a fighter."

"Literally," her dad added.

"Maybe you'll introduce me to Clarice sometime," Zach suggested. "We have a few barn cats at home. Last count I think we had seven. Levi brings them inside when it's cold, which is most of the time, so they're not truly barn cats if you take that into consideration." He laughed. Emily grinned and caught Kylie smile in her peripheral vision. Maybe she was coming to her senses.

"I might," Emily said, adding, "She isn't the friendliest cat, just as Dad said. If you're willing to get involved in a catfight, I'll introduce you when the time is right." Emily directed her gaze at Kylie, hoping she got the message. Their friendship could possibly turn into a full-fledged catfight if she didn't back off and stop acting like she'd escaped from the loony bin. Or could Kylie truly be suffering from some sort of breakdown? Until Emily knew for sure, she would back off.

"I've had my share of cat scratches. Not that big a deal," Zach said, then turned to look at Kylie, really looked at her, as though he were seeing her for the first time. He leaned as close to Emily as he could without drawing any unnecessary attention. "Isn't Kylie your friend, the one I saw at Benny's?"

Emily had forgotten about that night. Sort of. "She is." If Zach asked if she were also the friend who was his biggest fan, Emily couldn't lie.

"I thought I recognized her. Is she always so . . . spirited?" he asked, a grin lighting up his handsome face.

"Most of the time, yes," Emily answered truthfully. Just not in the way she was behaving now. Kylie had a temper, was always passionate about whatever her current hang-up happened to be. Maybe Zach was her current fixation and it would pass just like all the others.

"She wouldn't happen to be that girl who claims to be my biggest fan, would she?" Zach whispered in her ear. Emily smoldered with irritation and humiliation. Once again she was in the position where she had to decide between the truth and a lie. Or something in between, she thought. "If you want to know that, you'd have to ask her yourself." At least that wasn't a lie.

"Okay, I will, but I don't believe the timing is in my favor, given where we are," he said, again in her ear. If he didn't stop, Kylie might think they had some sort of weird conspiracy against her.

"True," Emily said in a normal tone, hoping Zach would pick up on the no-more-whispering hint.

"I can't wait to ride the summit, Mr. Ammerman," Zach said, out of the blue. Emily knew he was trying to make small talk for her sake and she truly appreciated the effort.

"Call me Mason. It's been a while since I've spent a night grooming the mountain. I'll enjoy your company. I remember the days when I groomed full time. It's a lonely profession."

Surprised, Emily said, "I don't remember you ever being a full-time groomer."

"It's because you weren't born yet." He laughed. "There's plenty of stuff you don't know, kiddo."

"And I'm sure I don't want to know," Emily added, looking at Zach with a grin. "So stop now before my nosy side comes out." Her family called her nosy all the time, but she considered herself anything but.

"Kiddo, your nosy side is always out. Frankly, we should have named you Rudolph, or some female version of the name, emphasizing your nose. Rudy, I suppose." Emily's dad always teased her about her inquiring mind. She really wasn't nosy in the true sense of the word, just curious. If she wanted to investigate a cause, she took the initiative to do so. Some called this attribute being nosy.

"She doesn't look like a Rudy to me," Zach offered.

Mason made the final turn onto River Run Way, though a river was nowhere to be found. "We're just a couple of miles from here," Mason said.

Emily wanted to know what Zach thought of her nickname but didn't dare ask. No way could she see herself as a Rudy. In her mind that name was reserved exclusively for one of Notre Dame's most well-known players, Rudy Ruettiger, even though he had only played in one game.

Kylie remained quiet, occasionally glancing at Emily, then at Zach. Emily dreaded explaining the situation between her and Zach to her. It was hard to imagine falling in love with a star without getting to know them first. Yes, Emily enjoyed Zach's movies and thought him very handsome, but until she'd met him she absolutely wouldn't say she was "in love." She would do her best to treat Kylie with kid gloves.

Mason rambled the giant machine over to the maintenance garage area, where all the Cats and snowmobiles were stored. The building had been added on to throughout the years and was now large enough to hold all their equipment. Papaw wanted to build a new garage from the bottom up, but they'd been so busy running the resort, it'd been a piecemeal sort of project throughout the years. However, it was in decent enough shape to continue to use for a few more years. Once Mason shut the engine down, Kylie, being as small as she was, could stand up inside the Cat without hunching down.

Mason and Zach jumped out of the Sno-Cat and Emily followed, then turned so she could help Kylie down. Refusing her offer, Kylie jumped to the ground, landing on her knees. The garage was cement, so Emily knew her friend was hurt. She raced over to her, leaning down so she could help her to her feet. "Are you hurt?"

"No, just leave me alone," Kylie said; then, with as much dignity as one could muster in such a situation, she managed to push herself into an upright position without wincing.

"Kylie, did you hurt yourself?" Mason asked. "Can't have one of my best instructors down for the season."

"No need to worry. I'm able to do my job." She gave Emily one last dirty look before leaving the garage. Emily was sure she'd find a ride back to her condo, or maybe she'd take the lift up to the top of the mountain and ski off her anger. It was what Emily did when she was angry, the angriest she'd ever been: when her mother announced her so-called engagement to Harold.

Mason and Zach watched Kylie storm out, clueless as to the drastic change in her mood.

"Emily, what's going on with her?" Mason asked.

"She's certainly acting odd. I don't know. You'll have to ask her. Maybe she's upset because you wouldn't let her drive the Cat. She does like to be in charge."

Zach and her dad both laughed.

"That's never going to happen. Her feet can barely reach the floorboard," Mason said.

"Dad, she can't help her size. She'll be fine. I'm going to speak with her later. For now, I told Zach we could get him outfitted. Maybe then he can ski down Maximum Vault so I can get a feel for his skills," she said.

"I can't wait," Zach said, winking at her.

"Your camera crew is in the lodge. There's going to be a few difficulties getting their equipment positioned when they film your scene on The Plunge. It might be a good idea for the three of us to go inside, warm up and listen to what they have to say," said Mason.

Emily hadn't had the first thought about all the filming equipment needed. When they'd filmed The Plunge for the website, she'd simply attached a GoPro to her helmet and let the webmaster do their thing. It would be good to have a rough idea of what they'd soon be dealing with.

Chapter Seventeen

The lodge was buzzing with skiers hanging out. Knowing the slopes were closed for the day hadn't deterred them; most of them already knew, as the lodge always posted information on their website, plus the local news usually reported openings and closings. This time of year, ski people like Emily often hung out at the lodge just for the holiday atmosphere. Emily's mother made sure the place was decorated regardless of whether the slopes were open. At the least, it was a nice place to hang out and watch the snow fall.

The lodge was filled with the fresh scent of pine. Knowing her mother always chose a variety of Christmas trees, Emily picked out her favorite, a balsam fir, its scent permeating the air. From what she could see, at least eight or nine trees were already completely decorated, the themes a bit of anything and everything. One tree was decorated in all peppermint decor. Red and white ribbons trailed throughout the trees branches with ornaments made to appear like giant pieces of peppermint candy. Large candy canes with giant red bows were placed strategically to catch one's eye. Emily knew her mother and her team of decorators had spent all night putting up the trees. They did this yearly, and this was just the beginning. Emily and Kylie, her mother's "bonus daughter," would decorate even more trees together throughout the lodge, as they'd been doing for years. However, this year Emily wasn't sure if Kylie would be able to do much of anything, let alone spend unlimited time with her doing up the trees.

Zach motioned to a group seated by the fireplace. Emily and Mason tagged behind him. "Hey, guys," Zach said, acknowledging the group of six.

After several "heys" and "his" and "nice to meet yous," Zach took Emily's hand and said, "This is my instructor, Emily Ammerman. Her father, Mason, owns the Summit. You're going to be seeing a lot of these two over the next few weeks."

Emily could feel her face turning several shades of red, but she tried to hide it, figuring she could blame it on the cold. With a display of confidence, she said, "Nice to meet all of you. We have our work cut out for us over the next few weeks; The Plunge isn't very forgiving." She tried to take charge as she normally would if she had a group of regular folks to train. "It's tough terrain," she added, wanting to emphasize they weren't talking about a tough black run. The Plunge could be life-threatening given the slightest mistake.

"Have a seat," said Joseph Carlson, introducing himself as the executive producer.

Emily and Mason brought over chairs from another table while Zach took a chair for himself, sitting next to Emily.

After the rest of the introductions were made Zach spoke up, all business. "Okay, give me the details."

As Zach and the crew members discussed getting their equipment to the top of The Plunge using the chair lifts,

Mason interrupted them. "I can take all of your equipment up in one trip with the Sno-Cat. Plus eleven people,"
he explained. "If that'll help, just say the word."

"Perfect," Joseph said. "I'll accept your offer, Mason.
Thank you. I'll make sure you're compensated for this."

Mason held out both hands, palms up. "No need; it's on
the house."

"Take the money—it's in the budget," Zach said.

"I can't, so let's leave it at that."

Emily watched her father. She was quite familiar with
the expression on his face. Jaws clenched, eyes narrowed.
They'd be wasting their time trying to persuade him to
take their money.

"We need a figure, Mason. What would this normally
cost if you were to take payment? It's very standard. There
are guidelines we follow. Basically, we have to cover our
rears. If one of us is injured on the Sno-Cat, we'll need
something to show the insurance company. If we reported
an injury that's 'off the books,' so to speak, we'd be in hot
water." Joseph looked to be in his early forties, with light
brown hair combed away from his forehead and pulled
into a long ponytail that teased the back of his chair. He
was cute in a hippie sort of way. Emily wondered if he
wore Birkenstocks, surfer shorts and Ray-Bans in the summer. He seemed the type, she thought. Not that it was a
bad thing.

"He's right, Dad." Even though she agreed with her
dad, Emily knew there must be contracts with stipulations
to cover everything, from a skiing accident to a dangerous
ride up the mountain. The lodge had to cover their butts
as well; they, too, had risks to consider. Though she expected nothing too terrible would happen. They were well
equipped, professional and up-to-date.

"If it helps to have it on paper, I'm fine with that," said
Mason.

"Perfect." Joseph turned to the young man seated beside him. "Noah, you'll take care of this contract?"

"Yes, sir, I'll get on it immediately." In his midtwenties with short hair, Noah wore khaki slacks and a yellow shirt with a navy North Face ski jacket. He stood up and nodded to the group, preparing to leave the lodge.

"Noah's my assistant. You can trust he'll have the contract in your hands before the end of the day," Joseph explained.

"Fine," Mason said.

Now Joseph focused his attention on Zach. "Your stunt double will have a high tech GoPro Omni camera strapped to his helmet. Plus, we're going to use drones to film your scene on The Plunge, and I've contacted Ron Hammond. He's a local guy, an excellent ski cinematographer, and he'll be with us all the way. Of course, all of this depends on how—" Joseph paused and nodded toward Emily— "she instructs you. If the footage is bad or if you can't get the hang of it. And of course this is also all dependent upon the weather. We'll cut the scene if we have to, or use the double based on numerous factors."

"Why am I just now learning we're using a double? What's the point of weeks of training if you don't have faith in my ability to ski The Plunge?" Zach asked. He stared at the executive producer, not wavering.

"Zach, you of all people know there are various reasons we plan for the worst but hope for the best. If your girl is as good as Wynn says she is, I'm confident you'll wrap this up before Christmas."

"Emily," Zach turned to her, "is this timeline realistic?"

Talk about putting her on the spot. "Honestly, I'd like to see you ski first. I'll take you up to Maximum Vault."

"We haven't groomed the area yet," Mason told her.

Emily smiled. "That's the point, if Zach's willing to give this a try."

"I'm not sure that's advisable," Joseph told her. "I don't want him hurt before we begin filming."

"Then you don't need my services," Emily told Joseph. Pushing her chair aside, she took her jacket from the back, preparing to leave.

"Wait!" Zach said. "This is all part of the training, Joseph. Right, Emily?"

Slipping her arms into her jacket, she contemplated the audacity of her suggestion. "Given the short amount of time I have, I wouldn't suggest starting at the bunny hill."

"She knows what she's doing, Joseph. If you have any doubts about her capabilities, maybe you should use Watters's instructors and forget about filming here," Mason interjected.

"Enough," Zach said. "I'll practice with Emily. I trust her. End of story. You guys know I don't take unnecessary risks."

Joseph nodded. "All right, if you're sure."

Emily hoped she hadn't exaggerated her abilities. She didn't want to be responsible if something were to happen to Zach.

Zach stood as well. "Emily has offered to let me use their ski equipment, just so you know. If you need an inspection, I'm sure Emily can arrange it." He turned to her.

"No need; we do this daily. However, if you have any issues, you all are free to inspect our equipment for yourselves," Emily said.

"Mark, can you check this out?" Joseph asked. "Just following protocol," he told Emily.

Clueless as to what Mark's title was, she replied, "Of course." Having never been in this particular situation before, she assumed this level of scrutiny was normal. "If you want to go with me to the rental area, I'm ready now."

If she wanted to get Zach on the mountain, she didn't want to spend the rest of the afternoon dillydallying around, waiting for everyone to get their i's dotted and their t's crossed.

"Mark?" Zach asked. "Are you coming with us? We don't have all day here."

"Uh, sure," Mark told Zach, then spoke to Joseph. "We need a waiver on this?"

"I'll have Noah take care of it later. Go ahead. If you're unsure about their equipment in any way, it's a flat no until we have our own."

Emily watched the men spar back and forth, but kept her peripheral vision on Zach.

"Mark, you're the prop master, I would think you'd have skis, suits, anything I need ready. Am I right? If not, I don't need Mark to follow me around making sure my bindings are properly fitted. I'm sure the folks here at the Summit know what they're doing."

"Yes, we're extremely cautious with all of our rental equipment," Emily added. "We put ourselves at risk if we don't adhere to specific guidelines."

"That's good enough for me," Zach said. "You won't need to tag along then, Mark. Emily has this."

Joseph nodded. "Go ahead, Zach. Just be careful. Don't let your emotions override your common sense again."

Chapter Eighteen

Emily waited for Zach to respond, to defend himself, to say anything to counter Joseph's assessment of his emotions. But all he said was, "Em, I'm ready to hit the slopes. So let's get what we need before the sun sets." He turned towards her, yet all she could do was stare at him.

What had Joseph meant when he'd told Zach not to let his emotions override his common sense *again*? She so wanted to ask, but now wasn't the time. Maybe the time would never be right. Forcing herself to focus on her job, she nodded. "Yes, let's get out of here and get to work."

As they were about to leave, Mason called out to Zach, "I'll be at the lodge at seven if you still want to ride with me tonight."

"I'll be there. I'm looking forward to seeing the summit," Zach said.

Before Zach could reach for her hand, or even worse, place his arm around her waist in front of everyone, Emily hurried to the double doors, pushing them aside. A sudden gust of wind caused her to lose her balance. Zach came up behind her, wrapping his arms around her. He turned her so that they were face-to-face. "Em, careful! There's something going on with you. You'd tell me if we're not okay?"

She looked away; she didn't want him to see the doubt in her eyes. "I'm good. I just wasn't expecting that sudden gust of wind. Now I'm not so sure it's a good idea to take the lift up the mountain."

What did he mean by "tell me if we're not okay"?

"So I'll go ahead, get fitted for boots and skis, and then if it settles down, we'll be prepared. Sound good?" His tone let her know he wasn't fooled by the sudden change in her personality.

"Makes sense," she said. It was getting late, but she didn't have an adequate explanation to offer him for her lack of planning. Since they'd left the Taggart farm, she hadn't bothered to check the weather, so this was on her. Being so focused on Zach, and Kylie's obsession with him, Emily had tossed caution to the wind—quite literally in this case. And now she appeared unprofessional, and the crew probably thought she was starstruck.

"We can use the back entrance," she said, bowing her head down and jamming her hands into her pockets.

Zach walked alongside her, not bothering to button his coat. "Emily, please wait a minute," he said, the wind muffling his words.

Hearing him despite the wind, she stopped. Beside her, he pulled her close to him, tucking her head close to his chest. "If I've said or done anything to offend you, tell me now. Please, you're not acting like the Em I've been falling for."

Leaning back, she gazed up. His blue eyes were powerful, intense. "Let's go inside where we can talk. I'm freezing out here."

"Of course," he said, "I'm sorry."

Tromping through at least two feet of snow to get to the back entrance of the rental shop, she opened the door, the wind forcing the heavy metal to slam against the building. Zach yanked the hefty steel door behind him as he en-

tered, making sure it was properly closed, then returned his attention to her.

The back of the rental shop was scattered with ski boots, skis, helmets and ski poles, all in need of repair. Wet leather and the fruity scent of ski wax filled the air.

"Jeremy, it's just me," Emily called out before he thought someone was breaking into the ski shop.

Dressed in fluorescent green ski pants and a red shirt with the Summit's logo, which stood out against his long, blond dreadlocks, Jeremy peered out from the back of the shop. "No worries, Emily. Hey," he said to Zach, "dude, you look familiar."

"Zach, this is Jeremy. He manages the ski rental shop. Anything you want or need, ask and he'll make sure you get it. Zach Ryker is filming a movie here. I'm surprised no one told you."

"Cool," Jeremy said. "I've seen all of your movies about ten times each." He held out his hand to Zach.

"I appreciate that. Crazy line of work, but somebody's got to do it. Emily brought me here to get fitted. You think you've got something I can fit into?" Zach asked. He was personable with Jeremy, just as he'd been with all the other people Emily had seen him interact with. So far, Zach had proven her initial expectations wrong. He was a guy who just so happened to be an actor. He wasn't full of himself— or at least she hadn't seen that side of him if he was.

"You're a lot taller in person, dude, but sure, I'll fit you," Jeremy said, "if I have to drive to Denver myself."

Zach laughed and Emily couldn't help but join in.

"Jeremy, come on. I am not that big a deal. Em says there's a place in town that sells ski clothes for big guys. Right now I just need boots and skis, maybe one of those rental suits?" He nodded at the long row of ski pants and jackets hanging on the opposite wall.

"They haven't been cleaned yet. They were brought in yesterday afternoon, but with this storm, Pickles didn't pick up this morning."

"Get a new suit for him," Emily instructed.

"Can do," Jeremey said, disappearing into the stockroom where they stored all the new items.

"Pickles?" Zach asked, a huge grin on his face.

"His parents own the cleaning service we use."

"I won't ask about the name," Zach told her. "I can only imagine."

"It's not what you think. It's a Christmas tradition in his family, hiding a pickle in the tree. Apparently he's the champion of pickle-finding in his family, hence the nickname."

"I see," Zach said. "Other than more trees than I've seen in one place in a very, very long time, do you have any particular Christmas traditions in your family?"

"Where to start? My birthday celebration the day after Christmas is off the charts, or rather it was when I was younger. I've forced my mom to tone it down, but she loves to throw parties, and her idea of 'toning it down' is cutting the guest list down by two or three people."

"My mother wasn't a party planner, but she had a way of making me feel extra special on Christmas. Not so much with dozens of gifts, but in her own way she thought it was an honor to have been born on such a special day. Personally, I don't like any extra hoopla. Don't get me wrong: parties are great, but they're not at the top of my priority list."

"I thought actors attended all kind of parties. Movie premieres and the like. At least that's what outsiders like myself are led to believe." Emily wanted to remind Zach they were from different worlds. Too far apart to pursue a real relationship. Kylie would also be smart to back off before she tried to get close to Zach, though she'd have to find that out for herself. Emily wouldn't tell her what she and Zach had shared, brief as it was.

"Sometimes the premiere is a requirement, included in the contract. I'm known for not attending them, though. When we wrap, I'm finished. There are times when a public appearance is required, and I don't mind as long as it's not expected too often."

Emily knew he spoke the truth. Kylie had said that according to Zach's online fan club, he didn't make many public appearances.

"I like parties as long as they aren't a surprise. Growing up in a party atmosphere, I couldn't help but join in the fun. On my sixteenth birthday my mother decided not to have my party the day after Christmas. Instead, she told me we were going to Denver to shop. Said I could buy anything I wanted. Being sixteen, I'd asked for a car, but I was told that was out of the question until I'd had my license for a least one year. I understood that. So we're heading toward Denver, and the next thing I know my mom parks the car and tells me she has a big surprise and I have to wear a blindfold. Dad was waiting with my grandfather in the parking lot at Apple Jacks. I go along with it, thinking maybe I really was getting a car and my mom just wanted to make a big deal out of it. She's that way about most things. Instead, I'm led to a van with six of my good friends, who didn't say a word. Long story short, we're heading to the airport. We flew to New York City and spent three days there, going to the theater, shopping, see the Rockettes, all the touristy stuff. I didn't enjoy myself because I was terrified knowing that to return home, I'd have to get on an airplane again."

"That's certainly a birthday to remember."

"A few friends still talk about that party. My poor

mom; she had no idea I was afraid to fly because I'd never been on an airplane until then."

"Did you get the car?" Zach asked.

"Who told you?" Emily asked.

"No one. It's just obvious that your family would do whatever they could for you."

"Actually, I did eventually get the car, but I was only allowed to drive if one of my parents was with me for the first year." Emily wondered what was taking Jeremy so long. Zach would know her entire life story if he didn't hurry it up.

"What about now? Are you still afraid to fly?"

Emily grinned. "No, not at all. I think at the time it was just a fear of the unknown, not having control. My mom is like that. She refuses to ride in a Sno-Cat; says it makes her feel claustrophobic."

Jeremy finally came out of the storage room with a handful of ski attire. "Sorry it took so long. I had to open a few boxes, but I've got everything you'll need here. Follow me! Let's go use the dressing room so I can see better. It's too dark in here."

Emily made a mental note to add more lighting for the shop when she returned to her office duties. The shop windows allowed for plenty of light, yet the snow continued to fall. It wasn't quite as heavy as before and the wind had died down. Emily remained hesitant about taking the lift up to their private ski area or Maximum Vault, knowing the wind at the top of the mountain would be much worse. She would check the reports before making a decision. She'd let her emotions override her practical side earlier. She wouldn't allow it to happen again.

Jeremy gave Zach undergarments that would prevent him from freezing, a pair of ski pants and a jacket. All black.

"Thanks," Zach said to Jeremy. "My character's favorite color."

Emily knew Gunner West always wore black, but she'd never given it much thought. Now she knew one more fact about Zach: black wasn't his favorite color. She supposed this was part of getting to know him . . . but no—she reminded herself she was not going to allow her emotions to get out of control. Yes, she liked Zach, maybe too much, but they lived different lifestyles. If she had to pinch herself each time she thought of him in a romantic way, she would.

Zach stepped out of the dressing room wearing the latest ski gear. Emily's heart hammered in her chest at the sight of him. She pinched her neck because it was the only visible skin she could reach with her so bundled up.

"Fits great," Zach told Jeremy. "What do you think, Em?"

Wishing he would stop with the "Em" stuff, she had no choice but to answer; she didn't want Jeremy to suspect there was anything unprofessional between them. "I'm glad we're able to fit you. Jeremy, your ordering is spot-on."

Jeremy took the boots and skis, adjusting the bindings as he chatted. "You guys aren't gonna ski today, I hope?" he asked. "I don't think the weather is gonna get any better."

"Have you heard a current weather update?" Emily asked.

"No, can't say that I have, but let me check." Jeremy went behind the counter and turned on the small television set to a station that gave an updated ski report every fifteen minutes.

In his very cheery voice, the forecaster announced that there was more snow due tonight, though the winds were expected to die down, and tomorrow would be cold and sunny.

"We'll start training tomorrow, Zach. With this wind, I

wouldn't feel comfortable taking the lift to the top of the mountain."

"I trust you know best," he said. "So we'll go out to dinner? To Fiesta Jalisco in Silverthorne? The Mexican restaurant we were planning to go to?"

Emily watched Jeremy, a grin on his face. She wanted to force the words back into Zach's mouth, knowing as soon as the slopes opened tomorrow, news of her and Zach going out for dinner would spread throughout the lodge like hot chili on a cold day.

Should she just go with it to avoid making a bigger deal out of it? Taking a deep breath, she said, "Dinner will be fine. I want to go over a few techniques I'd like you to try."

Jeremy burst out laughing, Zach joining in.

"What's so funny?" she asked.

Chapter Nineteen

It took a few seconds for Emily to realize what they were laughing at, and when she did, her face blossomed with embarrassment.

Zach quickly spoke up. "I knew I could get you to go to dinner with me, I just wasn't sure how. Jeremy, I know you'll keep this to yourself. I don't care too much for the public knowing what I do privately. Since you're a friend, I'm sure I can count on your cooperation?"

"Dude, my lips are as tight as these boot laces," Jeremy said.

"For the record, this isn't a date as in a real date," Emily told Jeremy.

Zach removed his jacket, placing it across his arm. "So if it's not a date, what are we calling it?"

"Dinner at the same place," Emily quipped. "Separate checks."

"Not happening. When I take a lady to dinner, I also take care of the check. End of discussion."

"Maybe I'm not always a lady," Emily couldn't help saying, though she was smiling.

"And that's not always a bad thing, if the time and place are right."

"You two need to get out of here. Go get a room or something. You're making me gag," Jeremy said.

"Jeremy, that's not necessary," Emily chastised him.

"I'm renting the Taggert farm," Zach said to Jeremy. "You should pop over, have a beer with me, and I'll show you around the place."

"You're serious, dude?"

"Only if you bring your best girl and stop calling me dude," Zach said, a huge grin on his face. "I'm thinking about getting a Christmas tree and having a party, but you'd have to keep it to yourself."

"I thought you hated parties?" Emily asked Zach. "Did I miss something?"

"I don't like parties, but if I have a party of my own, on my terms, I'm good with that. A tree-trimming party, isn't that a thing?"

"Yes, it is," she said.

"It'll be fun. I'll make dinner, then we'll decorate the tree. I'm sure there's a store where I can purchase a few ornaments and lights," Zach said.

Emily knew him well enough now to know that he was serious. She thought about Kylie and how she would feel if she knew what Zach was planning. She was feeling guilty because she knew Kylie would give anything to trade places with her. Emily decided it was time to tell her the truth. Whatever happened, she would have to deal with it the best way she knew how. Love and kindness had always worked in the past.

"Zach, I need to talk to you privately. Jeremy, loose lips sink ships. I'll see that you get better lighting in the store as soon as possible. I'm sure Zach will let you know when he's having his tree-trimming party."

"Sure thing, Emily," Jeremy said. "But I don't know about ships, only snow. Sorry."

"It's just a figure of speech. I'll see you later," she said, then headed to the back entrance with Zach following behind her.

When Zach pushed the heavy door aside, a rush of icy cold air hit her face. It felt like a thousand tiny pins poking her. Keeping her head down to avoid the pinpricks of ice, Emily waited while Zach closed the door behind them. Before she could take another step, he reached for her, not giving her a chance to pull away. The light touch of his lips on hers sent a wave of warmth throughout her body. Then he deepened the kiss, her lips expressing things she couldn't say in words. Zach's mouth was warm on hers. The kiss, and the snowfall, created a dreamlike intimacy she'd never experienced before. Zach slowly eased his mouth from hers and, as he did before, kissed the tip of her nose, her cheeks and the top of her head.

"Em, tell me you didn't feel anything more than just a kiss and I'll accept it. I won't pursue a relationship with you."

Emily was stunned, a bit weak in the knees, and shivering, though she wasn't sure if it was from the cold, his kiss or a combination of both. She couldn't deny what she felt any longer. She'd kissed a few guys in her lifetime, and enjoyed every minute, but this was more. It wasn't a kiss she could just walk away from. This went much deeper than pure physical attraction, though she hadn't ever been this attracted to a man. It had nothing to do with his movie-star good looks or his killer blue eyes—but they didn't hurt. Rather, she felt him in her heart. A yearning for more of him, a desire so strong it frightened her. She wanted to know everything about him, his real self and not what he portrayed on the screen.

"Em?" he asked gently.

"Yes," she said. "I do feel something more."

He smiled at her. Joy burst throughout her body, then tears began streaming down her face. She could blame it on the bitter cold, but she knew that wouldn't be the truth. They were simply tears of happiness. So very cliché but true.

He cupped her head in his hands, using his thumbs to wipe away her tears. "These are happy tears, I hope?"

Emily nodded. The knot in her throat prevented her from speaking.

"Does this mean you'll let me pay for dinner tonight?"

Again, she nodded.

"I think it's time to get a cup of hot chocolate," Zach suggested, "from the lodge."

She used the sleeve of her jacket to wipe away her remaining tears. "It's not very good. It comes from a packet poured in a paper cup of hot water." She wanted to prepare him because his hot chocolate was so delicious. She didn't want to get his hopes up.

"As long as it's hot, I don't care," he said. Taking her hand in his, together they trekked back to the lodge.

Before they went inside, Emily cleared her throat. "Can we keep . . ." She paused as she tried to form the words. "This quiet. For a little while."

"What about if I make Thanksgiving dinner for you, your family and friends? We can tell them then. Maybe I'll invite Jeremy and we can do the tree-trimming thing afterward. Mom always decorated the house on Thanksgiving Day after the big meal. Said it helped her work off all the calories." He had a distant look in his eyes. Emily let the moment pass, knowing this was personal for him. "Dad has continued the tradition ever since."

"So you'd be breaking tradition if you did this, right?" She hoped he didn't pick up on the apprehension in her voice. Her mother would never share a holiday with someone she didn't know, let alone one of those dreaded "movie people."

"No, Dad and Levi would come here. We'd do the same as usual, just under a different roof. As long as we're together, that's all that matters."

He was right, but she couldn't accept his offer. There were way too many variables. They'd had Thanksgiving dinner at her parents' home for as long as she could remember. Only a few friends were invited. It was one holiday where she didn't have to worry about Harold or Lucille making a surprise visit. She was actually unsure of why her mother never overcelebrated that particular holiday. Hearing Zach speak of his family so lovingly, about sharing the holiday anywhere as long as they were together, made Emily believe that was what real family love was. She didn't doubt her family's love for a moment, but there were strings attached to certain events that she was no longer comfortable complying with. At her age it was time to start some holiday traditions of her own.

"I'd love to meet your family," she said, meaning every word.

"They're going to adore you, Em," Zach told her. "I'll call Dad later and tell him what I'm planning. Give him enough time to get the horses prepared. Thanksgiving is just around the corner."

Emily raised her eyebrows. "Does this mean he'll bring the horses, too?"

Zach laughed. "I don't think so, but with Dad, who knows? It might be a good time to test out those fancy stables. Just in case," he added.

"In case of what?" she asked, curious about everything that came out of his mouth.

"In case the Taggart farm goes up for sale."

He opened the main door to the lodge, motioning for her to go inside before him. Emily couldn't remember when a guy she'd dated had opened a door for her, let alone picked up the dinner tab. Her heart gushed just a tiny bit more.

The movie crew was gone; only a few diehard ski bums remained in the lobby. It was odd to see the lodge this empty, especially given all that beautiful powder they had.

"There's someone I want you to meet," Emily said, feeling brave. "Follow me."

Inside the industrial-size kitchen, with only a few employees working, it was unnaturally quiet. Kathryn rarely took a full day off even though she had the freedom to do so. She was the happiest when she was in her kitchen. Kind of like Emily and the mountain, which was her happy place. "Kathryn," Emily called out.

"In here," she called from the back.

"She must be in the freezer," Emily told Zach. "Wait here. I'll be back."

Grinning, he said, "I'm not going anywhere." His sexy smile caused her to tingle all over, and it wasn't from the cold.

Emily returned with Kathryn trailing behind her. "Oh my gosh! You weren't lying," Kathryn said, her Spanish accent more noticeable when she was excited.

"Zach, this is our chef and my good friend, Kathryn Diaz Espinosa."

"It's an honor to meet you. I have seen all of your movies. More than once," Kathryn said. "If you film with Emily, you'll have the best of the best. She can teach a rabbit to ski."

Zach leaned in and gave Kathryn a hug, "It's my pleasure. Glad you enjoy Gunner West. He's a tough guy, though I have to tell you, I am nothing like him in my everyday life."

"No? You look much taller in person," Kathryn teased. "Emily needs a tall man. She's tall for a girl."

"Good grief, Kathryn, I'm not a girl, and you're just jealous because I can reach all of your secret hiding places." Emily turned to Zach. "She hides some of the best brownies you'll ever put in your mouth. I've seen you with your stepladder."

"Then I will have to find another hiding place. Zach, it's been a true pleasure to meet you. I can't wait to tell my friends back home in Spain. They won't believe me."

"Then let's take a picture together." He reached inside his jacket for his cell phone. "Stand beside me, Kathryn. Em, use my phone and take a few shots for our friend to share."

Surprised at his willingness to take pictures, Emily took his cell phone and took several photos, all of them perfect. Kathryn had taken off her white apron for the pictures. "I'll forward these to your phone," Emily told Kathryn.

"Thank you. What a surprise! Emily, maybe I will make a pan of my special brownies for you and Zach to share." She winked. "I'm expecting us to be slammed tomorrow, so I'm preparing enough food for the entire town. I hope to see you two soon. Now it's back to work for me." She put on her apron and gave a little wave before returning to her freezer.

"She's a character," Emily explained to Zach. "More like a member of the family. She spends Thanksgiving with us every year." She wanted Zach to know Kathryn was more than just an employee.

"Then I'll ask her to join us for Thanksgiving, too. The more the merrier," Zach said. "The crew will leave for the holiday, so I'll have a few days off to spend with my family, and then, hopefully, I'll get to know your family. This is perfect timing. I can't believe this is happening." He pointed to himself and to her.

Emily was unsure how long she could put off telling her parents, Kylie and Kathryn about her Thanksgiving plans.

Even worse, she had to figure out a way to tell Zach she couldn't invite her family. Her mother had such a strong distaste for his profession, it would ruin the time with his family.

"Emily, I'm not wrong, am I?" Zach asked.

Shaking her head, she said, "No, it's not us. There are issues in my family. I'm afraid they would spoil your Thanksgiving if I were to invite them, that's all. Let's get that hot chocolate and talk," she said, heading to the café. Filling two paper cups with hot water, she took two packets of chocolate mix, then found a table away from the entrance where they could view the mountain and have some privacy.

"This is serious?" Zach queried once they were seated.

"That depends," Emily said, emptying a packet of powder into one of the cups of hot water. Stirring it with a plastic spoon, she slid the cup across the table to Zach. As she prepared her own, she had no idea where to start or how to explain her mother's dislike for actors without offending the man she was falling in love with.

Wrapping his hands around the paper cup, Zach said, "It can't be all that bad. You look like you're about to cry. Please, whatever it is, if it hurts you, I don't want you to . . . I don't know. Suffer?"

Taking a sip of the hot chocolate, which tasted fake to her now that she'd had the real deal, Emily knew this would be her last cup of the nasty stuff.

"It's not that bad. My mother—she's a sweet, adorable woman. I can't tell you how much I admire her. She's quite ornery, yet she's smart and wise. But she has this . . . thing. I don't know why, though I have my suspicions." She took a deep breath before continuing "Mom doesn't like—and these are her words—'movie people.' She thinks the profession is silly. When Hollywood comes to town, she gets angry. Says the town turns into a paparazzi nightmare, that people stare and treat actors like they're royalty. To sum it up, she doesn't approve of me training you, though I haven't told her your name, and she doesn't approve of filming here regardless. If she gets wind of . . . us, who knows what will happen?"

Now that it was all out in the open, she tensed up as she waited for Zach to walk out of the café, to tell her to forget training him, let alone having a relationship.

Instead, he offered up a wry smile. "Then I've got my work cut out for me, don't I?"

"You're serious?"

"Emily, we're both adults. I care about you very much. Having your family's approval isn't going to change what I feel. This is important to you, so I will use some of my best acting skill and see if I can win your mother over to the 'movie people's' side. If not, we still have each other. It's that simple."

Put that way, Emily agreed that it *was* simple. He hadn't met her mother yet. She may be in diehard opposition against his profession, but what if she met him first, not knowing what his profession was? She didn't even know his name, and Emily was sure she hadn't seen any of his movies.

"Why don't we ask her to join us for dinner tonight? Maybe we can get away without anyone noticing you. Let her get to know you; then, when she discovers who you are, she might have a change of attitude."

He laughed. "That's sneaky, especially given our circumstances. She's bound to discover who I am, and then what? Movie people are liars, too? But, if you think this will work, I'm all for it. I don't care too much for the deceitful part. I like being up-front and honest with folks. Especially folks who are in my family."

What did *that* mean? That she was in his family?! No, it was way too soon to even think about the "m" word.

"I'm sorry. It was a bad idea," Emily said.

"Now wait, don't put the cart before the horse. I didn't say it was a bad idea. I said I don't like being deceitful. Is there possibly another way around this? Not dinner, but something private where we won't have to worry about anyone recognizing me."

"Dad invited you to stay at their house. How could I have forgotten? Let's go to their house now. I'm sure my mom is there and Dad had to tell her he's invited a guest. He's that way. So they're likely expecting you."

"Makes much more sense than lying," Zach said.

If he only knew how many lies she'd told over the past few days, he wouldn't have anything to do with her! She would do her best to never lie to him again.

"It's just around the mountain. I'll see if Dad's still around. He can drive us over in the Cat. I'll call him—be right back." Emily went behind the café counter to use the landline. She called her dad's cell phone.

"Mason here," he said after picking up.

"Dad, I need another ride, this time to your house. Zach's going to stay there, so I thought I'd go along and introduce him to Mom as my friend. Will you go along with us?" She knew he caught her drift.

"You still at the lodge or the rental shop?"

"We're in the lodge."

"I'll be around back in ten minutes to pick you two up."

"Thanks, Dad."

Back at the table, Emily saw Zach had finished his hot chocolate. He probably had to force it down, but now wasn't the time to debate the pitfalls of real versus fake chocolate. "We can ride over in the Cat. Dad will be here in ten minutes. He's going to introduce you as my friend. Which you are," she said, a mischievous grin on her face.

"More than a friend, but we'll leave it at that for now," Zach said.

When they heard the Sno-Cat, they went through the rear exit just in time to see Mason pulling up in the giant machine. Zach, being so tall, opened the door with ease, then helped Emily in first. As soon as they were inside, Emily's stomach turned into knots.

She was dreading what was about to happen, yet also excited she was about to step fully into adulthood. As far as her mother was concerned, she would cut the umbilical cord to her mother's strict rules against "movie people" and begin a new chapter in her life.

Chapter Twenty

The Ammerman family homestead was a two-story log home. With five bedrooms, five and a half baths and a four-car garage, at first appearance it could be a bit overwhelming. All of the rooms had views of the mountain. The porches downstairs and upstairs were decked out with heaters and gas firepits. Inside the great room were two large, rock fireplaces across from each other. The kitchen and dining room spanned out onto a large, closed-in sunroom. It was all decorated in soft white leather and rustic tables and chairs designed to blend in with the surroundings. Emily had been around nine when it was built. The home had been her mother's dream. They needed room for parties, her mother said. And she'd had plenty of them throughout the years.

Emily found herself grateful that her childhood home was over five thousand square feet. If Zach and her mom didn't hit it off, there was enough space in the house where they'd never have to see each other if it came to that. Or, Emily thought, Zach could stay at her place and she'd stay with her parents.

Mason stopped the Sno-Cat before heading to the

house. "Hope you don't mind footing the rest of the way. Julia will have a fit if I park in her drive."

As soon as they made the turn leading to the drive, the house rose above them like a glorious gold mountain. The lights were on in every room, which was Julia's way of welcoming a guest to their home.

"Whoa," Zach said when he saw the house. "This is where you grew up?"

"For the most part," Emily said. "I spent a lot of time with my grandparents. They're closer to the resort and have a private lift that takes you to the main lift."

"I have to say I am beyond impressed. This is beautiful." Zach smiled. "Fits in with the natural landscape, too."

"Yep, Julia wanted it this way," Mason told him. "But it's just a house, Zach. Maybe too much house for us now, but Julia does like to throw a party, so it's rare that it's not filled with folks celebrating one thing or another."

They went through the main entry, which was the best way to experience the enormity of the place. Inside the foyer were tall, built-in shelves where Julia kept framed photos of Emily at every stage of life: all of Emily's school photographs from elementary school to her high school and college graduation. From family outings at the resort to vacations, Emily's entire life was right before her eyes. Nothing extraordinary at all, except the pictures reminded her just how protected she'd been as a child. Other than her sixteenth birthday trip to New York, she had no bad memories, nothing to compare to those who had. Almost a perfect life—though uneventful, she thought.

Zach walked around the great room, taking it all in. He stood in front of the fireplace that faced the dining room. "This is just out of this world. My dad would croak if he saw this place."

"Well, I certainly wouldn't want to be responsible for his demise," Julia said, making her grand entrance as she came down the stairs. "You must be Emily's friend. I'm Julia Ammerman. And you're?" Julia wore white wool slacks with a light blue angora sweater that brought out the blue in her eyes. She knew how to make a first impression.

"You look fantastic, Mom! What's the occasion?" Emily asked before this became too formal.

"Your friend's visit of course." Julia smiled at Zach. "I don't believe I caught your name?"

"Zachary William Ryker, ma'am," he said, smiling the ever-so-sexy smile he was famous for.

"Mr. Ryker, it's nice to see Emily with a friend. She's been such a loner for most of her life. All that time on the mountain; she's missed so many opportunities. She's even turned down a marriage proposal, so I'm very excited to see she's not giving up on men."

Now would be the perfect time for an avalanche, Emily thought.

"Mother, please." If she even hinted at Harold's name, Emily would leave. Zach could stay at her place. She didn't care what her mother or her friends would think. She knew introducing Zach to her mother would be risky.

"Mrs. Ammerman, trust me, I'm the lucky one. Emily is a dream come true. I can't believe we hit it off so well and so fast. I can't wait to introduce her to my family. I'm sure they'll adore her as much as I do."

"Of course they will. Emily is the perfect catch. I don't know if she's told you that she's taking over the lodge next year. Mason and I are ready to travel the world. It would be such a relief knowing she won't be alone. I understand you're going to ride with Mason tonight and get to know the summit. Have you any experience with this newfangled Sno-Cat he recently purchased?"

Emily's eyes bulged like a cartoon character. "Mother! Zach isn't here to work at the lodge. He's my friend." She wanted to add more, but now wasn't the time. Sometimes her mother was such a snob without really knowing she was being one. Plus, she was a little nosy, just like her daughter.

"No, ma'am, I can't say that I have. Mason offered to let me tag along tonight, and I accepted."

"Of course. How silly of me. I'm sorry if I offended you."

"Not at all," Zach said a bit too sweetly.

"I've made a Mexican lasagna. I hope you'll both have dinner with us. Mason, you aren't leaving for a while yet?"

"No, Julia, I'm going to sit in this warm house and eat dinner with my girls, and Emily's new friend. I offered Zach a place to stay for tonight. I assumed dinner was included," he teased. "We should be finished after midnight."

"Of course. I was getting his room ready when you arrived."

"This is so sweet of you, Mom." Emily leaned down to give her a peck on the cheek. "Making Zach feel right at home."

So far, so good, Emily thought. How was it her mother didn't recognize Zach? Not being a movie buff was a good thing, she reasoned. She promised herself she would talk to her mother later and find out why she had such distaste for "movie people."

"Any friend of yours is a friend of ours," Julia said. "Zachary, Emily, let's go into the sunroom where we can have a drink before dinner. It should be ready in half an hour."

"Sounds perfect," Zach said.

"It smells delicious," Emily told her mother. Mexican lasagna had been one of her favorites as a child and continued to be as an adult.

The sunroom sported more white leather with rustic tables, wooden lamps made by local artisans, and a scattering of colorful throw rugs on the shiny oak floors. The room was far less intimidating than the rest of the house.

The beams were not quite as high as those in the main room and were made of logs from the original house on the property, giving it a cozy vibe. It was Emily's favorite room in the house.

Mason sat on the sofa while Emily and Zach sat in recliners opposite the large sofa. At a small bar off to the right, Julia took charge of the drinks. "Margaritas or sangria?"

"I'll have a soda, if you have one. I don't drink much alcohol," Zach said. He looked at Emily, a sneaky grin on his face. She knew exactly what he was referring to.

"Mineral water for me. I need to be at my best tomorrow," Emily said without mentioning what she would be doing.

"Let's forget the alcohol, then. Mason, a soda okay with you?" Julia asked.

"Sure is," he told her. "I can't drink and run the Cat up the mountain."

Emily watched her mother, her face turning red just as her own did when she was embarrassed. "Clearly I wasn't thinking straight," she told them. "Sodas and a mineral water it is."

While she poured the drinks, Julia asked Zach about his family. "What is your family's business?"

Talk about getting straight to the point. Leave it to her mother to cut straight through the flesh and go right to the bone, thought Emily.

"Ranching, at one time. Now Dad trains horses for handicapped children. My brother does most of the hard work, managing the stable hands and groomers and all that goes along with the care of our horses."

"So, is your family's ranch here in Colorado? I don't recall knowing a Ryker family working a ranch with handicapped children—which I must add is a very noble deed."

"Wyoming, and yes, ma'am, it's the noblest of deeds.

My dad enjoys the kids, the horses, and Levi, my brother, is in his element as long as he's around a horse."

So far so good, Emily thought. She wondered if Zach's family would scrutinize her the same way her mother was slyly worming information from Zach.

"What is your job on the ranch?" Julia asked.

Emily cut in. "Mom, I think you're being a bit too inquisitive."

"No, Emily, she's fine. Honestly, I earn money outside the ranch so Dad and Levi can continue doing what my family loves," Zach explained.

"I like that. You don't see many family businesses now as you did back in the day. Mason and I try to use locals for the needs at the lodge. For the most part, we've been able to stick with that policy."

Julia came around from the back of the bar with a tray. A bit overkill, Emily thought, but her mother liked to make a good first impression. Once everyone had their drinks, an awkward silence hung over them for a few seconds.

Zach was the first to speak. "I appreciate you all allowing me to stay here tonight. I'm renting a place just outside of town. All the snow made it virtually impossible for me to return, so Mason was kind enough to offer to put me up for the night. I'd like to return the favor and invite you all to my house for Thanksgiving dinner. My dad and Levi will be there, though I haven't actually spoken to them about it yet. It's a family thing, you know? As long as we're together, it doesn't matter where we celebrate the holiday."

Emily thought Zach deserved an Oscar for his performance. She'd make sure to tell him that later.

Her mother had a surprised look on her face. "That's very kind of you, but we always celebrate at home."

"Julia, we should consider it. Emily is our daughter.

She's never brought a friend home . . . a *male* friend. It might be time to break with our old tradition and let these two start a new one." Mason must've caught on to the plan.

Emily felt her cheeks flame. Her parents were assuming way too much. She and Zach barely knew each other, but in her heart she knew she would be friends with Zach even if their relationship didn't continue to move forward as it had thus far. She liked him as a person; he truly was a kind man. Add in all his other attributes and she could see a future with him. Hopefully, he felt the same.

"I appreciate the offer, but we can't. I'm sorry," Julia told Zach again. "It would be lovely if you and your family would spend the holiday with us. We've plenty of room. Would you both agree to that?" Julia smiled, believing the issued was settled.

Zach glanced at Emily. She gave a slight shake of her head before speaking.

"That's kind of you to ask Zach's family here, but I'm going to pass. I want to meet his father and brother, so count me out this year. I doubt anyone will notice I'm gone." She'd finally said what she should've said years ago. Even before meeting Zach, she should've started her own traditions, which still could've included her family. But she wanted the option to choose, to decide for herself. Now was the perfect time.

"You're sure you want to abandon our traditions?" Julia sounded confused and a bit hurt.

"Mom, I'm not 'abandoning traditions' at all. I've been invited to spend the holiday with a friend."

"What about your best friend Kylie? Are you going to just . . . leave her out in the cold?"

Emily rolled her eyes. Shaking her head, she looked at her mother, not bothering to hide the irritation she felt. "No, I can't forget about Kylie, even though she's flipped out on me, won't speak to me and is acting like she's bumped her head one time too many. Something is wrong with her, but her being your 'bonus daughter,' I'm sure you can find out and direct her life as expertly as you've been guiding mine."

"Mason, do you know anything about Kylie? Has she been injured?" Julia asked, ignoring Emily's sarcasm.

"We're not sure. She's been acting very odd—a bit hateful to Emily, if I'm being honest. She called earlier today and said she hadn't seen Emily and was worried. I told her I was headed to the old Taggart farm to pick her up. She couldn't drive down the pass with all the snow, and Kylie insisted on riding along, which was fine with me. We enjoyed the picnic you sent; then, when she saw Emily with her friend, she started acting, well, a bit crazy."

"Emily, did you two have a disagreement? That isn't like Kylie."

"Nope, we did not, Mom."

"I'll call her later. It's possible she's hormonal right now."

Again, Emily wanted a big black hole to swallow her up. She felt like a thirteen-year-old with her first boyfriend. She had to put a stop to this. "Why don't you let me work out my problems myself? I'll speak to Kylie later. If I need you to help, you know I'll call you. Zach, I'm sorry you have to hear this drama. It's embarrassing."

He chuckled. "No worries. I understand. I have disagreements with my brother and father. There isn't a perfect family on this planet, or none that I've ever met. Emily, maybe you should ask your friend to join us for Thanksgiving. See if that helps ease the tension between the two of you."

Emily just nodded, then released her breath. This wasn't going as planned. Actually, it wasn't as bad as she'd thought. As long as her mom didn't figure out who Zach really was, she could take a bit of hammering. She knew her mom didn't mean any harm. It was just her way. She'd always been overprotective, with Emily being an only child.

The only way out of this crazy dilemma was to tell her mom who Zach was, and then also tell Kylie they were in the beginnings of a relationship. Both of them needed to know. The only decision left was who to tell first.

Chapter Twenty-one

Surprisingly, dinner was as close to perfect as one could expect. All talk of Thanksgiving was forgotten as Zach told them stories of his youth. His inexperience with horses when he was seven, and how his brother Levi used to sneak out and sleep in the barn because he was afraid the horses were lonely. He never mentioned his film career. Emily enjoyed learning about his childhood. When it was time for Mason and Zach to ride the Cat up to the summit, Emily decided she'd spend the night with her mother. They needed to talk.

In her old room, Emily kept a set of pajamas and a couple of pairs of jeans. Her old Mac was still on her desk. She walked over and wiggled the mouse, surprised when the monitor came to life. The screen saver, pictures of her and Kylie when they were much younger, was just as she'd left it. Leaning in, she couldn't help but laugh at their silliness. She would hate to lose Kylie's friendship after all these years. Like sisters, they'd shared just about everything.

So, as adults, why couldn't Emily share her true feelings with her best friend? Only because Kylie had told her she had a crush on Zach Ryker, the movie star. She didn't know Zach Ryker, the man. This had to end. Emily had a landline in her room. Before she could change her mind, she quickly dialed Kylie's cell phone, knowing if she were physically able, she'd answer on the first ring.

"Hello," Kylie said in a cheery, singsong voice,

"Don't hang up," Emily said quickly.

"Where are you calling from?"

So far this was typical Kylie; she sounded like her normal, nosy self. "I'm staying at my parents' place tonight. I wanted to talk to you and clear the air."

She could hear Kylie's nails tapping on the countertop, which meant she was in the kitchen, most likely baking. "Go on," she told her.

"It's about Zach."

"Duh, I figured as much."

"I can't believe you still use that word," Emily said, though she was grinning.

"What is it you want to tell me?"

"Why were you acting so weird today? You were mean," Emily told her. "Like you used to be when we were ten."

"I was . . . jealous."

"Of what?"

"Of you and Zach! An idiot could see there's something between you two. It ticked me off, especially after I told you all that childish stuff about how he was mine, blah, blah, blah. I hope you didn't tell him what I said. If you did, I'll die of humiliation."

Emily released a breath she didn't realize she'd been holding until now. "No, I wouldn't do that to you, Kylie. I was concerned about your odd behavior. You were embarrassing yourself and beginning to scare me."

"No kidding. Why do you think I stormed off as soon

as we got back to the lodge? I don't think I'll ever be able to look the guy in the face again. More so knowing you've got the hots for each other."

"It wasn't planned, Kylie. It just . . . happened. I don't know how, but I fell for him, and I'm pretty sure he feels the same. I don't want to lose your friendship."

"Bull—you know that's not going to happen. I'm happy for you, seriously. Just give me a little time to get over humiliating myself before you formally introduce us."

"I will. Listen, Zach invited me to the Taggart farm for Thanksgiving dinner. He's invited his family, too. His dad and brother," she said, wondering if Levi was as good-looking as Zach. She was already doing a little matchmaking in her head.

"I'll bet your mom will croak," Kylie said, sounding exactly as she should. Ornery, sarcastic and just a wee bit mean-spirited.

"I told her tonight. She wasn't that upset, believe it or not. Zach actually asked her and my dad to dinner, but she refused. It's okay. Or, at least, it is right now. Most of all, I wanted *us* to be okay. We're okay, right?"

"Of course we are," Kylie said. "You know how I romanticize every guy I see, even the ones I read about. I am not in love with Zach, Em. Seriously, I don't even know the guy."

"He's nothing like Gunner West. We can talk about that later. As long as we're still BFFs, that's all that I care about."

"No, duh," Kylie said, "I'll see you later."

" 'Night, Kylie."

Emily was so relieved when she ended the call she reclined on her bed, dozing off before she even bothered to change into her pajamas.

A light tap on her door jolted her awake. It took a few seconds to remember where she was and why. "Mom?"

The door opened and her mother stepped in. She'd removed what little makeup she wore, her tiny body wrapped in her old red robe.

"I can't believe you still wear that old thing." Emily sat up in bed and patted a spot to indicate her mother should come and sit beside her.

"It was a gift from you. I'll never stop wearing this 'old thing.' It's comfortable, and I think of you when I wear this, kiddo. Listen, I need to talk to you. We've had a rough couple of weeks, nitpicking at each other. I don't like myself when I'm this way."

"I understand. There's a lot going on at the lodge. I'm sorry I ruined your retirement. I'm just not ready to give one hundred percent of myself now. I know how hard all of you worked throughout the years to make Snowdrift Summit a success. I don't want to take a chance on ruining that, at least not at this stage in my life."

"You might find it hard to believe, but I admire you for standing up for yourself."

Surprised, Emily sat up a little straighter. "Why?"

Her mother looked down, her small fingers intertwined in her lap. "You're not afraid to go after your dream."

"My dream? What do you mean?" Emily thought her mom might've had a couple of drinks before coming upstairs, but she didn't smell alcohol.

"You aren't afraid to speak up for yourself, Emily," she told her.

"No, I'm not. I believe I might've inherited that from you. I don't recall you holding back whenever the occasion required."

"I'm not talking about being confident." Her mother raised her eyes. Emily saw they were filled with unshed tears.

"Mom, is there something you're not telling me? Are you ill? Is Dad? Mimi or Papaw?" She recalled a similar conversation the night of the retirement party, or the day after. She'd been so smashed that night.

"You love being a ski instructor, don't you? But, if you had your choice at another career, what would it be?" her mother asked. Emily took a tissue from the box on the nightstand, giving it to her mother.

"I don't know. I guess since I majored in business, I'd be working in some office. I wouldn't like it, if I'm being honest. I hate being cooped up inside. I've always liked the outdoors. I guess I already have my dream job," she said, thinking she did at least until next year. Yes, she would still be able to ski the mountain, but she was a realist. Most of her time would be spent indoors, taking care of the inner workings of the resort.

"And if I'm being honest, I'm not ready to retire. I never said that to your father. I suppose you rejecting what we planned for your future gave mine back to me."

"Then I'm glad I spoke up. Mom, you're still young! You need to tell Dad how you feel. I don't think he's ready to call it quits yet either. When he was driving the Sno-Cat today I could tell he enjoyed every minute. He told me he used to groom the mountain before I was born."

Her mother smiled. "He did, and I hated him being gone at night. I forced my father to put him in another position where he wouldn't have to leave me alone. I wanted him with me all the time. I was such a spoiled young woman."

Just like me, Emily wanted to add, but her mother wanted to talk, so she wouldn't interrupt her.

"Mason hated being inside, just like you. I took that away from him, but he never complained. I, on the other

hand, had a laundry list of complaints I would report to my mom and dad just about every day. 'Mason didn't do this,' or 'Mason didn't do that.' You know, we were so young when we got married. I'd just returned from California heartbroken just a few months before the wedding. I took my anger out on your father."

"California? What does California have to do with this? I'm stumped." Emily had an inkling, but kept it to herself.

"Oh, it's nothing. It doesn't matter now, but at the time I was an angry young woman who didn't realize how fortunate I was. In so many ways." She blotted her eyes with the tissue. "Seeing you tonight with your friend, it reminded me of my younger days."

"Mom, are you and Dad having troubles? Marriage-wise?"

"Emily Nicole, you can't be serious. Why would you ask that? Do we seem unhappy?"

"Not really." Emily thought about them when they were together. Her father adored her mother. But were his feelings reciprocated? "Dad's head over heels in love with you. Do you feel the same way about him?"

"If I didn't know better, I'd swear you've had too much to drink. Your father and I are wonderful together. He's my knight in shining armor."

"So nothing's rusty?" Emily couldn't help herself.

"Oh, you are a rotten young woman," her mother said, then burst out laughing. "You are my daughter, that much is for sure."

"I should hope so." Emily stopped laughing and stared at her mother. "I am Dad's too, right?"

"You can't tell when you look in the mirror? If you weren't his, I wouldn't have married him. Good grief, you make me sound like a . . . floozy. Mason is the best man in

the world. My life wouldn't be complete without him. We had a few rocky moments in the beginning—nothing serious, just immaturity. As I said, I was spoiled and, well . . . you get the idea."

Emily nodded. "I suppose so." She needed to know about her mother's time in California. What did that have to do with everything? She couldn't wait any longer.

"Mom, tell me what happened in California."

Chapter Twenty-two

"What makes you ask about California?"

"I'm not a child and I know you might've wanted to work there at one time," Emily said, careful not to reveal to her mother what she knew, even though it wasn't all that much.

"Why on earth would I want to work there when my family was here?" Julia said. "I had already met your father and we were dating." She took a deep breath, then turned to face Emily. "I received a callback from a movie audition three months before the wedding."

"Mom, that's . . . fantastic! Tell me more." Emily feigned some of her enthusiasm, but not too much. Finally she would learn the truth about her mother and her extreme dislike for "movie people."

"It was a dream of mine. To become an actress. I kept it to myself until my sophomore year of high school. I was in a few high school plays. We did a horrific version of *Bye Bye Birdie*. I loved acting so much, I begged my mom to let me go to California, where I could study the craft. My parents were dead set against it, so we compromised. I could go a couple times a year to audition as long as

Mother went along with me. I didn't care as long as I could go. I knew it would only be a matter of months before I was 'discovered.' Then I wouldn't have to worry about returning home.

"Then I met your father after high school. He was as handsome as any Hollywood movie star. More so, actually, because he wasn't aware of it. I fell fast and hard. We both did. Mom was ecstatic because it would keep me close to home. Mason knew of my love of the stage and screen, said he would never get in the way or force me to choose between him and a career." Julia had a dreamy look in her eyes. Emily could only imagine how she must've been as a young woman with stars in her eyes and a young man she was in love with.

"I received a callback from John Harris, the director. I was excited. Mom and Dad were, too. So much so, they took out a front-page ad in the *Loveland Weekly* to announce to everyone that I'd been given a part in a movie. For me, life was perfect; all my dreams were becoming a reality. Your dad didn't say much, but I knew he was sad that I'd be leaving. I assumed we would just postpone the wedding until I became famous; then we would have the biggest wedding Hollywood had ever seen. I returned to California, your dad with me this time. I went through a second audition. The director said he'd call me. I returned home, told everyone I came in contact with I had a part in the movie. It was a small part, but still, I was beside myself. I waited for the call from the director. And I waited and waited. Finally I found the nerve to call back myself; I didn't have an agent to make the call for me. I waited on hold—mind you, this was long distance back then—the minutes ticking away. The director's assistant finally picked up the call and told me, 'Nope, kid, you didn't get the part. Good luck next time.' "

"I'm so sorry. That had to be horrible for you."

"It was the most embarrassing moment in my life. To this very day."

"So that's why you don't care so much for 'movie people'?"

Her mother nodded, blotting a fresh round of tears.

Emily waited while her mother dried her eyes before she spoke. It must've been extremely traumatic for her after she'd told everyone she had a part in a film. What kind of person could be so mean and cruel to a young woman? No wonder her mom felt this way. She understood her so much better now.

"You must think I'm a nuisance, a silly old woman." Julia gave her a wan smile.

"No, I don't think you're either. You were young and hurt. I'm guessing you never really had an opportunity to deal with your true feelings, given the entire town was witness to your ordeal."

"Thank goodness for your father. I couldn't have gone on without him. We married as planned, and honestly, I don't have one regret. No, that's not true, I do have one—sort of a wish, I suppose. I would like to personally give Mr. John Harris a swift kick down Maximum Vault."

"That's pretty drastic, but I understand why you would feel that way. It might be a liability, but I can see why you'd want to do it. Maybe try Willie's Way. It won't hurt so much if he soars down the bunny hill," Emily said. A plan began to form in the back of her mind. One that might benefit them both. She knew just the person who might be able to grant her mother's wish.

Zach Ryker.

She'd heard the director's name before; maybe she'd seen it in screen credits. It didn't matter; she'd ask Zach if he knew him. Maybe she could arrange for Mr. Harris to have an entire week's paid vacation, a ski trip with all the amenities, courtesy of Snowdrift Summit. What would happen if he were to accept her invitation? Emily would let her mother take care of those details.

"I would never do such a thing, but it's nice to fantasize. He was a hateful man. Always smelled like old whiskey and cigarettes, if memory serves correctly. Now that you know this about me, I hope you'll understand why I feel so strongly about folks in the movie industry."

"Mom, I understand you were embarrassed beyond imagination. But I do believe there are some folks in the business that are good, kind people."

"How would you know? You haven't started training Wynn's actor, have you? I'm sure he's an oddball just like the rest of them."

"No, I haven't begun to train him yet. We're starting to-morrow morning. The weather is going to be perfect. Sunny and cold. And I'm pretty sure he isn't an oddball," she added.

"For your sake, I hope not. They're all so full of self-importance. People like us are nothing but gum on their shoes."

Emily chuckled. "I hope my trainee doesn't see me that way, but I'm going to take a chance. Mom, have you ever thought of talking to a professional about what hap-pened? Someone who knows how to help you resolve or at least come to terms with your feelings? Maybe an outsider who isn't biased?"

Her mother's head jerked around so fast Emily thought she'd break her neck. "No, I am not seeing a shrink if that's what you're referring to. You sound just like your grandmother. I am just fine, Emily. I'm fifty-seven years old. It's a little too late for that. Besides, my mother tried to get me to see a therapist at the time and I refused. I married your father and, as you can see, we did quite well for ourselves."

"It's not that, Mom. It's all about your internal feelings, I think. I'm not a professional; I'm only suggesting an unbiased ear, that's all. I'm sorry if I've upset you."

"Emily, I'm not upset with you, I'm ashamed of myself for acting so childish all these years. I'd be lying if I said there wasn't a bit of lingering embarrassment. A few of the folks still live around here. If I get a smirk now and then, I can live with that."

"I'm glad you felt comfortable enough to tell me your story. Personally, I think you're one tough lady. Holding your head high, marrying Dad; then, of course, a few years later I came along." She laughed. "I wouldn't worry too much about any lingering people who can't let sleeping dogs lie. At the very least, you tried."

Nodding her head, Julia responded, "That's one way of looking at my silly past. Thanks, sweetie. Now, I am going to bed, and you'd better get a bit of rest, too. If you're going to train that actor, you'll need to be in tip-top shape tomorrow. Want me to get up early and make you pancakes before you leave?"

When she was a child, before going to church, Emily's mother always made her pancakes. "I'd love that, Mom. Thanks."

"Good night, Em."

"See you in the morning."

Emily knew she would never be able to sleep after learning what she had tonight. She sat down at her old desk, where she'd spent hours doing homework and hanging out on MySpace, chatting with Kylie and other friends from school. Clicking on to the Internet, amazed her parents still used the same password, a memory emerged at the back of her mind. Why now, she had no idea, but the brain was a remarkable machine.

Going to a genealogy site, she typed in her father's full name, *Mason James Ammerman*. Several Ammermans materialized on the screen. Seeing some of the dates went as far back as the late eighteenth century, she searched the twentieth century, then added her father's date of birth. A window popped up asking her for a credit card number if she wished to continue her search. Rolling her eyes, she found her purse on the edge of the bed and typed in her credit card information, purchasing one month of the service. It took several minutes to complete the process; high-speed Internet hadn't made it to this household yet.

A graphic of a tree with several branches appeared on the screen.

"Okay, so we have a tree," Emily muttered as she waited for an answer to her inquiry.

Leaves slowly appeared on the branches of the tree, each with a name on them. Emily impatiently twirled her hair while the images finished loading. When the leaves on the tree were all filled with names and dates, she clicked on a John James Ammerman. From there, she learned John James Ammerman married Nicole Helina Tomski. Emily clicked on Nicole Helina Tomski's name and saw she was a young woman of Russian descent who came to the States in the early fifties. She had two sons: William James Ammerman and Mason James Ammerman. It was odd that both had the same middle name, but not unheard of. She clicked on what she was sure was her father's name, and she was right. It had his date of birth and he'd been born in Wyoming. Next, she clicked on William James Ammerman. His date of birth was two years earlier than her father's, and he, too, was born in Wyoming. Clicking out of the site, she did a search on William James Ammerman, who could possibly be her uncle.

For the next hour Emily clicked her way through several websites until she was almost sure she'd located her uncle. She'd found a service that stated they could locate anyone. A bright green bar on the screen loaded with all sorts of letters and numbers, then she hit pay dirt.

William James Ammerman still lived in Wyoming. He was married to Lenora Elise Hartford-Ammerman. They had three daughters and two grandsons.

"Son of a gun," Emily whispered. She had an entire family out there that she'd never met.

The holidays were about to change.

Chapter Twenty-three

Unsure of what time it was when she'd finally fallen asleep, when Emily woke up, her eyes were gritty and her mouth dry as a bone. Untangling herself from the covers, she couldn't believe she'd actually slept in her clothes. Having a bathroom connected to her own room hadn't seemed like a big deal when she was growing up, but now she appreciated having it close by. Checking the time on the computer monitor, she saw it was after six. Remembering Zach had spent the night, she wasn't sure what time he and her father had returned from the summit, as apparently they'd been extra quiet. She didn't want Zach to see her like this. Thankfully, as she opened her dresser drawer, she saw she had more than just a couple of pairs of jeans stored at the house.

Hurrying before her mother came upstairs, Emily took a quick shower, then changed into fresh jeans and an old sweatshirt she'd had since high school. She brushed her hair, letting it hang to her waist. Later, when she suited up for Zach's first day of instruction, she'd braid it. Searching through a couple of drawers where she used to keep makeup, all she found was an unopened tube of ChapStick and a small container of hand lotion.

After she brushed her teeth and used the ChapStick, she put a small amount of lotion on her face. Winters were so harsh on her skin. She almost always had a tube of sunscreen with her, but today she didn't. Someone at the lodge would have a tube she could use, she was sure.

She could smell coffee brewing downstairs. Had it only been twenty-four hours since she'd been with Zach and he'd made coffee while she slept? It seemed like a lifetime ago. Excited to see him, she pinched her cheeks to add a little color, then forced herself to walk at a normal pace downstairs to the kitchen.

She was surprised when she only saw her mother in the kitchen. Emily took a mug, filling it with coffee, and asked "Where's Dad and Zach?"

"Your dad should be down any minute. Zach didn't return with him last night. Apparently, your dad was able to drive him back to the Taggart farm. He said he would pick you up this morning in your car."

"How did he get my keys?"

"Remember you gave Dad a set?"

"Yeah, I forgot about that."

"Were you able to get much sleep last night after hearing my crazy story?" Her mother was mixing pancake batter.

Emily wanted to tell her about finding her father's long-lost brother, but now wasn't the time. "I slept pretty well. I messed around on the computer for a while. I can't believe you still have the same password. Might want to change that, and update your service."

"We never use the Internet here, only at the office. I've never bothered, but if you think it's important, I'll look into it."

"Just change your password now and then," Emily said. She walked over to the large window overlooking the mountain. The sun would be up soon, though the icy morning air was bitter cold. She couldn't wait to get to the mountain and glide back down it, free as a bird.

"Emily, your pancakes are getting cold," Julia said.

"Sorry, I was lost for a few minutes."

"You can't wait to get out there, can you? You remind me of your dad."

"It's that obvious, huh?" Emily sat down at the table in the kitchen. They only used the formal dining room for Thanksgiving, Christmas and, of course, all of her mother's parties.

"It sure is, young lady," said Mason, entering the kitchen. " 'Morning, sugar plum," he said to his wife, then to Emily, " 'Morning, kiddo."

" 'Morning, Dad. I hear you're having Zach return my car. I appreciate it. I wasn't sure how I'd get back out there now that I'm going to actually have to work for the next few weeks."

"It was his idea. I just so happened to have your keys on my key ring."

"It will work out perfectly. I need to go by the condo to check on Clarice before I start work. I've been away for two nights. She's probably thinking I've abandoned her."

"I hope you have one of those automatic feeders I saw on TV," Julia said.

"I do, Mom. If I didn't, I'd have Kylie feed her."

"So you two are on speaking terms again?" Mason asked.

With her mouth full of food, Emily nodded and swallowed before answering. "We're good. We're like sisters, Dad. We never stay mad at each other very long."

"Good to hear. I wondered what you two were arguing about." Mason dived into the plate of pancakes Julia set in front of him.

"Do you want more, sweetie?" Julia asked Emily.

"Three was enough! Thanks, Mom. Your pancakes are

the best." However, Emily's thoughts were elsewhere. How should she approach her father with the information she had pulled from the Internet last night? Contemplating the various ways in which she could approach the topic, she decided to just tell him outright.

"Dad, I know you have a brother. Why don't you two speak?" There, she'd said it.

Mason placed his fork across the top of his plate. Taking a deep breath, he wiped his mouth with one of the cloth napkins Julia insisted on using, no matter the occasion. "Hmm, so what exactly do you want to know?"

Stunned by his casual reaction, it took Emily a couple of seconds to answer. "Why haven't you stayed in touch with him? He's your brother. Is he . . . horrible?" She didn't know what else to say, or any kinder way of asking.

"No, he is many things, but horrible isn't one of them."

"Dad, come on. I'm not a child. What's so tragic that you've spent my entire life ignoring your own brother?"

"Emily, this is not the time or place," her mother said. "Maybe when the holidays are over, you and your father can sit down together and talk it out. Mason?"

"It's all right, Julia. She's old enough to know, and I don't see any reason to keep this from her any longer."

Just then, the doorbell rang.

"I'll get it," Emily said, knowing it had to be Zach. Her mother was right; she would wait for a better time to talk with her father about William. Maybe there was a good reason to keep him out of their lives.

Smoothing the wispy hair around her forehead before opening the door, Emily's heart fluttered like a humming-bird's wings. When she opened the heavy wooden doors, Zach was standing on the other side, holding out her keys for her. As soon as she reached for them, he pulled her outside, using his free hand to quietly close the doors. He wrapped his arms around her and she placed her arms around his waist. They didn't speak. Emily didn't care if anyone saw them. This was where she was meant to be—in Zach Ryker's arms. He leaned back to gaze into her eyes. "You're beautiful, Em."

She didn't respond, but hearing him say those words for the first time, she believed them. She had heard them many times from others, yet brushed them aside, as if they had no meaning. Zach's compliment wasn't about her looks. She knew it came from his heart, and to her that meant more than she could put into words.

"Mom made pancakes. We'd better go inside before she forms a search party," she teased.

"Is she really that overprotective?" Zach asked, his tone no longer lighthearted.

"Not really. She's just a bit nosy, if I'm being honest. So is my grandmother. It's just their way."

"At least I know what I'm in for," he said as he opened the door.

Inside, Emily heard her parents, their voices louder than normal. "Zach is here," she announced, giving them a moment to gather themselves. Whatever they'd been discussing would have to keep.

When they came into the kitchen, both of Emily's parents pasted smiles on their faces—phony smiles, Emily knew, but they were trying.

"Zachary, it was so nice of you to return Emily's car. I hope you'll stay and have breakfast with us?" Julia asked. She was in her prim and proper mode.

Emily realized that, like Zach, her mom was an actress, too. No, she didn't have any movie credits, but she knew the craft. How had she missed that all these years? Until recently she'd had no idea her mother wanted to become an actress. After hearing her story and seeing her in action, Emily decided she was pretty good at this acting thing.

"Breakfast sounds good. I'm going to need all the energy I can muster today. I have no doubt Emily is going to push me to my limit once we're on the mountain."

No one said a word.

Emily realized she should have told her mother the truth.

"Am I missing something?" Julia asked Emily while she plated a stack of pancakes for Zach. "Coffee?"

"Black," Zach said. "Thank you."

"My pleasure."

"Julia, that's enough, all right?" Mason said.

"I don't know what you're talking about, Mason," she said ever so sweetly.

"Mom, come on, I know you're ticked. Frankly, I am beyond caring. Zach is the actor I'm training. He's one of those tacky 'movie people' you dislike so much. So like it or get over it because I plan to spend as much time training him as the weather allows. And then, when the weather stinks I'll either be at my place. Or his," she added, just to tick her mother off further. She was embarrassed that she had to chastise her mother like this in front of Zach, but it had to be done. She was too old to sneak around and hide their relationship—if he stuck around that long—from the world.

"Hey, let's not get too excited. It's just a job," Zach said to both of them. "I don't want to cause any problems between you two."

Julia sat down in the chair opposite Zach. "You're a fine young man, Zachary, and a fine actor, too. Yes, yes, I knew who you were the minute I laid eyes on you. Who wouldn't? So my secret is out." Julia had such a look of defeat on her face that Emily felt guilty for being so hateful.

"You knew who Zach was all along? You've actually seen his movies, too? When? Who did you see them with? Dad, did you know?"

"Of course. We might be old, but we're not *that* old. We

do go to the movies now and then. Your mother adores them. We go to the theater over in Breckenridge. Just our own little secret." He smiled at his wife then, and somehow Emily knew through all the craziness of the past few weeks, she would survive and be a better person because of this.

Chapter Twenty-four

"Are you sure I'm not overdressed?" Emily asked Kylie for the tenth time. "I don't want to look like I'm trying too hard to impress his family." She looked in the mirror again. "I don't know . . . maybe I should stick with jeans."

"No, you will wear these slacks and blouse just like I told you. Do you want them to think you're just a ski bum?" Kylie asked as she adjusted the belt on Emily's high-waisted slacks. Black, wide-leg satin slacks weren't her usual style.

"I kind of *am* a ski bum. You too."

"You know what I mean." Kylie tugged the belt tighter.

"Ouch! I'll never be able to eat if you keep yanking on this belt."

"You need to emphasize your waist. You're tall and gangly. Show off what you have. Your waist is one of your best assets."

"Thanks."

"You know what I mean," Kylie said, stepping back to admire her work.

Emily looked in the mirror, too. The dark green silk

blouse she wore brought out the green in her eyes, plus it happened to be her favorite color.

"They'll like you—you look like a sophisticated lady who's about to trap their famous son and brother into a lifelong relationship. With at least four kids in the not so distant future."

Rolling her eyes at Kylie's overly descriptive words, Emily couldn't help but laugh. "No way am I ever going to have four kids. I'll be lucky to get married, let alone have kids. And no, Zach and I have not discussed marriage, despite this being one of those whirlwind romances you read about. I'm nervous, Ky. What if they hate me?" She plopped down on her bed, and Clarice chose that moment to pounce on her new slacks, dumping a pound of cat hair all over her. "Oh, Clarice, you are jealous, aren't you?"

"Meow, meow."

"I bought a filet of trout for this stinker. I've been leaving her alone so much, I think she's mad at me."

"Trout? Come on. Who buys trout?" Kylie said.

"You don't like fish, remember?"

"So? I still wouldn't buy trout for a cat."

"Clarice isn't just any ordinary cat, Kylie. She's my friend. My furry child, sort of. She knows when I'm upset or anxious. That's why she jumped in my lap. Right, little girl?" Emily rubbed her nose against Clarice's.

"That's so gross. Do you know where her nose has been?" Kylie asked.

Emily had to laugh. "I could probably guess, but it would ruin my appetite."

"Do you have one of those lint roller things? You look like a giant ball of fur."

"Somewhere, I think. In the nightstand," Emily said as she gently removed Clarice from her lap.

"Stand up," Kylie ordered.

Emily stood towering above her bossy friend as she

rolled the lint thing up and down the front and back of her slacks.

"Okay, much better. Don't pick up that cat again—don't even go near her. You look fantastic, Em."

"Thanks. Are you sure you don't want to ride with me? I could use the company."

"No, I told you the only way I would go was if I drove my own car. If I humiliate myself again, I'll have a way out. Look at it like a blind date. Remember? We always meet them in a public place, with an escape phone call? This is just like that in a way."

"Have it your way, then. You know how tired you get after a heavy meal? I doubt driving down that treacherous mountain while you're half asleep is going to be in your best interest, but you do you," Emily said as she searched for the new tube of lipstick she'd bought.

"Did you ever ask Zach if he liked lobster?"

"No, it hasn't come up in conversation yet, but I'll make sure to ask him. Are you thinking about the Lobster Lady restaurant? Isn't that where you were going to take Zach for dinner?" Emily teased. "And to think you don't like seafood."

"Oh stop it! You're never going to let me live that down, are you?" Kylie said, but she was grinning.

"Sorry, I couldn't help myself. Seriously, I'll ask just for the heck of it. See if that fan club of his knows what they're talking about." She looked at her cell phone. "We should leave now, just in case the weather turns to crud."

"Three hours early? I don't think so, unless you plan on pushing your car. Besides, I still have to get dressed. You're a nervous wreck, Emily. Relax—if Zach's family doesn't like you, it's a sign. Everyone likes you. If they don't, something is wrong with them. Remember that, just in case."

"In case of what?"

"I don't know. Maybe the dad slobbers or wears socks with sandals. The brother—isn't he a bit old to still be living at home? You need to be aware of folks these days. People aren't always who they say they are. For all you know, Zach could hire actors to portray his family."

"Good grief, Kylie, stop it! You're making me more nervous than I am already."

"That's good; it'll keep you on your toes. Stay alert. Aware of the world around you."

"I'll try to remember this much-needed advice," Emily shot back.

"Just looking after my bestie," Kylie said.

"I know, and I appreciate it, too. Just don't act like my mom. She's been so smothering since she confessed she knew who Zach was from the get-go. Calling daily, asking a dozen questions."

"Speaking of, how is the training going? Think he'll be able to complete his own stunt?"

Emily had wanted to keep their progress to herself, but she was willing to tell Kylie. "I haven't told this to anyone yet, but Zach's been down The Plunge twice already. He's a much better skier than he told me. Honestly, they could start filming the scene at this point if they knew his capabilities. His crew left town for Thanksgiving weekend, so we have four days to ourselves to ski and do whatever we want. We're getting to know each other very quickly. Just keep this between us for the rest of the weekend if you can."

"Absolutely. My lips are sealed. I can't wait to get up there myself. I spoke to that guy Noah; he's an assistant or something. My three-second scene is insane. When Zach goes through the tunnel, I'm at the end. I fall and he skies over me. Some movie scene, but I can't wait."

"So I hear, but they're getting a good shot of your face, according to Zach."

"Good to know. I'm going to start working with their

crew on Monday. According to Noah, they should be able to get this shot in a few takes. Unless Zach hits me in the face with his skies or I fall. Anything could happen, but I doubt it will."

"You'll be perfect. You know The Plunge as well as I do. I can't wait to see you in action. You're still going to hang around for the tree-trimming party tonight, right?"

True to his word, Zach had arranged for a freshly cut balsam fir to be delivered yesterday. They'd gone into town twice, when Emily had helped him pick out lights and decorations for his tree. He insisted he had to buy her a special ornament, though she'd yet to see what he'd chosen for her. In turn, she'd made another trip into town, when she found what she hoped to be the perfect ornament for him.

"Depends. If I humiliate myself, no. I'll have to see how the day plays out."

She could count on Kylie to be honest most of the time. "Sounds reasonable to me. Mom is waiting until tomorrow to decorate the trees at the house. Not her usual style, but this year hasn't been normal for any of us. Are you going to help decorate the lodge again this year?"

"Think I'm going to miss out being the 'bonus daughter'?" Kylie asked her.

"No, you love Mom as much as I do. What about KiKi? She staying in Florida this year?"

"Yep. I think she has a boyfriend, too. Can you believe that? She deserves to be happy after putting up with me all these years. I told her I'd try to visit after Christmas, which will be tough for you as far as work goes. You'll handle it, I'm sure."

"You should go. We'll be fine here. I have a list of part-timers we can call in a pinch if we need them."

"Good to know. Now it's my turn to primp," Kylie said as she removed the plastic from the hanger covering her new outfit. They'd spent an evening looking at Nord-strom's website together. It was as close as they could get to actually driving to Denver and shopping together. They were busy and made use of modern technology.

Kylie had chosen a burgundy, V-neck jumpsuit, with dolman sleeves and a sash waist that tapered down to a fitted bottom, showing all of her curves. "You think this is too racy?"

Emily sat back down on the bed. "Are you serious? No, it isn't racy. It's dressy. Admit it: We're both not comfort-able in dressy clothes. We're jeans and T-shirts girls, or ski suits. The color looks good on you, Ky."

"I know," Kylie agreed. "And as you know, the green looks perfect on you, with all that blond hair, and your eyes. People pay big bucks for hair and eyes like yours— do you realize that?"

"So you've said."

When Emily had searched for her dad's brother online she had found it interesting that her grandmother was Russian. Weren't Russian women often tall with blond hair? She hadn't spoken to her dad about the topic since she'd confronted him a week ago. The timing wasn't right. He was busy, she was busy, her mother was busy. Maybe after the holidays, when all the excitement was over, they could sit down and he could tell her the story of his brother.

"I can tell you no one pays to be short with dark hair," Kylie said.

"Oh, bull! Would you stop already? We go through this every time we get ready together. You just want me to tell you how gorgeous you are, how men like tiny, petite women with muscles and enough hair for three people."

"You forgot the 'dark, sexy eyes.' "

"Yep, that too," Emily quipped. "Seriously, you look fantastic in that outfit."

"Thanks. You always build up my confidence. It's been a tough road growing up beside you."

Kylie had never admitted this to her before. "Kylie, I'm sorry, I had no idea. Did I do or say something along the way to make you feel . . . inferior or bad?"

"Nope, you didn't. It's me and my insecurities. No parents, all that stuff . . . sometimes it gets to me. Watching you grow up with a family, even though I know I am a very big part of it, there were times when I felt resentful of you. Pretty, well-off, with perfect parents. And here I am with just KiKi, and well . . . you get the idea."

"We'll have to work on that. Make danged sure you are involved with the family more often. And here I want to get away from all this family stuff at times. I'd love for my bonus sister to stand in for me now and then. Mom loves it when it's just the two of you."

Kylie grinned. "Really?"

"Yes, really. Now finish up and let me brush your hair for you."

Kylie tossed the brush to her. When they were teenagers, they would take turns brushing each other's hair while they discussed their latest crush, or who they would never speak to again. Emily thought they were still doing the same thing—they were just adults now.

Chapter Twenty-five

Emily hadn't been this nervous since she'd taken her final exams in college. She shut the engine down and took a deep breath before she opened the car door. Jeremy's truck was parked beside another truck with Wyoming license plates. "Great," she said to herself. Unsure if Zach had been serious when he'd invited Jeremy for Thanksgiving dinner, now she knew that he was. She peered into her rearview mirror just in time to see Kylie pulling into the drive. She'd wait so they could go inside together.

She pulled the visor down to take a last look at her makeup and make sure she didn't have lipstick on her teeth. She flipped the visor back and picked up her purse with the small gift inside. She'd wrapped it herself, something she was horrible at, but thought it would be more personal doing it that way. Usually she had her mother and Mimi help her wrap her gifts—they were both experts at it—but not this time.

Kylie knocked on the window. "Hey," she said, a huge grin on her face.

Startled, Emily practically jumped in her seat. She opened the door and said, "You just about scared the pants off me! If you plan on acting like that today, I may mention all those little things to Zach you don't want me to."

"Geez, I was just letting you know I'm here." Kylie tossed her hands in the air. She, too, had brought a wrapped package that was tucked under her arm.

"Who's the gift for?" Emily asked, getting out of her SUV.

"Santa Claus."

"You are such a smart-ass," Emily told her. "I should hit you with my purse, then wrap the strap around your neck and yank it as hard as I can."

"Aren't you a jolly old elf."

"Hush. Now walk with me to the door, and don't act like an idiot. Please?" Emily asked.

"You just called me an idiot!"

"You're not, okay? I think I am an idiot."

"Okay, then let's go," Kylie said, linking her arm with Emily's.

They walked up the steps to the front door. It was cold, but not miserably so. Emily wore her dressy, black Michael Kors full-length coat. Kylie wore a white wool Stella McCartney coat she'd paid a small fortune for last season. Emily thought it looked perfect against her olive skin, but she wasn't about to tell her that now.

Emily tapped on the door, hoping she didn't have to stand out on the porch too long. She wanted Zach to be as nervous and anxious as she was about meeting his family. He'd seen hers, kind of at their worst, so it could only go uphill from here, she thought. As she was about to knock a second time, Zach opened the door.

Neither she nor Kylie said a word. Zach, all six five of him, wore a white dress shirt, having left the top two buttons open. The sleeves were rolled up, revealing his muscular forearms. In his black dress slacks, he looked exactly like Gunner West.

"Come on in! I can't have the two prettiest ladies in Loveland freezing at my doorstep," he said and stepped aside to let them in.

The house was warm, with delicious smells coming from the kitchen. "Let me take your coats," Zach said. "Dad's in the kitchen, basting the turkey, and Levi is trying to explain farm life to Jeremy. Your timing is perfect."

"The tree is huge," Kylie said. "It'll take all day to decorate."

Zach laughed. "We've got plenty of helping hands. Dad and I put up the lights last night. That's always the toughest part."

Emily gave Zach her coat. He leaned down, giving her a kiss on her cheek. She could feel her face turning red. She gave a side-glance at Kylie, who looked surprised. Zach took her coat, too. "Wait here, I'll be right back," he said.

"Don't say a word," Emily whispered to Kylie.

"He really is crazy about you, huh?"

Emily smiled. "It's mutual."

Zach returned minus their coats. "I've got all sorts of drinks in the kitchen. Come on, you two—I want you to meet my family."

Emily's stomach flip-flopped.

Kylie gave her a look meaning, *remember what I said.* Emily gave a slight nod, then rolled her eyes.

The kitchen was bustling with activity. Jeremy and Penny, his current ski bunny, sat at the U-shaped bar, where a man, a couple inches shorter than Zach but a replica in the looks department, was mixing drinks.

Good grief, Levi was as hot as Zach, Emily thought. She glanced again at Kylie.

"Guys, this is Emily Ammerman and her best friend, Kylie Esposito. This is my brother, Levi, and over there with the fancy apron on is my dad, Robert Ryker."

Levi wiped his hands with a kitchen towel, "It's an

honor to meet you," he said, coming around from the bar to shake their hands. "Zach's talked about nothing else since he's been here. I must say his words didn't do justice to either of you."

Emily didn't know what to say.

"He sure as heck never mentioned you were his twin either." Kylie didn't seem to have the least bit of trouble making her thoughts known.

"We get it all the time," Levi said. "Pain in the rump, especially when one of his movies hits the big screen. I have to go into hiding for a bit," he teased.

"You love it," Zach told his brother.

Robert Ryker was as tall as Zach. With his thick white hair and the same startling blue eyes as his son, Emily could not believe how handsome the three men were. She couldn't stop staring. They could all be movie stars as far as she was concerned.

"Nice to meet you, Levi," Emily said. She'd needed to ask Zach if Levi was spoken for. If not, maybe he and Kylie might be interested in one another. It would be the perfect setup.

"My pleasure, Emily," Levi said, giving her the same sexy movie star smile as his older brother. "Kylie, what would you'd like to drink?" Levi cupped Kylie's elbow in the palm of his hand, directing her to the bar. Zach winked at her and then led her to the kitchen island, where his dad was washing his hands. "Dad, this is Emily, my friend and ski instructor."

"My dear, it's a fine time to meet you." Robert dried his hands on his pair of faded jeans and walked around the island to give her a hug. "Zach's never introduced me or his brother to a lady friend, so this is a big deal in our family." He stood back to look at her. "You're as stunning as Zach said."

All thoughts of being humiliated or nervous flew out the

window when Emily met Robert. He made her feel at ease instantly. "It's been fun helping him on this movie, though honestly, he could've skied The Plunge without my help," she told him.

"All those movie folks, they gotta have everything just so and cover their backsides, if you know what I mean. It's part of his job. Why don't you have a seat?" He nodded at one the stools at the kitchen island. "Levi, get Emily something to drink. Sorry—I think he's mesmerized by your friend."

"Sure thing, Pop," said Levi from across the room. "What can I make? This place is stocked with more alcohol than a Jim Beam factory."

"I'll just have a glass of cranberry juice, thanks," said Emily. A few seconds later she had a tall glass with cranberry juice in front of her. Taking a sip, she had a zillion questions she wanted to ask Robert about Zach, all the usual things a woman would want to know about the guy she was falling for.

Zach returned to the kitchen, taking out a set of pot holders before removing a pie from the oven. "Pumpkin. Homemade by the one and only, except the crust."

"One of my favorites, with lots of whipped cream," she told him. The smells coming out of the kitchen were making her stomach growl.

"I suppose I should tell your girl a little bit about the family," Robert said while he stirred something in a large pot.

"Sure, Dad. Emily and I don't keep secrets from each other," Zach said, winking at her again.

The secret that she was already a huge fan of his before they met would have to keep. Maybe later she would tell him, but now it seemed silly to even bother to bring it up.

"Zach's mom died when he and Levi was just in their teen years," began Robert. "We had a rough time for a while, then life got a little better. I started working with the handicapped kids, the boys took good care of the horses and the house. Did pretty darn good in school, too. We made a life for ourselves, didn't we?" he said to Zach.

"We did," Zach agreed.

"A few hard times hit us, but we managed and got through them. Zachary was ranching at the old Hartford place. All the bigwigs from Hollywood were filming a movie there. I think my son was more interested in hooking up with one of the rancher's daughters, but that's another story. Some fancy producer asked him if he wanted to earn a few bucks as an extra. Zach was too smart to say no. He had to join a few organizations before they'd let him on set, but they paid him good money. How long was that job?"

"A couple of weeks, I think," Zach answered, a sly grin on his face. "Like Dad said, I was interested in the three daughters, but I liked earning my keep, too. I wasn't getting any younger, so when Samesh Mangal called—he was the executive producer of *Hard Knocks*, the indie western I worked on—and told me about an upcoming movie and that I should audition, I said what the heck. That was the beginning of the Gunner West movies. Sam and I are good friends now. His wife just had twins a couple of months ago. Cutest little gals you've ever seen. That pretty much sums up my movie career."

He really wasn't a Hollywood type, thought Emily. His brother and father were proof of that. He acted as natural with them as he did with her and all the folks she'd seen him with.

"Do you mind if I ask about Zach's mother?" Emily said.

Robert shook his head. "Not a bit. Miriam was almost as close to a saint as I've ever seen. We worked the ranch, had a few cattle at one point, but as I said, we fell on hard times off and on, even before she got sick. I thought she was gettin' too thin and told her she needed to see the doctor. She wouldn't go, said it cost too much money, that she was fine. I think we fought back and forth a couple of months before I took her to the hospital myself. By then, there wasn't much they could do for her except try to keep her comfortable. The cancer had spread throughout her body. I was in a state of shock. Had to tell the boys their momma wasn't going to be around much longer." He stopped and turned to face Emily. "Worst day of my life, but it had to be done. I went home and told the boys it was time for a talk at the kitchen table."

Zach interrupted. "We only had kitchen table talks when something was important."

"Both were old enough to know their momma wasn't well. We talked about the future without her." Robert's eyes shone with unshed tears.

"Robert, you don't have to talk about this," Emily said.

"No, it's okay, hon. You need to know. As I said, I discussed the future with the boys. We had just a few weeks left with Miriam. She wanted to come back to the ranch and be with us as long as she could. We had a nurse come in and out, but for the most part Miriam's last weeks were spent with the boys. Preaching to them on all she thought they would need to know to get by in the world. I think she did a mighty fine job."

"She did, Pops," Levi called out. He, Jeremy, Penny, and even Kylie had all stopped talking when Robert spoke of Miriam. He had a soothing voice, with a trace of a Southern accent, but not so strong it could be narrowed down to a specific state.

"You had a hand in raising us as well," Zach reminded his father. "We led a simple life. Work the ranch, take turns making dinner. It wasn't a bad life," Zach said.

"Because you work your tail off to make it easy for me and Pop. Don't deny it or I'll have to whip your butt," Levi chimed in.

"You mean you could *try*," Zach teased. "There isn't any butt whipping happening today. It's a special day for me and Emily. Our anniversary."

Emily raised her brow in confusion. "What are you talking about?"

Zach came up behind her, placing his arms on her shoulders. He whispered in her ear and she felt herself blushing again.

"What? You have to tell us now! Emily's face is as red as Penny's hair," said Kylie. "I mean, uh . . . Robert's apron. No offense, Penny—your hair is beyond cool, especially the shaved side."

Penny was a cute girl with hair that matched her name. She only had hair on the right side of her head; the left side was shaved.

"It's all Gucci. No worries," Penny said.

"Uh, sure, of course," Kylie said, turning away from Penny so she wouldn't see her grinning and crossing her eyes at the slang speak. "So, Zach, what's the anniversary you're celebrating?" Kylie wouldn't stop until she had an answer. She took a drink from her glass.

"It's been one month since we had our first Coke together," Zach answered.

Brown liquid spewed from Kylie's mouth, her eyes as large as the glass she drank from. "Crap, sorry." Levi made fast work of helping her clean her drink off her chest. "It's just that Emily doesn't drink soda. If she does, she burps the most disgusting burps you'll ever hear," Kylie explained.

Mortified, for a couple of seconds Emily couldn't get her mouth to work. Then it did. "I can't believe you said that in front of . . . people! You have the manners of a . . . hog!"

"Yeah? So, I learned from you," Kylie tossed back.

Levi and Zach were doubled over laughing. Robert's

grin stretched across his face like a half moon. Jeremy and Penny were laughing, too.

Emily wanted to strangle Kylie, but when she saw how everyone was laughing, she couldn't help but start laughing, too. It was funny. She might as well let it all hang out, let them get to know the real Emily. Though she had excellent manners. With a mother and grandmother like hers, she'd be in big trouble if she displayed bad manners as a child or now.

"Dad, didn't you bring a case of Coke? For the Jack Daniels later? Maybe Emily could try it out. Maybe it would cure the burping real fast." Levi laughed so hard there were tears in his eyes.

"Enough, Levi. Don't get him started. He will act like a twelve-year-old and start making flatulence noises with his armpit," Robert said.

Kylie burst out laughing, "You can do that? I have to admit trying, but I didn't have much success. I think it's my deodorant," Kylie said to Levi.

Emily was ready to die. Kylie was seriously talking to Zach's brother about arm farts. They were all adults—Jeremy and Penny barely, but still. Thank goodness Emily's mother hadn't accepted Zach's invitation.

"Come on, guys, there are ladies present. Your mother is probably spinning in her grave about now." Robert turned to Emily. "This is what I've had to put up with all these years. I keep thinking they'll grow up and then . . . boom!"

"Being an only child, with Kylie as my 'bonus sister,' I understand," Emily said. Later she was going to pinch Kylie's butt so hard she wouldn't be able to sit down for a week. But then, she would be playing right into her game. Kylie was loving this.

"I think it's time to serve up those appetizers we made

this morning. Stuff our faces for a bit," Robert said, taking a large, foil-covered tray from the refrigerator.

The Ryker family was the total opposite from hers, Emily thought. She absolutely loved this back-and-forth teasing. Though she didn't like Kylie embarrassing her, she was still enjoying every second of this day.

Two hours later, Robert called them all to the formal dining room for Thanksgiving dinner. The table was set with Wedgwood blue china plates. White linen napkins with flatware placed inside sat neatly at each place setting. It wasn't perfect, like Emily's mother's tables, though being not-so-perfect made this dinner even more special. They all took their seats—Robert at the head of the table, Emily and Zach beside each other, Jeremy at the end, and Kylie and Levi across from him with Penny between them. An odd group, but fitting, Emily decided.

Robert asked them to bow their heads as he gave thanks for the food, the friends and the family. Zach carved the turkey, giving each of them their preferred portion. The menu was vast: mashed potatoes, gravy, corn bread stuffing, yams with brown sugar and candied pecans. The homemade cranberry sauce with oranges and walnuts mixed together tasted like dessert. Emily would ask Zach for the recipe so she could give it to her mother. The freshly baked yeast rolls with butter were the best Emily had ever had—another of Zach's recipes, she learned. There were green beans, a squash casserole she passed on, a green salad with fresh tomatoes, cucumbers and tiny sprigs of spring onion that tasted as though they'd been picked fresh from the garden. They ate, they laughed, they had dessert and drank hot chocolate, and then it was time to decorate the tree.

Chapter Twenty-six

All the ornaments Emily and Zach had purchased were now out of their boxes, each with a hook and ready for its place on the twelve-foot balsam fir. It was after five, so it was already dark outside. The multicolored strands of lights on the tree reflected in the windows and the lingering smells of dinner still filled the great room. Tired, but in a good way, Emily remembered the gift in her purse. "I'll be right back," she said to the group, which wasn't paying attention to her. Except for Zach. He followed her back to the kitchen, where she'd left her purse. From inside she removed the ornament she'd bought for him. "This is for your first tree in Loveland," she said, handing him the small box.

"Hmmm, a sneaky one, aren't you?" He removed the gold bow carefully and picked at the tape so he wouldn't tear the wrapping. She, on the other hand, would rip right through the paper; she was always impatient when she opened gifts.

He placed the wrapping paper on the counter, then carefully removed the ornament from its box. It was a miniature version of The Plunge with the title of his movie, *Down and Deadly*, engraved at the bottom. She had also added his name and the date of his first trip down The Plunge with her.

He grinned. "I like this, Em. It's . . . cute."

Just cute? Emily thought to herself.

"I have a gift for you, too. Stay put," Zach said, heading to his bedroom. A minute later, he came back with two gifts, each wrapped in red foil paper with emerald green ribbon. "The color of your eyes," he said.

"Thank you," Emily said. Wanting to rip the paper, she instead slowly removed the ribbon, then, using her thumbnail, removed the tape. The box was an odd shape for an ornament, she thought, as she removed the last piece of tape. Lifting the lid off the box, she gasped when she saw what was inside: a thin, gold bracelet lined with emeralds and diamonds. It looked so delicate she was afraid to remove it from the velvet-lined box. "Zach," she whispered, "This is . . . I love this, but it's—"

He placed his finger on her lips. "Shhh. Let me slip it on your wrist."

Stunned, she lifted her right arm so he could fasten the bracelet on her wrist.

"There," he said, then kissed the inside of her wrist. "My gift to you. And this." He handed her the other box, which was the size of an ornament.

She wondered if he'd wrapped the gifts himself. Again, she took her time opening the gift. When she took the ornament from its box, she almost squealed like a little girl. "How did you know?" she asked.

"Kylie took a picture for me."

"She hates Clarice, so you must've bribed her." It was a round ornament with Clarice's face hand-painted on it. It looked identical to her furry friend. Her name was painted below in fancy lettering. "I love this, Zach. Both gifts. Truly."

"I know you do."

For a minute she thought she would cry, but he didn't give her a chance. Instead, he lowered his mouth to hers, his lips warm and sweet-tasting. She melted into him, careful not to drop the glass ornament. She draped her free arm around his waist and pulled him closer to her, intensifying the kiss. Emily was the first to pull her head back, though she didn't want to. "They'll miss us," she said, still wrapped in his arms.

"Let them."

"Zach." But truly, at this point, she also didn't care who saw them. Everyone here knew they were dating, if you could call this "dating." Her family knew, too. Her mother and father didn't seem to care, so any awkward feelings were hers alone.

"What's going on in that beautiful head of yours?" he asked, then kissed the top of her head.

"Not much," she lied. "No, that's not true. I *was* thinking. About you and me. Together."

"Same here."

"We've known each other for less than a month," she said, not moving an inch from his arms.

"Is that important to you?" he asked.

She didn't think it really mattered and told him so.

"Me either. It's simply time. What's the time limit on love?" he asked. Emily felt his heart racing in his chest, pressed against her.

Zach was right. There wasn't a rule or a time limit. When you knew, you just knew.

"I've never felt this way before," she said truthfully.

"I'm glad."

"You?" she asked, knowing at his age he must've had at least a few serious relationships.

"Not like this," he said. And she believed him.

"I'm glad, too."

"I can live anywhere in the world—you know that, right?"

"I do now," she answered.

"Keep that thought close to your heart tonight."

"I'll try," she said, stepping away from his arms. One of them had to or they'd be there all night.

He took a deep breath, then raked his hand through his messy hair. He was so easy on the eyes it hurt. "Let's go put our ornaments on the tree. Let's save the bracelet for us. Keep it as a special gift. If you're okay doing that."

"I am. I don't want to share our private moments with anyone."

"Then we're on the same page?" He looked at her with that sexy grin again. If this was what the rest of her life might entail, she was in for one heck of a life.

"What are you two doing in here? We're almost finished decorating the tree!" Kylie stomped through the kitchen, searching for something. "Have you seen my purse? I have a gift I want to give Zach." Kylie looked around the room and then spotted her purse at the bar, where she'd left it earlier. "Never mind, here it is."

When she was out of earshot, Zach said, "Levi likes her. What are your thoughts on the two of them?"

"They're perfect for each other at this point. Maybe he can teach her how to do that arm thing. She really does those things," Emily said and laughed.

"Come on—let's go join them all before they think we're hiding."

Kylie hadn't been kidding. The tree was full of decorations. Some Emily didn't recognize. "Did you buy more ornaments? I don't recall getting so many." She walked over to the tree to get a closer look. There was a yellow star made from flour. On the back it read "Zachary, Second Grade." Another ornament appeared to be a nutcracker made from construction paper and maybe a paper towel roll. Written on it in crayon was "Levi, third grade." Emily looked at all of the old ornaments—the bubble lights, clip-on birds and glass beads. She guessed they all belonged to Zach's family. She turned to Robert and asked, "You brought the family ornaments?"

"Yep. Zach asked me to. Said this was going to be a special Christmas. Some of those belonged to Miriam's mother, so I was careful with them. The boys always brought them out every Christmas, so why not now? Pretty little things, aren't they?"

"They are incredible."

"Me and Penny brought this one," Jeremy said, directing her to a pair of skies with a character on them whose hair blew in all directions, with arms held up against its face.

"Crash skiing. That's very encouraging, Jeremy. I like it," Emily said.

"Penny made it for me to give to Zach," he said sheepishly.

"I love this," Zach told Penny. "You used a kiln to make it?" he asked, taking the ornament from the tree to have a closer look.

"No, I have this rad thing I use in the microwave. Kinda a kiln, I guess," Penny explained. "It melts glass. I painted the rest."

"You're very talented, Penny. I promise I'll take care of this," Zach said as he put the ornament back on the tree.

"I'm tired," Kylie said, standing up to stretch. "I have this to give you, Zach, and then I'm heading home." She handed him a package. As he had with Emily's gift, he took his time opening it. When he saw what was inside the box, he tossed back his head and laughed. "Only you, Kylie. Thanks. These will entertain my grandchildren one day."

He lifted the box to show them Kylie's gift: DVDs of his

Gunner West movies, taken unknown to Emily from the top shelf in her hall closet.

"Kylie's right—I'm tired, too. All that turkey. I should get going. We can follow each other and make sure neither of us runs off the road," Emily said.

"Us too. I have to open the ski rental early. We'll be crazy after the holiday," Jeremy said. "Zach, dude, this was awesome. I'll tell my grandkids I had Thanksgiving dinner with you. Thanks, man."

They shook hands, and Zach walked with them to the door. "I'll see you around, Jeremy, Penny. Drive safe."

Emily waited for Zach to finish saying goodbye to the couple before she said, "I need to go, Zach. I have a zillion things to do myself, plus the drive. I want to make sure ding-dong doesn't run herself off the side of the mountain."

"I don't want you to leave, but I also don't want you or Kylie driving too late," Zach said.

"I'll follow them, Zach," Levi offered. "Make sure they get home safely."

"Really? You'd do that? You hardly even know us," Kylie said. "I think you two guys might be the real thing, like gentlemen. Right, Em?"

"I agree. Thanks for the offer Levi, but I think we'll be just fine. There isn't a snowstorm out there and Kylie and I are familiar with the roads. We'll be fine."

By this time Robert had joined them. Kylie and Emily put their coats on and got out their keys, preparing to leave. "You two girls come up and visit us on the ranch. It's an easy drive or flight. Something's been nagging me all day since I first met you, Emily. You remind me of Bill and Lenora's middle daughter . . . what's her name?"

"The tall blonde. Her name is Nicole, Dad," Levi said. "Isn't she in medical school now?"

Emily's heart started pounding. "This Nicole, you say I remind you of her?"

"Both of you remind me of each other. What's that they call it—a doppelgänger? Yes, she could be your sister."

Emily's mouth was now dry, a sure sign she was nervous. "How old is this Nicole?" she asked.

Robert brushed his hand over his face. "Let's see, Helina is the oldest—she's probably thirty-three or thirty-four. Has a couple of little boys. Nicole is the middle girl, so she'd be about thirty, and Sasha is in her late twenties. They were all pretty close in age. Never mind me. I'm just an old man rambling. You just had an expression on your face earlier, and it's been nagging me all day. I knew there was someone you reminded me of. They own the old Hartford farm where Zach was working when Sam found him."

"What did you say their parents' names were?" Emily asked.

"Bill and Lenora."

"Well, it's good to know I have a doppelgänger out there. Maybe I'll get to meet her sometime in the future. Robert, I've enjoyed this day more than you can imagine. Mother wants me to invite you all to the house tomorrow evening for her tree-trimming party and dinner. If you can't, I understand."

"I would like to meet your family, sweetie. Levi, Zach?"

"I'm in," Levi said. "Kylie, are you going to be there?"

"Yes, I'm the bonus daughter," she said and laughed.

"You don't have to ask me twice," Zach said. "I know where your family lives, so let me know what time and we'll be there."

"Around seven?" Emily said.

"We'll be there. What can we bring?" Robert asked.

"Just yourselves," Emily said. She reached up and gave him a hug. "I'll see you fellows tomorrow. Ky, you ready?"

"Boys, walk these ladies to their cars," Robert instructed.

After Zach and Levi walked Emily and Kylie to their cars, Zach leaned in to give Emily a light kiss. She wanted to be nosy and see if Levi was doing the same with Kylie but given Robert's revelation, she had more important things to think about.

"I'll see you tomorrow evening," Zach said.

"I can't wait," Emily said, a full-blown, happy smile on her face.

She cranked the engine over, backing up, then heading down the drive leading to Snowmass pass. They'd cleared the roads, plus she was on the safer side of the road now. She spied Kylie behind her. When the opportunity presented itself, Emily was going to give her a piece of her mind for sneaking into her house and stealing her DVDs. Then she'd ask her what Zach had used to bribe her to take a picture of Clarice. Maybe Clarice had scratched Kylie while she took the picture. If she had, it would serve her right.

Chapter Twenty-seven

As soon as Emily returned to her condo, she hurried inside before Kylie could tease her about stealing her movies. When she opened the door, Clarice pounced off the back of the sofa, rubbing her head against Emily's legs.

Emily picked her up. "Poor Clarice. I know I've been a bad mommy, but I promise you are going to have the best kitty Thanksgiving to date."

Emily went to the freezer and took out the trout she'd bought as a special treat for Clarice. She put it in the microwave to defrost. "Just a few minutes, okay?" she assured the cat as she refilled her dry food, which still had plenty left. Her fountain needed a little water. She rinsed it out in the sink, then refilled it with bottled water. Kylie always teased her about giving Clarice bottled water. She was more of a dog person who had yet to make the decision to adopt one.

The microwave beeped. She took out the trout, rinsed it off, then removed the skillet she used for scrambling eggs. Adding a half cup of water, she placed the filet in the skillet. Normally she knew enough to use butter, or olive oil, maybe some lemon, but not for Clarice. Plain would be just fine. She turned the burner to low while she went into her bedroom to change clothes. At least Kylie had been right about the clothes they'd picked out. They were comfortable and dressy, but not too much.

In her room, she put on a pair of sweatpants and a T-shirt. She'd take off her makeup in the shower. She grabbed her laptop from her office/Clarice's room and took it with her to the kitchen.

"Meow, meow, MEOW!" Clarice grew louder on the last meow.

"Coming right up," Emily said as she took the trout from the skillet, putting it on a paper plate. "Give it a couple of minutes to cool off, sweet girl." At the table, Emily booted up her laptop, returning to the website that located people. She'd paid for a month's worth of service, just as she had on the genealogy site. Thankfully, her laptop was much faster than her old Mac desktop, and she typed in the names of the girls Robert had mentioned.

Once the fish was cool enough for Clarice, Emily used a fork to smash it up, then ran her fingers through to make sure there were no small bones.

"MEOW!"

"Clarice, this is for your own protection," Emily said, putting the paper plate down next to her water fountain. "Enjoy, Miss Prissy."

Emily took a bottle of water from the fridge for herself, then sat down to wait for the search results. The green bar was moving super fast, but patience was not her best trait.

Finally information filled the screen. Emily couldn't believe what she read:

Nicole Michelle Ammerman, MD, thirty-two. Attended medical school at the University of Wyoming.

Helina Anja Ammerman-Patrickson, thirty-four. Attended the University of Wyoming.

Sasha Renee Ammerman, twenty-eight. Attended the University of Colorado, Denver.

Emily typed in *Lenora Hartford-Ammerman*. She only had to wait a couple of minutes for the results:

Lenora Hartford-Ammerman, fifty-eight, married to William James Ammerman.

She clicked out of the site. She didn't need to know anymore. She was 100 percent sure these were her cousins. Robert had said she reminded him of a Nicole, and she was pretty sure Nicole was their grandmother's name. What were the odds? It was her middle name. She was pretty sure that Helina was part of her grandmother's name, too.

Next she needed to know what had happened to her grandparents. The only thing she knew about them was that they'd died young. She did a bit of math in her head, then began her search. She was unsure if the older newspapers were online; many were still on microfiche, if at all. Emily began typing in names, followed with the words "accident" and "death." After a couple of hours, she gave up. Her eyes were gritty and she needed a shower.

She would ask her dad about it all tomorrow. Armed with this new information, he couldn't avoid the subject much longer. After Zach's family left, she would have a sit-down with her dad. Or a kitchen table talk, like Zach's family.

After she showered and brushed her teeth, Emily practically fell into bed. She made sure her cell phone was on the charger but turned off. The last thing she needed was Kylie calling her in the middle of the night or popping over.

"Crud," she said, getting up to make sure she'd locked the front door. She put on the chain lock. Normally she didn't bother; Kylie had a key or just walked right in. Tonight she wanted to sleep. Back in her room, Clarice waited for her on the bed. "You going to sleep in here with me tonight?"

"Meow." Clarice made herself comfortable on the extra

pillow next to her. Emily turned the lights off, falling into a deep, sound sleep.

Emily woke up to Clarice's sandpaper tongue licking her face. "Ugh, you need a breath mint." She rolled onto her stomach, then dozed off again. She wasn't sure how long she'd been asleep when her she heard someone pounding on her front door.

"Shit," she said, not caring for the word but finding it fitting in the moment. It had to be Kylie because no one else would beat on her door this early. She glanced at the clock. Seven thirty. Hadn't she'd told Kylie she planned to sleep in?

"Hang on," she called out in a grouchy voice.

She stumbled out of bed and into the living room. After looking through the peephole to make sure it was Kylie, she unlocked and opened the door. "Geez, Kylie, I told you I planned on sleeping in. I'm tired. What do you want?"

"Good morning to you, too," Kylie said, heading to the kitchen. "I'll make a pot of coffee."

"Sure, make yourself at home. I guess this means you're not leaving so I can go back to bed?"

"Sleep is overrated," Kylie said as she rinsed out the coffeepot, filling it with bottled water. Emily wouldn't drink it otherwise. Emily sat at the table, her elbows on the table, her chin in her hands. "I know you're dying to tell me something, so spit it out. Seriously, Ky, I am super-tired. Maybe I'm coming down with a bug or something."

"I got an email from Noah, the movie guy. They want to film my and Zach's scene Tuesday."

"Okay. And how does this concern me now?"

"I wanted you to know because you'll have to be with us to make sure your lover boy doesn't goof up."

"Speaking of, I think it's pretty rude what you gave Zach yesterday."

"I think it's pretty rude you didn't tell me you had all those movies."

"I didn't think it was your business, Kylie. I'm serious. Coming into my home and taking my things, then giving them as a gift to Zach. Exactly what was your point?" Emily really was mad at her about it. She would never do something like that to her. Privacy was important to her.

"I wanted you to know I knew you'd seen Zach's movies, that's all."

"What if I told you I hadn't even watched them yet? Maybe I just bought them recently and was planning on watching them until you stole them from me. Zach and I are together, so it's only natural that I'd want to see his movies." No way would she tell Kylie the truth. Maybe when they were eighty, but not anytime soon.

"Shoot. I'm sorry."

"You should be. I can't believe you would do that to me. I'm having the locks changed, too." She wouldn't, but it didn't hurt to give her a scare.

"I said I was sorry. Really I am, Em."

"I don't like you nosing through my things. Let's leave it at that. Pour me a cup of coffee since you woke me up for nothing."

Clarice pounced into the kitchen, meowing superloudly at Kylie.

"I had to break in to get a picture of that furball for Zach," Kylie explained.

"Okay, but just don't go through my stuff, okay?"

"I won't," she promised as she poured them both a cup of coffee. Then Kylie's eyes doubled in size as she grabbed Emily's wrist. "What's *that* all about?"

Emily hadn't wanted to remove the bracelet the night before when she got into the shower because Zach had put it on her wrist. "None of your biz, Kylie, okay? You need to get a life. What about Levi? He's a hunk. Do you like him?"

"What's not to like? Of course I do. He's so sexy, I had a hard time not jumping his bones last night. He's as polite as Zach, plus he has a warped sense of humor like I do. I think he likes me too."

"He does. Zach told me so last night when he walked me out to the car."

Kylie sat down in the chair across from her. "Nice. I'll make sure to look extra sexy tonight. What are you wearing? Your mom probably expects you to wear a dress as usual."

"Then she's in for a rude awakening. I'm going to wear a nice pair of jeans and a sweater with boots. I'll be comfortable."

"Good, then I'll do the same so you won't feel out of place. Your mom is a proper lady; I do like that about her."

"Yes, I do, too, but sometimes she takes it too far." Emily saw her laptop on the table. Thankfully she had closed it before going to bed. Otherwise, Kylie would be going through her search history.

"Listen, I've found out some things about my dad's brother, the only family he has left. I was up late doing some research. I found out so many things and I want to tell you, but I owe it to my dad to discuss it with him first. It's mind-blowing. Now I'm going to finish my coffee. Then I want you to leave and come over at five thirty. We can ride over to my parents' place together, unless you've made other plans. I have some business I need to take care of first."

"Now you're throwing me out?!"

"I am, but take an extra cup of coffee on your way out. I'll see you here at five thirty."

Kylie saluted her and filled her mug, leaving by slamming the door behind her. As soon as she left, Emily locked the door, put the chain lock back on and closed the blinds in the kitchen before going back to bed. She rarely had the opportunity to laze around. It was Black Friday and the traffic would be insane. The lodge would be so busy, she wouldn't be able to get anything accomplished, plus she'd had no other students while she'd been training Zach. She needed a good rest. She set her alarm for noon in case she was lucky enough to sleep that long. Clarice hopped on the bed with her, found her spot on the pillow and curled up into a ball. She flopped her tail back and forth like a pendulum, lulling Emily into a deep sleep.

Chapter Twenty-eight

"Are you excited to see Levi?" Emily asked as she backed out of her parking space.

"Duh, of course. Who wouldn't be?" Kylie replied.

"Listen, you need to stop with the 'duhs' and the arm farts. At least for tonight. If you and Levi get a good laugh out of it, I don't care. Just try not to do it tonight. I can only imagine the 'just a few people' Mother's invited. Probably half of Loveland, so watch your mouth."

"You sound like your mom."

"Sorry, I do. I guess I want to make sure everything goes off perfectly with Zach's dad and Levi. They're so down-to-earth, I feel like I've known them forever, and I just met them last night."

"Me too. I like Robert. You know, he must've been a real stud in his day. Just look at him now! I bet your mother will bend over backward to make a good impression on him."

"She's not too bad herself, Ky."

"True, and she doesn't look her age. Think she's getting Botox?"

"I don't think so, but if she is, I think it's okay to do those things if it makes you feel better about yourself. It's not in my cards just yet, but when the time comes, I would certainly consider having a session."

"Look at me," Kylie commanded.

"I'm driving and it's dark."

"I had Botox in my elevens two weeks ago."

"What are your 'elevens'?"

"The frown lines between my waxed eyebrows," she said. "That you never noticed."

"I did notice, I just didn't say anything."

Emily turned onto the road that led to her parents' house. When she pulled into the long drive, she was surprised to see only a few vehicles. "Something's going on. There aren't a lot of cars here." Emily took her purse along with her keys and got out of the car. With Kylie trailing behind her, she rang the doorbell just as a formality and then stepped inside the house. She saw there were three balsam firs in the middle of the great room waiting to be decorated. The smell of something yummy was coming from the kitchen. "Mom, Dad, we're here," she called out.

"Your dad and I are in the kitchen," Julia called back. "Come and join us."

Emily's parents were seated at the kitchen table. They looked a bit surprised to see their daughter and "bonus daughter."

"We weren't expecting you yet," Julia said. "The party doesn't start for a couple hours."

"There's something I wanted to talk to you about," Emily said. "Before everyone else gets here. Something I wanted to talk about just as a family."

"Should I go?" Kylie asked, looking from Emily to her parents and back again. She sensed that whatever was coming was serious.

"Of course not," Emily assured her. "You're part of the family. I wanted you here for this."

"Emily, what is it? What's wrong?" asked Julia.

"Nothing's really wrong. In fact, things are suddenly going so well between me and Zach. I've been thinking a lot, and after meeting his family and hearing about how much they still miss his mom ... it got me to thinking about our own family. About the missing pieces. About how life is short and we shouldn't waste any more time. And then, out of the blue, Robert said I looked exactly like someone he knew back home. And I did some research on-line—actually, I had already started doing some research, but what Robert said was the final piece of the puzzle."

"What puzzle?" asked Mason, but the look in his eyes suggested he understood more than he was letting on.

"The puzzle of your family, Dad. Your brother."

"Emily, I don't think this is the right time ..." Julia began, but Mason interrupted her.

"No, let's just get this out in the open so we can all enjoy the rest of the evening," Mason said. "I've suspected this was coming anyway. I've kept things a secret for too long. What do you want to know, Emily?"

"I want to know the truth, Dad. About why we have all of these relatives in Wyoming that we never see or talk about."

Mason sighed as the three women looked at him expectantly, waiting for him to begin. "My parents married young. Mom was from Russia. She was just a girl when she came over. Dad wasn't much more than a boy himself. They purchased a small ranch in Wyoming after they'd been married a few years. I'm not sure how much long after, but Will came along, then I followed two years later. My mother was the hardest-working woman. I remember, even though I was young, that she could do as much work as my dad, if not more. They had a few cattle, a couple of horses, some chickens. Mom would sell their eggs once a week. Dad would always get mad when she did that because he wanted eggs for his breakfast on Sunday morning.

"Will and I grew up. Will had just met his future wife, Lenora, and I was working the ranch to carry my weight. It happened late one night. Dad wasn't home. I remember Mom pacing the floor, speaking in Russian. I'm sure they weren't nice words, but it is what it is. She went out to look for Dad. He'd started drinking a lot back then. She found him passed out in the stables. Stormy, a wild stallion Dad brought home a few weeks before, was kicking and bucking, trying to break free of his stall. Mom went inside the stall to drag my dad out before the horse stomped him to death. But Mother was no match for the horse. After I went out to check on her and found them, I went to get Will and a gun so we could put the horse down. Will wouldn't have any part of it. He moved Stormy to the Hartford ranch. Afterward, I couldn't forgive him. I left town and never looked back."

No one spoke. What could they say? Finally, Emily broke the silence.

"Dad, I am so, so sorry." Emily came over and sat beside him.

"I'm sorry I didn't tell you sooner. Sometimes it was easier to forget, to pretend none of it ever happened. I made my own family, with your mom and her parents and you and Kylie."

"Are you going to be okay seeing Robert tonight? He might ask you about all of this."

"I can handle it," Mason said.

"But why don't you try reaching out to your brother?" Kylie blurted out, unable to contain herself any longer. "All that stuff happened so long ago—"

"Kylie!" Julia admonished her.

"No, it's all right, Julia. She has a point. Emily too, about life being short. So many changes are happening, what with retiring and Emily taking over the lodge. And now her new young man, who has this connection to my past. What are the odds? Maybe fate is trying to tell me something."

"Will you at least think about it, Dad?" Emily asked him.

"I promise I will," he said, taking her hand in his. "But for now, let's focus on the present."

Emily, her parents and Kylie spent the next couple of hours preparing for their guests. After Mason's story, everyone felt lighter, now that the truth was known. Kathryn arrived, lugging various containers of food and serving pieces. Once they were all in the kitchen, Emily gave Kathryn a hug.

"Where are all of your guests? Did they beg off this year?" Kathryn asked, looking around the room.

"I thought since Zach's family would be here tonight it would be nice just to have us. You and Kylie aside, as we all know you're also part of the family."

"I appreciate this, Mom. Truly," said Emily, surprised at her mother's restraint.

"Me too," Kylie said. "You aren't wearing a ball gown either."

They all laughed. "I was going to, but decided against it," Julia said, modeling her navy slacks with a cream-colored blouse. It was a very casual look by her standards. "Your grandparents are on their way. You want to help us with dinner? Kathryn suggested we set this up buffet style. A little more casual tonight."

"Perfect! What can we do to help?" Emily asked.

For the next fifteen minutes the four of them stacked plates, bowls and flatware in the formal dining room. Kathryn had brought chafing dishes over from the lodge— the fanciest ones, of course, with the gold handles. In the sunroom they'd added more white leather chairs taken from the main room. The fireplaces were lit and Christmas music played in the surround system Mason had installed. It was all quite cozy.

"Knock knock," Mimi called from the foyer. "Better not be doing anything I wouldn't want to see."

"Mother, we're in the dining room. Come and help. Is Dad with you?" Julia said.

"Yes, Julia, I'm here."

"Dad, can you please go find Mason and help bring in the box of ornaments?" Julia asked.

"Hey, Papaw," Emily said as she passed him while returning to the kitchen for another chafing dish.

"Hey, kiddo. You look exceptionally pretty tonight."

"Ella, I can bring the boxes in without help. I'm not dead yet," Mason said as he stepped into the hallway.

It took them all working together, but within twenty minutes they had the food in the chafing dishes and drinks at the makeshift bar set up in the dining room. The menu consisted of prime rib, scalloped potatoes, Caesar salad and freshly made French bread. For dessert Kathryn had made apple, pumpkin and cherry pies. Simple but perfect.

Emily and Kylie kept glancing at the clock. "We did say seven, right?" Emily said.

"Yeah, I believe so," Kylie confirmed.

The words were no more out of her mouth when they heard a car pulling up. Then came the sound of car doors closing and the doorbell.

"I'll get it," Emily said, hurrying over to greet Zach's family. She opened the door and said, hoping to keep the mood light, " 'Welcome to my parents' home." She stood aside to allow them to enter.

Robert gave Emily a hug, then Kylie. Zach gave Emily a loud kiss, and Levi picked Kylie up like she was a doll and gave her a long kiss before setting her down.

"Wow," Kylie said. "Do you greet all your dates this way?"

"No, they're usually too big," Levi joked.

"Mom, Dad, company's here," Emily called out a bit too loudly.

Zach had a shopping bag with him. "I made another batch of cranberry sauce for your mother. Since you asked me for the recipe I wrote it down. It's inside the bag, too."

"You are truly one in a million," Emily told him. "I'll take this to the kitchen."

Mason and Julia appeared from the dining room all smiles.

Robert stared at Mason. Mason stared back. Julia stared at both of them.

"I know you," Robert finally said, breaking the awkward silence.

"Yep, I think I know you, too." Mason shook hands with Robert while they all looked on, some of them a little mystified at how these two knew each other, while Emily, Julia and Kylie already knew, but waited to see how things played out.

"You're Will's brother," Robert said.

Mason nodded. "Damn, I can't believe this. Come on in—we've got a few years to catch up on."

"Mason?" Julia asked.

"Oh, sorry. Rob, this is my wife, Julia. You've already met my daughter and bonus daughter."

"Hello, Robert." Julia couldn't take her eyes off him. Or Levi. "You have two very talented and handsome sons. My goodness!" Julia was acting like she was going to swoon.

Luckily Kathryn came into the main room then and said, "I'm making drinks if you all would like to come out to the sunroom and relax."

After a lot of "yeses," "sures," and "okays," everyone followed Kathryn to the sunroom.

Suddenly Emily had a hideous thought. As soon as everyone had found a seat and was settled, she had to ask, "You guys aren't related to us in any way, are you?"

Robert laughed. "No. We knew each other in high school, and for a little while longer after the accident."

"Damn, Mason, I'm so sorry," said Robert. "I thought . . . never mind what I thought. Maybe we should just go."

"No, don't go. Emily has already given me a lot to think about tonight. And I think I'm done hiding from my past."

The two families—and their surrogate family members—spent the rest of the evening together. They ate, drank and got to know one another better. Then they gathered around the trio of Christmas trees and began to decorate. Slowly the trees began to sparkle as more and more ornaments were added. As everyone happily chatted around her, Emily was standing on a stepladder stringing a garland near the top of the middle tree when Zach tapped her leg.

"Can you come down here a second?" he asked quietly, giving her one of his most dazzling smiles.

An Ultrabrite smile, thought Emily. Once she had stepped down, Zach led her around to the other side of the tree, where they could be alone.

"I have another ornament for you," Zach said. "I already hung it up on the tree."

"But you already gave—" Emily began, but Zach cut her off.

"Just take a look," he said, nodding his head toward the center of the tree.

Emily leaned in, searching the sturdy branches. In the center she spotted the same ornament she had given Zach earlier, the miniature version of the ski slope. It was hanging from a branch of the tree, only this time there was a

delicate band of white gold embedded with diamonds nestled on top.

"Emily," said Zach, "will you take the plunge with me?"

It was as if time froze for a moment as Emily took it all
in—Zach standing before her, an expectant look on his
face, the sparkling ring nestled in the festive tree. But, also
the people milling around them on the other side of the
trees—her parents and grandparents, her best friend and
surrogate sister, Kathryn and Zach's father and brother. It
was overwhelming, but in the best way possible. She
wanted this feeling to last.

"Zach . . . it's all happened so fast. And I'm so happy it
almost feels unreal. But . . . I'm not ready to give you an
answer yet. I will someday, but I need some time."

"I understand," Zach said. "I can be patient. I'll hold
on to the ring and wait for your answer. And I'll be ready."

Emily thought back on everything she had experienced
and learned the past few weeks—her mother's past heart-
break, her father's rift with his family. Her parents' high
expectations for her, which she understood better now,
given their complicated, wounded histories. The random
twists of fate that brought her and Zach together, and his
family's connection to her father's past. Even their shared
Christmas birthdays. And she thought of everything that
still lay ahead of them. She felt like she did when she was
at the top of the mountain, ready to hit the slopes—the ex-
hilarating sense of freedom with a bit of uncertainty mixed
in. Only, this time, she wouldn't be alone.

Epilogue

Christmas Eve, One Year Later

Mason and Julia were thrilled to be celebrating Christmas at their house this year. "Are you just a little bit nervous?" Julia asked her husband.

"Nope, not at all. Will and I have spent more time on the phone and Zooming than I thought possible. I've come to terms with the past and I plan to leave it there."

"Then I won't bring it up again," Julia said. "Our lives have come full circle this year. I am so happy for our girls. And now one is about to be a mommy! Poor Kylie—she's like a little ball with legs, but Levi adores her."

"They're good people, the Rykers. Movie people, too."

"Zach invited John Harris to the Summit. I'm as excited as a little girl. I want to push him down Maximum Vault."

Mason laughed. "No, I don't think that's necessary. Once he sees you and realizes his loss, that will be enough. I wouldn't have it any other way."

They heard car doors opening, slamming shut, voices they didn't recognize calling names they knew, but hadn't yet seen the faces they belonged to.

The plan was to get the family settled into their rooms

and then have dinner, prepared by none other than Kathryn, who'd become very friendly with Robert. Then they would trim the tree later that evening. Robert was helping Kathryn transport the food from the lodge to the house.

The doorbell rang, then Julia heard several knocks. "Be right there," she called. They'd agreed she would answer the door, giving Mason a few minutes to observe his brother and his family before coming downstairs. "Go." She motioned to Mason.

As soon as Mason was upstairs, Julia pulled the wooden doors open. "You must be Will," Julia said, opening her arms and giving him a huge hug. "And Lenora. And your daughters and grandchildren. I'll let you all introduce yourselves, if you don't mind."

They came inside with grins from ear to ear. "We were thrilled when Dad told us we were going to finally meet the rest of the family. I'm Sasha, the youngest," said one of the girls.

"You are beautiful, sweetie. You look so much like Lenora. Tiny as a little bird."

"Julia, I'm the eldest, and most overworked, Helina. These are my boys, Timmy and James, and my husband, Charles."

"Nice to finally meet you, Julia. Hope you can handle having two rowdy boys around for the next few days," Charles said. He was of average height with blond hair and a beard. Julia knew he was a science professor at a university in Wyoming.

"Will," Mason said as he came down the stairs.

"Mason, damn, you look good." The two brothers shook hands, then Will grabbed Mason, hugging him so hard, Julia thought he would break his back. "I am so sorry I've missed all these years. I promise you, we will make up for them."

Both brothers had tears in their eyes. They stood side by side with an arm around each other's shoulders. "Isn't there one more daughter?" Mason asked.

"Yes, but she's on the phone. She's the doctor. Never a dull moment when she's around."

Just then, even though the door was open, Nicole tapped on it just to be polite. "Hello," she said.

Mason and Julia stared at her.

"I'm sorry, is something wrong?" Nicole asked.

"No, not at all, Nicole. It's just that you're a replica of Emily. I can't believe it. You two could pass for twins," said Julia.

Nicole smiled. "You had me there for a minute." She hugged Julia. "I've been looking forward to this all week. Uncle Mason . . ." She walked over to him and gave him a hug as though she'd been doing it her entire life.

"I'm so happy to have family here for Christmas. Emily and her crew should be here any minute. Follow me and I'll take you all to your rooms." Julia was in her glory, entertaining, even more so because it was family.

As soon as everyone was settled and Helina put the boys down for their naps, they all went downstairs to the sunroom for the drinks and snacks Kathryn had prepared.

Fifteen minutes later Kylie and Levi burst through the front door. "Bonus daughter and hubby here," Kylie called, knowing they were in the sunroom. Levi held her hand as they walked through the main room to the sunroom to join the others. "I'm Kylie, the bonus daughter," Kylie announced. "And this is my husband, Levi. And this . . ." She patted her baby bump. "Is Anna."

Everyone went through introductions again. When Kylie saw Nicole, her mouth actually dropped open. "OMG, you're Emily!" She hurried over to give her best friend's cousin a hug. "Where is Emily anyway?" Kylie asked. "I hope she's not bringing Clarice. Pregnant women and cats aren't a good mix."

"No, that's just a myth," Nicole told her.

"How do you know?" Kylie asked.

"I'm a doctor," Nicole said and laughed, sounding just like her cousin.

After an hour had passed they were all starting to wonder if Nicole's doppelgänger and her boyfriend were going to show.

There was a knock on the door. "It's just me and Robert," Kathryn called out.

"We're in here waiting for Emily. I have no clue why she's so late," Julia said.

"I think we do," Robert said.

It was then that Emily and Zach also came inside and found everyone waiting for them in the sunroom.

Emily's eyes immediately went to Nicole. "Holy moly!" She ran across the room to hug her cousin for the very first time.

"We are almost twins," Nicole said, amazed.

"Unreal," Emily replied. "Wait, Zach, come in a little closer."

He stepped into the room, and now all eyes were on him.

"Zach Ryker!" exclaimed Helina. "How great to see you after so many years!"

The conversation became noisy and overly excited. Everyone was talking over one another about which Gunner West movie they'd seen and which was their favorite. Then they all had dozens of questions for Zach, which he politely answered.

Emily whistled to draw everyone's attention. "I need a moment. Zach?"

After making sure everyone was assembled in the room, including Kathryn and Robert, she spoke. "I have an announcement to make."

"You do?" Zach said.

"Everyone," Emily began, "a year ago Zach asked me a question. And now I'm ready to give him an answer. Zach, my answer . . . is yes."

Zach picked her up and swung her around the room, knocking a glass off one table and a lamp off another.

"Dad, Levi, she said yes! Emily Ammerman has just accepted my marriage proposal!"

"Congratulations!" chorused the family members.

"Mimi, I see you upstairs—come on down now, it's safe," Emily said.

"Merry Christmas to my wife-to-be," Zach exclaimed. "And may our families blend together, with love for one another always."

Zach kissed Emily passionately. Her life was now permanently sealed with his kiss.

Benny's Peanut Butter Cookies

2½ cups of flour
2 teaspoons of baking soda
¾ cup of butter or margarine
1 cup of light or dark brown sugar
1 cup of granulated sugar
2 cups of peanut butter
¼ cup hot water
1 teaspoon vanilla extract

Sift the flour with the baking soda. Cream the butter, gradually adding the sugars and creaming until light and fluffy. Blend the peanut butter into the creamed mixture and then beat in the eggs. Add vanilla. Stir in the flour mixture, alternating with the hot water. Form the dough into small balls and place on ungreased cookie sheet. Flatten slightly with the tines of a fork, lightly dipped in sugar if you choose. Bake at 350° for about ten to twelve minutes. Makes about 5 to 6 dozen cookies.

Zach's Homemade Hot Chocolate

½ tsp sugar (more if you have a sweet tooth)
¼ cup cocoa powder
1 cup hot water

4 cups of milk
½ teaspoon vanilla extract

Mix sugar and cocoa in a medium saucepan, then stir in water. Bring to a low boil* over low to medium heat, stirring constantly. Keep at a low boil* for 2–3 minutes. Add milk; stir and heat until hot. Remove from heat, add vanilla.

*Do not fully boil